AMERICA'S FOUNDING FATHERS

ALLEN C. GUELZO, PH.D.

D0925714

Smithsonian®

THE
GREAT
COURSES®

PUBLISHED BY:

THE GREAT COURSES
Corporate Headquarters
4840 Westfields Boulevard, Suite 500
Chantilly, Virginia 20151-2299
Phone: 1-800-832-2412
Fax: 703-378-3819
www.thegreatcourses.com

ALLEN C. GUELZO, PH.D.

HENRY R. LUCE PROFESSOR OF THE CIVIL WAR ERA
DIRECTOR OF CIVIL WAR ERA STUDIES
GETTYSBURG COLLEGE

*A*llen C. Guelzo is the Henry R. Luce Professor of the Civil War Era and the Director of Civil War Era Studies at Gettysburg College in Gettysburg, Pennsylvania. He holds an M.A. and a Ph.D. in History from the University of Pennsylvania.

Professor Guelzo is the author of *Abraham Lincoln: Redeemer President* and *Lincoln's Emancipation Proclamation: The End of Slavery in America*, both of which won Gettysburg College's Gilder Lehrman Lincoln Prize and the Abraham Lincoln Institute's Annual Book Award. He is also the author of a volume of essays entitled *Abraham Lincoln as a Man of Ideas*, which won an Award of Merit from the Illinois State Historical Society. Professor Guelzo's other books include *Lincoln and Douglas: The Debates That Defined America*; *Lincoln: A Very Short Introduction*; and *Fateful Lightning: A New History of the Civil War and Reconstruction*. His book on the Battle of Gettysburg, *Gettysburg: The Last Invasion*, spent eight weeks on the *New York Times* best-seller list and won several awards, including the Lincoln Prize for 2014, the inaugural Guggenheim-Lehrman Prize in Military

History, the Civil War Round Table of New York's Fletcher Pratt Award, and the Civil War Round Table of Atlanta's Richard Barksdale Harwell Book Award. Professor Guelzo's most recent publication, *Redeeming the Great Emancipator*, originated as the 2012 Nathan I. Huggins Lectures at Harvard University.

Professor Guelzo has written for *The New York Times*, *The Washington Post*, the *Los Angeles Times*, *The Wall Street Journal*, *The Christian Science Monitor*, *First Things*, *U.S. News & World Report*, *The Weekly Standard*, *National Review*, *The Daily Beast*, the *Claremont Review of Books*, and *Books & Culture*. He has also been featured on NPR's *Weekend Edition Sunday* and *On Point*, *The Daily Show*, *Meet the Press's PRESS Pass*, and Brian Lamb's *Booknotes.*

From 2006 to 2013, Professor Guelzo served as a member of the National Council of the National Endowment for the Humanities. In 2016, he received the James Q. Wilson Award for Distinguished Scholarship on the Nature of a Free Society. He is also one of *Power Line*'s 100 top professors in America.

Professor Guelzo's other Great Courses include *Making History*: *How Great Historians Interpret the Past*; *The American Revolution*; *The American Mind*; *Mr. Lincoln: The Life of Abraham Lincoln*; and *The History of the United States, 2nd Edition*, which he team-taught with Professors Patrick N. Allitt and Gary W. Gallagher.

Professor Guelzo lives in Paoli and Gettysburg, Pennsylvania, with his wife, Debra. ■

ABOUT OUR PARTNER

*F*ounded in 1846, the Smithsonian is the world's largest museum and research complex, consisting of 19 museums and galleries, the National Zoological Park, and 9 research facilities. The total number of artifacts, works of art, and specimens in the Smithsonian's collections is estimated at 154 million. These collections represent America's rich heritage, art from across the globe, and the immense diversity of the natural and cultural world.

In support of its mission—the increase and diffusion of knowledge—the Smithsonian has embarked on four Grand Challenges that describe its areas of study, collaboration, and exhibition: Unlocking the Mysteries of the Universe, Understanding and Sustaining a Biodiverse Planet, Valuing World Cultures, and Understanding the American Experience. The Smithsonian's partnership with The Great Courses is an engaging opportunity to encourage continuous exploration by learners of all ages across these diverse areas of study.

Designed as a chronological narrative and richly supported by images and artifacts from the Smithsonian's unparalleled collections of historical Americana, this course, *America's Founding Fathers*, takes you from the closing days of the American Revolution to the opening decades of the United States under the newly created U.S. Constitution. The Founding Fathers highlighted in this course were each integral to what makes the Constitution the complex document it is today. Each profile of these historic figures is supplemented in the video with historic portraits from Smithsonian's National Portrait Gallery as well as important historical documents and artifacts from the National Museum of American History, giving a human dimension to such near-mythical figures as George Washington, Thomas Jefferson, Alexander Hamilton, and James Madison. This course offers something few other historical surveys can: the combination of a dynamic professor with the unrivaled American history collections and expertise of the Smithsonian. ■

TABLE OF CONTENTS

Introduction

Lecture Guides

Supplemental Material

THE ORDER OF HISTORY: THE IMPORTANCE OF POLITICS IN THE EARLY REPUBLIC

David C. Ward

SENIOR HISTORIAN
NATIONAL PORTRAIT GALLERY

*I*n 1776, that most significant year, the artist Charles Willson Peale relocated from his native Maryland to Philadelphia. The move was significant for Peale personally, as he expanded his practice of portraiture from the wealthy gentry to the political leadership that had gathered in Philadelphia to create the contours of the American republic. Peale was recognizing an opportunity to create public portraiture that would support not just the careers of individuals but the emerging American revolutionary cause.

Peale would soon become one of the foremost portraitists of American political and public life. He painted the first portrait of George Washington at Mount Vernon in 1772, and he built on this relationship to create several extensive portrait series on the Father of His Country. Peale was especially assiduous at commemorating Washington as a military leader, not least because the artist had fought under the general during the New Jersey campaign.

For Peale, the portraits were a means to a livelihood, of course, but they also spoke to his own commitment to the revolutionary cause: Peale was also active in Philadelphia and Pennsylvania politics. Peale's portraits of the revolutionary generation, while celebrating the personal virtues and heroic achievements of individuals, went far to the creation of a civic or public celebration of those men. Private and public ambitions and achievements merged in Peale's handsome effigies in a way that the Founders understood: The appetite for fame (or *fama*, to give the term its classical root in the political ideology of antiquity) was justified when it was directed to a larger societal purpose. Moreover, in a revolutionary ideology founded on individualism, the achievements of the individual would be given their full artistic appreciation within an evolving pantheon of American heroes.

When placed in Peale's Philadelphia Museum, which opened to the public in 1786, the

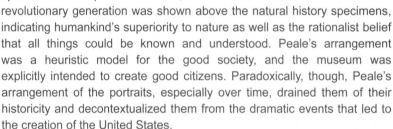

CHARLES WILLSON PEALE
(1741–1827)

revolutionary generation was shown above the natural history specimens, indicating humankind's superiority to nature as well as the rationalist belief that all things could be known and understood. Peale's arrangement was a heuristic model for the good society, and the museum was explicitly intended to create good citizens. Paradoxically, though, Peale's arrangement of the portraits, especially over time, drained them of their historicity and decontextualized them from the dramatic events that led to the creation of the United States.

So long as political history was the dominant mode of the profession, portraits served as illustrative signposts of the nation's political evolution for historians. But by the mid-20th century, political history had fallen dramatically out of fashion. By the turn of the 21st century, it was not even part of the history curricula at most colleges and universities. During the 1960s, as historians pursued a "history from the bottom up," paying attention to the lives of working men and women of all races, both free and enslaved, the very existence of fine art portraiture was taken as evidence of the rule of elite, privileged white men—the phrase "great white fathers" was not coined as a compliment. Political history had suffered the worst fate of all: It was dull.

After World War II, the humanities in America, especially history, undoubtedly needed a shake-up. Under the impact of the first American studies movement and then the influence of the new social history in England that pioneered the study of the lives of labor, the range and scope of historical inquiry was widened and deepened. However, that this should occur alongside and perhaps cause the decay of political history was unfortunate. The spine of political history, which had always provided an armature for scholars around which they could skein their narratives, was lost. But political history was partially culpable in its own demise: It had become a dry recitation of facts about seemingly arcane issues (the tariff, the coinage, political patronage) whose salience was inadequately conveyed to anyone outside a narrow range of specialists.

Fortunately, it appears that we are in the midst of a revival of the fortunes of political history, not least by historians who are eager to link political to social issues. Moreover, there has even been a revived interest in biography. The American public has always hungered to read about exemplary lives, and for scholars, the examination of a specific life is still the most efficient entry point into the past, charting the wider contours of a society against the index of an individual's trajectory.

This preamble necessarily simplifies (or even distorts) a complicated process in American intellectual history. But it is intended to give a backdrop to Professor Allen Guelzo's lively, insightful, and engaging survey of the people and politics of the formative years of the American Republic. First, what Guelzo's lectures confirm is the importance of style to the scholar—and the audience. As history, in the late 19th century, became more objective, "scientific," and professionalized, there was a conscious campaign to make scholarly writing dry, colorless, and certainly unemotional, encouraging presentations that actively discouraged a wider readership. Gulezo's lively, opinionated, and insightful pen portraits are evidence of a welcome reverse trend.

To say that Guelzo is opinionated is only to say that he argues forcefully from the evidence, not that he permits a personal political point of view to drive his narrative. He generally plays things down the middle, basing his narrative on the words of his subjects and explicating the specific arguments that animated the large questions that confronted the nation's leaders. (He also brings in artifacts of material culture and art, including portraiture, not only to illuminate specific points but also to establish more general linkages between the personal and the political.)

Such issues include, but are not limited to, the relationship between the city and the countryside, the beginnings of national fiscal and economic policy, and, above all, the overwhelming problem of slavery. That question would, of course, permeate the American 19th century, from politics to culture to manners and mores—the world that the protean revolutionary generation, so ably depicted by Allen Guelzo, brought into being. ∎

IN CONGRESS.

he unanimous Declara...

We the People

insure domestic Tranquility, provide for the common defen...
and our Posterity, do ordain and establish this Constituti...

Section 1. All legislative Powers herein granted...

SCOPE

*G*overnments, said Samuel Johnson, are "perpetually degenerating towards corruption" and must be rescued "at certain periods by the resuscitation of its first principles, and the re-establishment of its original constitution." The creators of the U.S. Constitution were contemporaries of the great Dr. Johnson, and they would not have disagreed. The question, however, is what method to use in paying that visit to our "first principles." It's been done by legal analysis, by comparative government studies, and even by philosophy. This course, however, uses a different method—biography—to answer the following questions: Who were the Founders? How did their lives shape their ideas, and how did those ideas get a hearing in the creation of the new American republic?

This course begins with George Washington, the indispensable man of our *novus ordo seclorum* ("new order in the heavens"). But it takes in the lives and contributions of both the prominent and the obscure, the brilliant and, on several occasions, the downright fraudulent. The course considers James Madison, often called the father of the Constitution, as well as Patrick Henry, who did his best to obstruct him. It also examines Alexander Hamilton, who almost singlehandedly laid down the architecture of the American economy, and Thomas Jefferson, who tried—and failed—to stop him. The course also includes important figures who have faded over time but deserve some dusting off: the hesitant Edmund Randolph; the rakish and one-legged Gouverneur Morris; Roger Sherman, simple but shrewd; James Wilson, the greatest lawyer in America; and Benjamin Banneker, the African American surveyor. Over the course of 36 lectures, there are preachers, such as Timothy Dwight (lecture 30); judges, such as John Marshall (lecture 34); and even printers, such as David Claypoole and John Dunlap (lecture 19), who printed the first broadside copies of the Constitution. But there are also the scoundrels: Aaron Burr (lecture 33), the chief of American scoundrels; Thomas Mifflin (lecture 2), a political scoundrel; and Daniel Shays (lecture 6), the Massachusetts rebel.

Each lecture that makes up this course takes one of these Founders as its target, using that individual's principles, ambitions, foibles, suspicions, and words to create a whole picture of the Americans who fashioned our "first principles." In the first six lectures, you will meet (in addition to George Washington), Thomas Mifflin, Robert Morris, Ben Franklin, Thomas Jefferson, and Daniel Shays and learn from them how the ending of the American Revolution in 1783 only seemed to increase the anxieties of these Americans about their future. The following four lectures set up the solutions proposed by James Madison, Alexander Hamilton, and Patrick Henry.

Over the course of lectures 11 through 18, the eyes of Edmund Randolph, James Wilson, Elbridge Gerry, Roger Sherman, William Paterson, and David Brearley will be used to watch the Constitutional Convention slowly weld together a new government for the republic and then move through the next four lectures to understand how and why people as well intentioned as Patrick Henry and Alexander Hamilton could take such violently different positions on whether to ratify the Constitution. For the next 14 lectures, you will discover how George Washington, John Adams, Thomas Jefferson, and James Madison struggled as presidents to bring the Constitution to bear on the problems of the republic. In the process, you will watch John Jay craft an important but controversial treaty (lecture 27), sober up with William Findley and the challenge of the Whiskey Rebellion (lecture 25), admire James McHenry for creating an army (lecture 31), and wince as Aaron Burr commits treason (lecture 33). The course will end with a retrospective, using the observations of a French visitor, Alexis de Tocqueville, to see what the finished product of the Founders' work looked like (lecture 36).

They are quite a gang: Rufus King, attacking slavery in lecture 17; Robert Morris, lending money in lecture 3; Hector Crèvecoeur, praising "this new man, the American" in lecture 29. Together, they form maybe the most collectively gifted lineup of saints and sinners that ever lived in one generation and in one place. You'll meet them all, and those "first principles," in this course. ■

GEORGE WASHINGTON'S DOUBTS

*T*he U.S. Constitution is the oldest continuously operating instrument of government in the world. Since the Constitution was ratified in 1788, we have undergone a civil war and two world wars, industrialization on a vast scale, and the emergence of a society whose sheer diversity exceeds anything since the days of the Roman Empire. Yet many believe that whenever we encounter some unprecedented crisis or problem in American life and develop a novel way of responding to it, the Constitution prohibits it. Indeed, those who wrote the constitution were all white, reasonably wealthy men, who wore knee britches and buckle shoes. We might well ask what mysterious power they should have over a generation six times removed from them.

WHO WERE THE FOUNDERS?

> ➢ Almost from the beginning, the men who wrote the U.S. Constitution—and the document they produced—have been accorded an almost mystical reverence, but who were these men who created the Constitution? Were they the offspring of the gods, like Hercules? Were they mythical progenitors of great dynasties and states, like Aeneas, or mighty conquerors, like Alexander? The answer to all these questions is: Don't be silly.

> ➢ Some of these men were dignified, but others were small and tending toward hypochondria, such as James Madison. Some were wise beyond their years when they sat down to write—and none more so than Alexander Hamilton—and some were a disaster almost every time they stood up and spoke off-the-cuff—which brings Hamilton to mind again.

> ➢ Some of them hated each other; John Adams and Benjamin Franklin had all the fellow-feeling of Sherlock Holmes and Professor Moriarty. Some of them saw friendships of many years break up over the Constitution, while others who disagreed violently over the Constitution somehow managed to remain close. They had both clay feet and golden minds, and it was the rare bird in this flock who was entirely one or the other.

> ➢ What may be a real mystery for us is who we should actually include in this unusual company. We speak of these men as the *Framers*, the *Founders*, or even the *Founding Fathers*. But the founding of the American Republic was a process that involved more than writing the Constitution; it included the Continental Congress, which guided American affairs during the Revolution, negotiated with foreign allies, and wrote the Declaration and the peace treaty that made us an independent nation.

> ➢ By various counts, such as signers of the Declaration, we come up with a variety of names of the Founders, including John Adams, Benjamin Franklin, Thomas Jefferson, Robert Morris, and John

Witherspoon. But we also omit some of those who seem to be vital, such as George Washington, James Madison, Alexander Hamilton, and others. And our list would also include some peculiar names we may never have heard.

➢ Putting together various signing lists, we end up with some overlapping areas that encompass a few prominent names intermittently popping up, surrounded by a large population of here-today-gone-tomorrow mediocrities. In this course, we will look at many well-known figures and some who are not quite so well-known but proved indispensable to the founding, including William Paterson, Elbridge Gerry, Thomas Mifflin, Daniel Shays, Edmund Randolph, and James McHenry. Each lecture will be built around a single Founder, will illustrate a particular challenge, and will show how that individual struggled to come to terms with it.

➢ We will cast our net widely in terms of a timeframe, as well, bracketing not just the Constitutional Convention and the ratification of the Constitution but the overall planting-time of the republic, from the ambiguities and dislocations at the end of the Revolution and the Articles of Confederation, through the Constitutional Convention, to the great tests of the "successful administering" of the Constitution in the presidential administrations of Washington, Adams, Jefferson, Madison, and Monroe.

➢ We'll close with a figure who wasn't even an American citizen, Alexis de Tocqueville, who toured the United States in 1831 to 1832 to gather material for his great study, *Democracy in America*. We will let Tocqueville be the voice who provides an answer to the question with which the course begins: Would the "experiment" in creating a republic—a government based on the consent of the governed rather than the authority of kings—really work?

➢ We'll hear first from a voice that posed that question once the battle smoke of the Revolution had blown away and a treaty of peace had been signed with Britain—a voice belonging to someone whose claim to be a Founder hardly even needs to be explained,

GEORGE WASHINGTON
(1732–1799)

much less defended—the voice of George Washington. But even Washington had his doubts about whether the whole enterprise might turn out to be a fool's errand.

WASHINGTON ON THE REPUBLIC

➢ Washington was ordinarily not a man given to much self-searching and was privately embarrassed in the company of lawyers and scholars. "I have not leisure to turn my thoughts to commentaries," he sighed in a letter in 1785, "a consciousness of defective education, and a certainty of the want of time, unfit me for such an undertaking." Yet at age 53, he soared above the reputations of all his fellow Americans as the soldier who had held off the British for seven long years and ensured American independence, then resigned it all to return to the life of a Virginia gentleman in peace.

➢ He might have remained in retirement at Mount Vernon, but in the two years that had passed since his resignation as the commanding general of the Continental Army, the "principles of republicanism" were not wearing well. It had been one of the cardinal tenets of the Enlightenment that republics, however much they be the most natural form of human society, are also the most vulnerable.

   ◆ For one thing, republics—unlike monarchies—are held together by the virtue, public-spiritedness, and self-denial of the people. Sovereignty, after all, rests in a republic with the people, rather than with kings or nobles, and if the people prove to be corrupt, selfish, and indolent, they will bring the roof of their republic down on their heads faster than any hostile emperor could.

   ◆ Further, republics were supposed to work only on a relatively small scale, like the city-state republics of Renaissance Italy, the cantons of Switzerland, or the ancient Roman Republic. Size dissipated the energies and fellow-feeling of republican citizens and left large-scale republics open to internal tumult and dissolution. It did not help, either, that the history of past republics was a history of failure, tainted by the persistence of hierarchy.

➢ What Washington saw in post-Revolutionary America made him afraid on all three counts. With the end of the Revolution, Americans found themselves released from the economic constraints placed on them by the former British colonial overlords and went on a binge of speculation and consumption. The bubble, as bubbles always do, burst in the spring of 1784.

- Five banking houses in London that had allowed Americans to buy on credit went bust because Americans ran out of specie (hard coin) with which to pay their debts; suddenly, American merchants could buy nothing further and closed their own doors. Credit collapsed, land values fell, mortgages defaulted, and worst of all, the people behaved like savages instead of republican citizens.

- Nor did the Articles of Confederation, which had been ratified as a governing instrument by the new United States in 1781, have much power to deal with this sudden evaporation of virtue. Based on the distaste for imperial rule they had experienced under the British, the members of the Continental Congress had deliberately created a minuscule government. This might have been acceptable in a small Florentine republic in the 15th century but did not promise much as a government for a nation that included around 3.5 million people and close to 900,000 square miles.

- The Congress created by the Articles of Confederation had no power to levy taxes on the states, which meant that the United States had no reliable way of repaying its wartime debts to bankers in Paris and Amsterdam; without that authority, no one would lend to Americans.

- Nor did the Confederation government have much sway even closer to home; the 13 colonies that had thrown off British allegiance in 1776 retained significant powers for themselves, even as they became member-states in the new Confederation—powers that they did not hesitate to use against each other in economic disputes, in printing worthless paper money to pay debts, and in enacting laws that prevented sellers and lenders from collecting what they were owed. This lethal combination of increased taxes and a deflated currency produced misery, but debt-relief laws passed by the state legislatures only jeopardized the future of capital borrowing.

➤ This was not the kind of republicanism that Washington had fought for. "Our Independence … our respectability and consequence in Europe … our greatness as a Nation, hereafter, depend upon … giving sufficient powers to Congress," he warned in 1781. Otherwise, "each Assembly, under its present Constitution, will be annihilated, and we must once more return to the Government of G: Britain."

➤ Even after the peace treaty with Britain was signed in 1783, Washington wondered whether "the want of energy in the Federal government, the pulling of one state and party of states against another and the commotion amongst the Eastern people have sunk our national character much below par" and "brought our politics and credit to the brink of a precipice."

GEORGE WASHINGTON

➤ The British government, incensed at American defaults, was threatening to retain control over forts on the frontier that it was supposed to have surrendered under the peace treaty. "Notwithstanding the boasted virtue of America," Washington wrote in dismay to John Jay, "it is more than probable that we shall exhibit the last melancholy proof, that mankind are not competent to their own Government without the means of coercion in the Sovereign."

> What Washington was looking at was a catastrophe not just for America but for the entire principle of government by a people competent to administer their own affairs. But if reason and virtue were not sufficient to guide the affairs of the American people, what was? By 1786, the need to answer that question had become the single greatest vexation of Washington's life.

SUGGESTED READING

Bernstein, *The Founding Fathers Reconsidered*, chap. 1 and appendix.
Diggins, *On Hallowed Ground*, chaps. 2–3.

QUESTIONS TO CONSIDER

1. What qualifies someone to be regarded as a Founder?

2. What made George Washington afraid for the future of the American republic?

Lecture 2

THOMAS MIFFLIN'S CONGRESS

*W*e do not have long memories of the first nine presidents, who all served under the Constitution of 1781. In fact, before the Revolutionary War was over, America had a different constitution and a succession of different presidents, who were, strictly speaking, presidents of Congress. They had been elected by the membership of the Congress created by America's first constitution, the Articles of Confederation. Each served only a year's term, and only one— John Hancock—was necessarily memorable. Third on this list was Thomas Mifflin. In this lecture, we'll learn about the problems Mifflin faced during his year in office.

BACKGROUND ON MIFFLIN

➢ Mifflin was almost 40 on the day in 1783 when Washington appeared before him in the Annapolis State House to resign as general-in-chief of the army. Mifflin had been born into a well-off family of Pennsylvania Quakers who were torn between the Quaker demand for simplicity and self-denial and a desire for Thomas to enjoy the fairly substantial collection of worldly goods his industrious father had won for the family.

THOMAS MIFFLIN
(1744–1800)

  ◆ Young Mifflin was educated at the College of Philadelphia. As soon as he graduated, he was suitably positioned with a Philadelphia merchant, married a well-connected cousin, and went into business with his brother George in 1765 in a store in Philadelphia.

  ◆ Money flowed into Mifflin's grasp with unQuakerly effortlessness, and by 1770, various high-profile public-service appointments were falling into his lap: city warden, manager of the Pennsylvania Hospital, director of the Library Company, and trustee of his alma mater.

➢ The coming of the American Revolution did nothing to disturb the arc of Mifflin's rise. He was one of the supporters of the embargo on British imports that protested the Stamp Act, was elected to the Pennsylvania Assembly in 1772, and was named to represent Pennsylvania in the First Continental Congress in 1774. When the news of Lexington and Concord arrived, Mifflin organized a military company of his own, and with the organization of the Continental Army, Washington tapped Mifflin as a staff member.

➤ Although Mifflin quickly climbed the ladder of rank, something about this man with the silver Quaker spoon in his mouth seems to have acquired tarnish for Washington. In 1775, Washington shunted Mifflin from front-line service to quartermaster-general of the army. This affronted Mifflin, who conceived of himself as a military genius; although he sullenly agreed to serve, he never ceased to agitate for restoration to field command. When front-line command failed to materialize, Mifflin turned his disappointment on Washington.

➤ Bitterly critical of Washington's failed attempt to defend Philadelphia in 1777, Mifflin resigned his commission and joined the agitators known as the Conway Cabal who were seeking to depose Washington as general-in-chief. The conspiracy failed, but Mifflin was soon back in the political saddle as a member of the Continental Congress, and in November 1783, he was elected the third president of Congress under the Articles of Confederation.

FINANCIAL DIFFICULTIES

➤ And there began Mifflin's career of woe. The American colonies had always had closer ties, individually, to Great Britain than they had had to each other; indeed, it had been no small achievement to even get the states send representatives to the Stamp Act Congress in 1765 and the Continental Congress in 1774 and 1775.

➤ As it was, the Continental Congress was merely a deliberative body: It had no official powers, no revenue to pay bills, and no means of enforcing its decisions apart from the army, which it paid in such a penny-pinching matter that it was twice on the edge of mutiny.

- > The states themselves sometimes seemed more intent on pursuing their own agendas than in a joint effort to fight off the British. Virginia sent militia beyond the Appalachians to stake claims to territory in the west; Connecticut and Pennsylvania fought over who had proper title to Wyoming Valley in northeastern Pennsylvania; and so on. It was only when America's French allies made it clear that they would do nothing more for the Americans until they submitted to a common government that the delegations in Congress adopted the Articles of Confederation.

  - ◆ Even then, the Articles stated, "Each state retains its sovereignty, freedom, and independence, and every power, jurisdiction, and right." And it took four years, from 1777 until 1781, before the states finally ratified the Articles.

  - ◆ The ratification was greeted with the discharge of artillery in Philadelphia and Delaware, but otherwise, the Continental Congress simply continued to conduct business as usual, now as the Confederation Congress. And the Continental Congress's presiding officer, Samuel Huntington, continued in that role until Thomas McKean was elected as the first president under the articles.

- > But the surrender of British forces at Yorktown in the fall of 1781 gave less cause for rejoicing than might be thought. The articles had provided no new means of raising revenue, and the wartime debts Congress had incurred to the French government, Dutch bankers, Americans, and others totaled more than $410 million.

- > By the time Mifflin had assumed the role of president, the Confederation Congress had tried to remedy its financial woes by proposing the adoption of a federal import tariff, known as an *impost*. This amounted to a 5 percent tariff on all foreign goods imported into the States. This was not a particularly onerous measure—the total proceeds would have done little more than keep up interest payments—but even so, the impost failed in 1782 and again in 1783.

THE CONTINENTAL ARMY

➤ Nor was this the only problem confronting President Mifflin when he assumed office on November 3, 1783. The Continental Army, underpaid and undervalued, had nearly taken Congress by the neck in 1781, when the Pennsylvania regiments, starving and shivering in camp in New Jersey, sent an angry delegation of sergeants to Philadelphia to meet with a committee of Congress about their grievances.

➤ A far more ominous outburst occurred at the beginning of 1783, when a delegation comprising General Alexander McDougall and two colonels showed up in Philadelphia to meet with Congress. Not only had they gone unpaid, but with the nearness of peace, they suspected that Congress would attempt to disband the Army and send it home with nothing more than promises.

➤ Washington himself would give no countenance to what was an attempt to frighten Congress into action, and he staged a showdown at Newburgh, New York, in March with his officers, to make it plain that he wanted neither part nor lot with any plans to use force on Congress. But in June, 80 men of the Third Pennsylvania Regiment took matters in their own hands, marched on Philadelphia, surrounded the State House (now Independence Hall) where Congress was sitting, and menacingly warned Congress to act.

➤ Congress promptly adjourned, with outgoing President Elias Boudinot wisely announcing that the next session would convene

on June 26 in Princeton, New Jersey. It did—after a fashion. It took another month, until July 29, for a quorum of Congress's 23 members to show up. Nor was it always possible to keep a quorum once obtained; thus, Congress resolved to move again, to Annapolis.

TREATY WITH THE BRITISH

➤ It was an omen that Congress had elected Mifflin as president the day before adjourning in Princeton—while Mifflin was not in attendance. On November 22, the newly arrived Treaty of Peace between Great Britain and the United States was delivered to Mifflin in Philadelphia, and if ever a topic should have brought a quorum to a congressional session, it should have been the vote ratifying the treaty, especially since the British had set a deadline of March for acceptance.

   ◆ But neither the treaty nor Mifflin could make a quorum happen; every state had to send at least two delegates under the articles, and seven such state delegations had shown up by December 13. But three days later, Jefferson, serving as a delegate from Virginia, complained that there was no certainty that the other delegations would appear.

   ◆ Mifflin had to prod by letter delegations from New Hampshire, Connecticut, New York, New Jersey, South Carolina, and

Georgia because "the safety, honor and good faith of the United States require the immediate attendance of their delegates in Congress."

♦ In fact, Congress would not have enough representatives on hand in Annapolis to take a vote on the treaty until January 14. Only because the British wanted peace as badly as the Americans was the deadline finally extended until May 12, when the ratifications were formally exchanged.

♦ Thereafter, even the feeble urgency summoned up by the peace treaty disappeared: Over the next four months in Annapolis, Congress was able to achieve a quorum on only three days; the others were passed in adopting "teasing resolutions."

♦ When Congress finally adjourned on June 3, it resolved to reconvene in Trenton. There, it would elect a new president to relieve the unhappy Mifflin. It proceeded to wait for nearly a full month before enough delegations showed up to elect Richard Henry Lee as Mifflin's successor. In January 1785, Congress would move again, this time to New York City, where it would end its days four years later.

SUMMING UP THE CONFEDERATION CONGRESS

➤ The Confederation Congress was not a total failure. It managed to head off further conflict between states with claims on western land, and it wrote trade agreements with Britain, France, and Spain. It struggled to recall a substantial portion of the valueless paper money and certificates it had put into circulation during the Revolution. It also successfully demobilized the Continental Army before it could turn on its creator.

➤ But none of those accomplishments could dispel the larger cloud of failure that hung over the Confederation and, perhaps, over the American cause itself. "It has already been spread throughout Europe by the emissaries of the British Court," wrote North

Carolina representative Richard Spaight, "that the United States are only united in name and that a little time will show that we are incapable of governing ourselves."

➢ Mifflin retired from his congressional presidency and spent most of the remaining 16 years of his life in Pennsylvania politics and in what one critic described as "a state of adultery with many women." Several towns and structures were named for him, but he also burned through most of his family's fortune and ended up hiding from bill collectors. One wonders, in that light, if Mifflin might not have seen a glint in Washington's eye as the general-in-chief handed over his commission in 1783: My troubles are now over, and yours have just begun.

SUGGESTED READING

Burnett, *The Continental Congress*, chaps. 28–30.
Jensen, *The New Nation*, part 4.

QUESTIONS TO CONSIDER

1. Why did the impost fail?

2. Are there any things that the Confederation Congress did right?

Lecture 3

ROBERT MORRIS'S MONEY

*T*he Confederation Congress was not the only government in America with money problems, or, for that matter, even the worst problems. That the Congress had no practical way of dealing with those woes was bad, but the states didn't have the means to deal with their money problems either, and the decisions they made about those problems almost make the paralysis of the Confederation Congress look appealing. In this lecture, we'll explore those decisions and, in particular, the contribution made by the Philadelphia merchant Robert Morris.

FINANCING THE REVOLUTION

➢ Financial problems appeared in the states almost as soon as the Revolution began. In the spring of 1775, the Pennsylvania Assembly began purchasing firearms and stores and established a 25-member Committee of Safety to oversee the purchases. Benjamin Franklin was named the committee's chair, but the real leadership fell to a Philadelphia merchant, Robert Morris, a partner in the Philadelphia trading firm of Willing & Morris.

➢ At the time, no one knew what the costs of the conflict with Britain might be, and the Pennsylvania treasury was, until new tax measures were passed and funds collected, wholly inadequate to the first demands made on it. Morris obligingly advanced to the state £25,000 from his own purse, but this amount didn't last long.

➢ When the Pennsylvania Assembly turned to consider raising new funds through tax revenues, it encountered the unpleasant legacy all the colonies had inherited from British policy over the previous quarter century. The fundamental problem was that America's most abundant asset was land; its least abundant was specie—hard coin.

  ◆ This was, in large measure, a product of British commercial regulation. Britain's transatlantic commercial philosophy was built around *mercantilism*, which assumed that national wealth was a zero-sum game: Every nation started with a piece of the pie of wealth and could only become richer by taking pieces of other's peoples' slices. The means for doing so were threefold: (1) Create financial reserves of hard coin; (2) regulate the nation's economy to produce goods for which other countries would pay hard coin; and (3) establish colonies in places with valuable resources that could be extracted.

  ◆ By these means, Britain starved its colonies of specie. Every piece of British commercial legislation from 1660 onward reached deeper into the colonial economies to ensure that the colonies served Britain's economic interests. The colonies got by for themselves by issuing paper currency and IOUs in the form of tax-anticipation notes and land banks, which lent money to farmers for improvements, taking their existing land as collateral.

♦ But Parliament forbade the creation of corporations or banks in the colonies; thus, there was no mechanism for accumulating significant reserves from what small amounts of specie came into American hands. For such merchants as Morris, business transactions were handled through privately written IOUs known as *bills of credit* or *bills of exchange*. By the outbreak of the Revolution, three-quarters of all the money circulating in the colonies was paper of various sorts.

PAPER CURRENCY

➤ Both Congress and the states were ill-equipped to meet the sudden demand for financing the Revolution. In both cases, the most familiar expedient was the issue of massive amounts of paper currency. By the end of the Revolution, 7 of the 13 states had authorized the emission of paper money.

➤ Thus, while the Confederation Congress limped by on grudging foreign loans and contributions from the states, the states themselves felt free to print their own money. Further, farmers and small-scale borrowers discovered that this a painless way to make their own commercial debts disappear. Loans and mortgages that had been contracted before the Revolution could now be effortlessly paid off in cheap paper currency. And if lenders and merchants balked at accepting the paper money, the legislatures passed penalty laws that criminalized such refusals.

➤ The depreciating paper currency also created a problem between states. When merchants in Massachusetts or Connecticut demanded payment for goods sold in Rhode Island and were presented with paper currency they knew was worthless anyplace except Rhode Island, there was nothing the Rhode Island legislature could do to reach across state boundaries and compel them to accept the money. Nevertheless, the legislature permitted Rhode Islanders to pay the amounts owed in Rhode Island currency to the Rhode Island courts, which then declared the out-of-state debts legally satisfied. This triggered an uproar in the Confederation Congress.

➢ The frustration felt over the behavior of Rhode Island and other states had a much more dangerous political corollary, because it suggested that republican forms of government, which lodged sovereignty in the people as a whole, would sooner or later prove that large numbers of those people were wholly unworthy to exercise sovereignty—that given political power, they would embark on increasingly reckless schemes for defrauding others.

➢ But in the state legislatures, such complaints were dismissed as the whining of the rich and propertied. In Philadelphia, the *Freemans' Journal* indignantly prophesied that without paper money, the people will "shrink in despair from the magnitude and frequency of the tax bills." Paper money is, in fact, "the traditional medium of America."

MORRIS AS SUPERINTENDENT OF FINANCE

➢ Robert Morris was originally from Liverpool and came to the colonies when he was 13. His father eventually apprenticed the boy to a merchant in Philadelphia, Charles Willing. When Willing died in 1754, Morris was made a partner in the company. He rose in wealth and standing, eventually being appointed as a port warden for Philadelphia and, in 1775, was tagged to represent Pennsylvania in the Second Continental Congress.

➢ Morris was dubious about the wisdom of independence but signed the Declaration of Independence anyway; he was also dubious about the wisdom of Pennsylvania's new state constitution. But none of these doubts prevented him from advancing money from

ROBERT MORRIS
(1734–1806)

his own pocket to pay the Revolution's bills, probably, all told, more than £1 million. Not surprisingly, when the Confederation Congress moved in February 1781 to create three "executive" offices to manage its day-to-day affairs, Morris was unanimously named superintendent of finance.

➢ Morris, however, did not accept the post until May of 1781, and even then only on the conditions that: (1) he concentrate solely on a new financial system, not the payment of old debts, (2) that he have full power to appoint and dismiss "all person whatever that are concerned in the official Expenditure of Public Monies," and (3) that he be permitted to carry on his own private business affairs at the same time.

➢ Morris achieved a series of small financial wonders for the Confederation Congress, including new loans from the French and the Dutch, but he also made enemies. The Virginian William Lee, whose brother Richard Henry Lee had proposed the original motion for independence in 1776, denounced Morris as the "most dangerous man in America" and accused him of plunging the country into "public Bankruptcy, while he at the same time amassed an immense fortune for himself."

➢ In July 1779, a congressional committee report attacked Morris for profiteering. But even more damning to his reputation was his opposition to paper money. From 1779 until his appointment as superintendent of finance, Morris fought the issue of paper money in the Pennsylvania Assembly, especially when it was suggested that Pennsylvania's paper money, like Rhode Island's, be declared legal tender, with penalties for non-acceptance. Morris was eventually acquitted of all charges, but not before they had almost cost him his life.

◆ On October 4, 1779, a street mob, whipped up by charges that Morris was at the heart of all their economic woes, attacked Morris and other members of a "Republican Society" at City Tavern in Philadelphia. Morris and the Society retreated to the home of James Wilson, and when the mob pursued them, they barricaded the doors.

◆ Someone began shooting, and in short order, the mob stormed the house, breaking down the doors and trading gunfire on the stairs. The mob wheeled up a small howitzer but was eventually dispersed.

➢ No one could have blamed Morris after the "battle of Fort Wilson" for washing his hands completely of public affairs; nor could anyone in Congress blame him for driving a hard bargain over his powers as superintendent of finance in 1781.

➢ William Livingston, the governor of New Jersey, tried to soothe Morris's disgruntlement with the assurance that "you have done too much for your Country not to create Enemies," but it was also true that the Revolution had spawned what one Boston newspaper complained about as a "private, selfish, and basely avaricious spirit … in the room of public virtue." It was difficult for Morris to insist on strict financial probity when American "commerce is so managed, as that it becomes a public nuisance, instead of a common benefit."

➢ But as clearly as Morris understood that America's chief peril lay in "the derangement of our Money Affairs," he could not get the states or the Confederation Congress to agree to any solution he proposed. On July 29, 1782, Morris submitted to the Confederation Congress an ambitious plan for restoring "the intimate Connection between the Commerce, the Agriculture and the Finances of a Country" that included:

- The approval of the 5 percent impost passed by Congress in 1781

- A national property tax on land

- The recall of paper money by exchanging it for a national loan offered at 4 percent interest

- The establishment of a Bank of North America.

➢ Rhode Island sabotaged the impost by refusing to approve it, and a renewed initiative for it in 1784 failed, as well. The Bank of North America was chartered by the Confederation Congress, incorporated by the Pennsylvania Assembly, and began operations in 1782. But in 1785, Morris's enemies in the Pennsylvania

Assembly engineered a repeal of the state incorporation of the bank.

➢ Morris damaged his own standing by egging on the Continental Army's mutiny in in the hope that he could somehow use the soldiers' threat to beat back his foes and critics. By October of 1783, the Massachusetts legislature was instructing its delegation to the Confederation Congress to "have the office of the superintendent of finance abolished."

➢ Disgusted, Morris turned in his resignation and left his post on November 1, 1784. "My Attention to the Public Debts," he wrote the president of Congress, Elias Boudinot, "arose from the Conviction that funding them on solid Revenues was the last essential Work of our glorious Revolution. … But other Circumstances have postponed the Establishment of public Credit in such Manner, that I fear it will never be made." And Massachusetts, ironically, would soon offer the first proof of Morris's dread.

SUGGESTED READING

Main, *The Anti-Federalists*, chaps. 4–5.
Rappleye, *Robert Morris*, chaps. 12–14.

QUESTIONS TO CONSIDER

1. What was specie, and why didn't Americans seem to have any?

2. What caused the "battle of Fort Wilson"?

Lecture 4

BENJAMIN FRANKLIN'S LEATHER APRON

"*A*merica has sent us many things," wrote the philosopher David Hume to Benjamin Franklin, "but you are … the first great man of letters, for whom we are beholden to her." Franklin had been awarded the Royal Society's Copley Medal for his experiments with electricity, named a member of France's Académie des Sciences, and showered with honorary doctorates. In 1774, his fellow Philadelphian Benjamin Rush marveled over Franklin, saying that his name would be "handed down to posterity among the first and greatest characters of the world." And no one had worked harder throughout his life to make himself into an object of honor, especially considering the low rung of the ladder of his birth.

FRANKLIN'S EARLY CAREER

➤ Benjamin Franklin was born in Boston on January 17, 1706, one of 17 children sired by Josiah Franklin. In 1717, Benjamin was apprenticed to his brother James, a printer. This initially satisfied Benjamin, who had always loved reading, but reading was not what James wanted from his brother, and in 1720, Benjamin ran away to Philadelphia.

➤ The city of Philadelphia was less than 40 years old when Franklin disembarked at the foot of Market Street, but it already was home to 2,000 people and the seat of government of Pennsylvania's ruling family, the Penns.

♦ William Penn, the founder of the Pennsylvania colony, had obtained his charter as an absolute proprietorship, which meant that he and his heirs literally owned Pennsylvania in the old manner of medieval lords. But Penn had not had a cheerfully medieval time managing the colony.

♦ Penn was a convert to Quakerism, which imposed on him an ethic of nonviolence and decision making by consensus that turned out to be poor instruments for governing a colony. Penn's sons and heirs, however, clung tightly to the family proprietorship, insisting on the right to collect quit-rents and name the colony's governor.

➤ In Philadelphia, Franklin found work with another printer, Samuel Keimer. He then traveled to London for a business venture with the governor of Pennsylvania, Sir William Keith, but found himself stranded abroad when Keith's letters of credit proved worthless. Two years later, Franklin returned to Philadelphia and set himself as an independent printer. He became a model of the industrious, leather-apron tradesman.

➤ Franklin produced a newspaper, the *Pennsylvania Gazette*; began issuing *Poor Richard's Almanac*; and in 1730, was named as the

Pennsylvania Assembly's official printer. Six years later, he was elected to a seat in the assembly and, in 1737, was named deputy postmaster for the colonies. Franklin also franchised his print-shop operations to other cities and, by 1743, had interests in three other firms. He bought shares in paper mills, purchased rental

BENJAMIN FRANKLIN
(1706–1790)

properties, and in 1748, had become wealthy enough to retire from active business. He had become a gentleman.

FRANKLIN AS A GENTLEMAN

> In the 18th century, a gentleman did not work with his hands, and Franklin, after 1748, turned his attention to his scientific experiments and to civic leadership. He also transformed himself, as befitted a gentleman, into a man of public affairs. He struck an "appearance of impartiality" in the ongoing struggles of the Penn family to cling to their proprietorship of Pennsylvania, and in 1757, he was rewarded with the lucrative appointment as the colony's agent (lobbyist) in London.

> Franklin served as Pennsylvania's agent until 1762, when he was recalled to become speaker of the Pennsylvania Assembly and lead the effort to have Pennsylvania transformed into a royal colony, with a governor appointed by the king. When that failed, Franklin was again dispatched to England as Pennsylvania's agent to continue the fight. The fight he became involved in, however, was about Parliament's new Stamp Act.

 ◆ It seemed logical to Franklin that the Stamp Act, which extended royal taxing powers into the colonial economy, should be greeted by Pennsylvanians as being of a piece with the effort to replace the proprietors with royal government. It wasn't, and Franklin's support for the Stamp Act caused ripples of outrage in Pennsylvania.

 ◆ Thus, Franklin promptly switched sides again, writing a series of articles for the London press that warned against the consequences of further efforts at imperial taxation. He also released a collection of six letters that had come surreptitiously into his hands, detailing the machinations of Massachusetts' royal governor, Thomas Hutchinson, for "an abridgement of ... English liberties" in the colonies. The Massachusetts Assembly demanded that the king remove

Hutchinson as governor, and hearings were scheduled before the Privy Council, to which Franklin was summoned as a witness.

- If up to this point Franklin believed that he had earned the status of gentleman, the Privy Council hearings soon disabused him of that notion. "Private correspondence has hitherto been held sacred," raged the solicitor-general and leader of the hearings, Alexander Wedderburn. Franklin's behavior stripped him of any pretense to the status of gentleman and returned him to what he was, a colonial laborer who dressed himself above his station, just as the colonies themselves were trying to do.

PENNSYLVANIA GOVERNMENT

➤ In 1775, in the wake of the hearings, Franklin decided to return to Philadelphia, just as the tensions between the colonies and the mother country exploded at Lexington and Concord. He arrived in Philadelphia on May 5, 1775, and within 24 hours, found himself selected by the Pennsylvania Assembly to sit in the Second Continental Congress. Twelve months later, he was appointed, along with Thomas Jefferson and John Adams, to the committee to draft the colonies' Declaration of Independence.

➤ The disruption of the colonies' ties to Britain had been accompanied by the disruption of all the colonial governments that represented British rule, including the overthrow of the Penns' proprietorship. A state convention with Franklin as president proceeded to tear down the old proprietary government and replace it with a government, not of gentlemen but of the people in the streets.

➤ The new Pennsylvania Constitution of 1776 began with a Bill of Rights that included several gems that would have stuck in the craw of both proprietors and gentlemen: "that all men are born equally free"; that "government is, or ought to be, instituted for the common benefit"; and that "the people have a right, at such

periods as they may think proper, to reduce their public officers to a private station, and supply the vacancies by certain and regular elections."

➤ By the time the convention finished its work on the new state constitution in September, it had produced a document that proposed to govern Pennsylvania through a unicameral assembly, abolished all property qualifications for voting (apart from paying "public taxes"), limited terms in the new legislature, and stipulated that elections be held annually.

➤ As radical as it was, the Pennsylvania Constitution of 1776 was a fair counterpart to the Articles of Confederation. It would have been more radical still if the convention had not agreed to delete its most explosive resolution, one allowing the states to discourage possession of large portions of property by individuals. Without the checks and balances provided by a bicameral legislature, the new Pennsylvania Assembly bolted ahead to revoke college charters, override judicial decisions about property, shut down Robert Morris's Bank of North America, and more.

➤ Critics of the Pennsylvania Constitution saw it as wielding too much power, and they found all the proof they needed that power had gone too much into the wrong hands when the street battle over "Fort Wilson" broke out in 1779. The Revolution had been waged on the assumption that power was the enemy of liberty, and while no government could do without some power, it had to be monitored.

➤ It was no consolation that the new assembly could be, by turns, both high-minded and whimsical; in 1780, it would inaugurate a phase-out of slavery in Pennsylvania, but it would also pass legislation that criminalized "profane swearing, cursing, drunkenness." It tried to fix prices, seize the property of suspected Tories and pacifists, impose loyalty oaths, and shut down the College of Philadelphia for "an Evident Hostility to the present Government." Cooler heads in a second house might have tactfully pigeon-holed such legislation but not in a unicameral legislature.

FRANKLIN IN PARIS

➢ In October 1776, the Continental Congress dispatched Franklin to the court of Louis XVI of France to recruit French support and recognition for the new republic. Set aside now were all the pretensions to gentleman's status, and Franklin transformed himself yet again into the very model of Poor Richard, the wise but simple, untutored but intelligent, purely American nobleman.

➢ The transformation was popular in France, and in 1778, Franklin was able to jockey the French into signing an alliance with the United States that turned the tide of the Revolution against Britain. Five years later, he signed the peace treaty that ended the Revolution and guaranteed an independent American Republic.

➢ From his perch in Paris, Franklin issued a stream of assurances to various European inquirers that the new American governments ensured "an enlightened People, with respect to our Political Interests." Yet when he finally returned to Philadelphia, Franklin was more than a little shaken by the results of the Articles of Confederation and the Pennsylvania Constitution.

RETURN TO THE COLONIES

➢ The Pennsylvania Assembly promptly elected Franklin as its president, but that only forced him closer to the oddball operations of the assembly. Robert Morris had been Franklin's chief ally in raising money in Europe for the United States, but Morris was now denounced as a criminal.

➢ In addition, the newspapers Franklin had founded had become unrestrained engines of "affronting, calumniating, and defaming one another." Franklin was also alarmed to find that the scaled-back voting requirements allowed immigrants a voice in

Pennsylvania's government. And it was no comfort to learn from Benjamin Rush that the Pennsylvania Constitution assumed "perfect equality, and an equal distribution of property … among the inhabitants of the state."

➢ Further, Franklin was chagrined that on his return from Europe, the government had made no provision for him as a retired foreign minister. It was, Franklin sighed, always "the reproach thrown on republics, that they are apt to be ungrateful."

➢ If a leather-apron philosopher-cum-gentleman like Franklin could gradually find fault with the new republican experiments he returned to discover on his doorstep, then the way clearly was open for a serious reconsideration of what the Revolution and the states had created in the Articles of Confederation and in state constitutions.

SUGGESTED READING

Isaacson, *Benjamin Franklin*, chap. 16.
Lyons, *The Society for Useful Knowledge*, chaps. 1 and 3.

QUESTIONS TO CONSIDER

1. Define the term *gentleman* in its 18th-century usage.

2. What convinced Franklin that English society would never concede the status of *gentleman* to him?

3. Why did the Pennsylvania Constitution of 1776 lack checks and balances?

Lecture 5

THOMAS JEFFERSON'S BOOKS

*T*homas Jefferson was born near modern Charlottesville, Virginia, in 1743. As an adult, he described his father as "being of a strong mind, sound judgment, and eager after information," and though "my father's education had been quite neglected … he read much and improved himself." The same defect would not be repeated in Thomas Jefferson, whose education began when he was 9. At the age of 17, he was packed off to the College of William and Mary. There, Jefferson studied a curriculum heavy on classical literature, rhetoric, logic, and ethics. In this lecture, we'll look at Jefferson's reading to see its influence on his thought and politics.

THE SCIENTIFIC REVOLUTION

➤ The first European universities offered their students a vision of the world that was wrapped around two principles: authority and hierarchy. The path to truth, wisdom, and beauty had been laid down for all to see in the Bible and the writings of Aristotle. Although the pious raised an eyebrow at Aristotle, both of these sources were understood, ultimately, to be compatible.

➤ The universe was viewed as a rational, reasonable place, in which all the parts fit together logically—a hierarchy. The physical universe was arranged with the earth at the bottom or center, and then, in ascending order of perfection, the moon, planets, stars, and the realm where God dwelled.

   ◆ All these parts of physical nature were, in turn, held together logically by certain relationships to each other based on their possession of certain intelligent or moral qualities. Why do stones fall to earth? Because they share a common moral quality of baseness with the earth that causes them to seek the earth's level.

   ◆ Human society followed the same pattern of hierarchy, like a pyramid, in which kings ruled over nobles and nobles ruled over the commons. Human society, too, was held in place by differing qualities and status: Why did more peasants than kings die of smallpox? Because peasants were inherently closer to the earth.

➤ These twin principles of authority and hierarchy gave European intellectual life stability for 400 years, but at the dawn of the 1600s, they cracked.

   ◆ By the beginning of the 17th century, new telescopes were available through which to behold the heavens. And when astronomical observers, such as Galileo Galilei, looked through those telescopes, they did not see much that looked like hierarchy.

♦ The earth, of course, everyone knew to be deformed by mountains, valleys, and so on, but when Galileo trained his telescope on the moon, he discovered that it was even more uneven and disfigured. By Aristotle's reasoning, the moon, since it was higher than the earth, ought to have been more perfect in shape. It wasn't; nor were the other planets.

♦ Nor, Galileo soon concluded, were the physical movements of the moon and the planets governed by moral relationships of superiority and inferiority to each other. Put a round ball on a flat plane, Galileo argued, and it will roll on forever, without any concern for the occult qualities possessed either by the plane or by itself.

➢ When Isaac Newton refined this to explain the movement of all physical objects in terms of a simple force ("attraction at a distance"), then the idea of the universe as a harmonious whole, with its various parts adhering to each other on the basis of their possession of intelligent qualities, went by the wayside. The universe became an assortment of material substances, governed only by indifferent physical laws and forces. And one no longer searched in the Bible and Aristotle for truth, wisdom, or beauty, but in the world. This was the start of the Scientific Revolution.

THE ENLIGHTENMENT

➢ It took no great length of time before Europeans began wondering whether the same rules that shattered the hierarchy of physical nature might not be applied to the hierarchy of human society. Were there natural laws of politics that paralleled natural physical laws? The task of discovering such social laws fell especially to John Locke, Adam Smith, and Montesquieu.

➢ Locke, for instance, asked readers in his *Two Treatises of Government* to perform a thought experiment. Suppose several of us were shipwrecked on a deserted island. In order to eat, we would need to begin harvesting fruit and berries, then plant crops for harvest. Investing our labor in producing food from the land is what sanctions our calling this land our *property*.

JOHN LOCKE
(1632–1704)

♦ But another fact would soon impress itself on us: Some people would rather steal other people's harvest or property than do the work themselves. Thus, it would become necessary to improvise some form of social organization or risk descending into cannibalism and murder.

♦ We are in what Locke called "a state of nature," and in that state, we are free to do what we wish. If we are successful, we manage to plant crops, hunt game, and build shelters, but to get security for our property, we must surrender a portion of the freedom we enjoyed in the state of nature and institute a political society.

♦ That, for Locke, explained the natural laws of politics. Every society emerges as an organized whole because people need to look out for their property—not because some royal law-giver imposes divine order. And whenever a society decays or is diverted from that basic purpose of protecting rights and property, the people who made that society can devise something new.

- ◆ Locke was happy for British society to remain a monarchy, because he regarded the British system as the mildest form of monarchy in the world. But there had always been more radical voices, arguing that monarchs of any sort were an unnatural imposition on the sovereignty of the people, and therefore, the only true and natural form of government was a republic.

➢ What was true for politics would also be true for economics. As long as society was conceived of as a hierarchy, kings were assured the top spot, followed by nobles and the commons. The idea that there might be another class, composed of tradesmen, merchants, and bankers, excited only disdain from the nobles and resentment from the commons. But to Adam Smith, if there was any virtue to be found in human society, it was in that much-despised commercial class, whose sober concentration on profit and trade was the real enrichment of everyone.

➢ Just as the protection of property explained to Locke the reason for government, trade explained to Smith what made societies happy and prosperous. Taken together, this new understanding of society and

ADAM SMITH
(1723–1790)

of the physical universe created what was known in English as the Enlightenment.

JEFFERSON'S EDUCATION

➢ James Blair, the first president of William and Mary, corresponded with John Locke, but little in the college's curriculum reflected that connection, and when Jefferson arrived there in 1760 as a student, its minuscule faculty was preoccupied more with adapting the new sciences to the rule of the old logic than emancipating them from it.

➢ Jefferson's real education came from two sources with only tenuous ties to the college: George Wythe, under whom he studied law, and Virginia's lieutenant-governor, Francis Fauquier. Jefferson became part of Fauquier's circle and learned much from him. How much that instruction revolved around Enlightenment poles can be seen from the booklists Jefferson compiled for purchase, which included Locke, Montesquieu, and Adam Smith.

➢ Enlightenment politics came easier for Americans than Englishmen because the history of the colonies seemed to follow precisely the stages of social formation that Locke had described. That the British government would not only fail to understand that but attempt to govern the colonies as though they really were an inferior segment of an imperial hierarchy propelled Jefferson into the colonial resistance movement.

➢ It also set him to work writing, in 1774, one of the resounding statements of that resistance, *A Summary View of the Rights of British America*. "Our ancestors," Jefferson wrote, "possessed a right which nature has given to all men, of … establishing new societies, under such laws and regulations as to them shall seem most likely to promote public happiness." They, and not the king, were the real sovereigns of America.

➢ The reputation Jefferson earned from the *Summary View* got him the ticket as one of Virginia's delegates to the Second Continental Congress, and it was there, in 1776, that he was chosen to draft the Declaration of Independence—his finest statement of Enlightenment politics.

JEFFERSON IN POLITICS

➢ The curious thing about Jefferson's political eloquence is that Jefferson the man did not particularly care for politics or commerce once they had to be translated into everyday affairs. "Science is my passion," he once said, "politics my duty," and it was not a duty he found very agreeable.

➢ He declined reelection to the Continental Congress but agreed to serve in the new Virginia Assembly from 1776 to 1779, when he unenthusiastically allowed himself to be elected governor of Virginia. He was right not to be enthused. The British staged a major invasion of Virginia during his tenure; the assembly printed paper money with abandon; and when he left office, the assembly resolved to hold an inquiry into "the conduct of the Executive of this State for the last twelve months."

➢ Nor can it be said that Jefferson was always consistent, or even generous, in his embrace of the Enlightenment's principles. In 1777, he had been the prime advocate of a statute securing freedom of religion in Virginia. But it was not always clear whether Jefferson meant freedom *of* religion or *from* religion.

➢ Jefferson was also less than enthusiastic about commerce. It was not merchants and trade but "cultivators of the earth" who "are the most valuable citizens," Jefferson insisted to John Jay in 1785, because landowning guaranteed virtue, and virtue was supposed to be the abiding concern of a republic.

➢ But a far more sensational departure from the Enlightenment's denunciation of hierarchy and despotism was the fact that

THOMAS JEFFERSON
(1743–1826)

Jefferson himself was a hierarch and a despot—a large-scale slave owner. He professed opposition to slavery, but that did not prevent him, after the death of his wife in 1782, from taking a slave woman, Sally Hemings, as his lover. He refused to free Hemings from bondage and sired at least five unacknowledged slave children by her.

➢ What Jefferson did see clearly, however, was that the ramshackle structure of the Articles of Confederation was doing nobody in America any good. He half-expected "some two States" to "commit hostilities on each other." In 1784, mourning the death of his wife, Jefferson agreed to become the American diplomatic minister to France, and he found there that "the nonpayment of our debts, and the want of energy in our government" had seriously damaged the "American reputation in Europe."

SUGGESTED READING

Israel, *Democratic Enlightenment*, chaps. 16 and 18.
McDonald, *Novus Ordo Seclorum*, chaps. 3–4.

QUESTIONS TO CONSIDER

1. How did the scientific revolution of the 17th century undermine authority and hierarchy?

2. How did Jefferson capture the spirit of Enlightenment politics in the Declaration of Independence?

Lecture 6

DANIEL SHAYS'S MISBEHAVIOR

*G*eorge Washington was not the only one to have doubts about the wisdom being shown by the Confederation, its Congress, and its presidents. But his doubts existed at one end of a spectrum; at the other end were the unhappy and contentious farmers of western New England. Although there had been comparatively little fighting in New England after 1776, new state governments still had to be formed to replace the provincial ones, the wartime economy completely redirected the usual flows of commerce, and there were soldiers to be recruited for the Continental Army and the state militias. In this lecture, we'll explore the fallout of this economic distress, Shays's Rebellion.

BACKDROP TO THE REBELLION

➢ Like the Confederation Congress and the other states, at the outset of the war, Massachusetts resorted to paying its bills by issuing paper. However, there was so little specie in the hands of the Massachusetts government to back up its currency that it was soon circulating at 1/4 its face value and, by 1781, at 1/40 its face value.

➢ Valiantly, Massachusetts pledged to redeem all of its paper at face value, which was awful for those who had exchanged handfuls of it earlier at the depreciated value, such as discharged soldiers returning to their farms. Conversely, it became a bonanza for speculators in Boston, who bought up state debt at 1/8 or 1/10 its face value and who now stood to gain hugely if and when the state ever managed to redeem the paper.

➢ And redeeming that paper was what the Massachusetts legislature, the General Court, set itself to do—by increasing taxes more than 500 percent and requiring payment in hard coin. Ten percent of the revenue from these taxes would come from state impost and excise taxes; the rest would come from increases in property taxes and poll taxes.

➢ The blow of these tax increases would fall hardest on those who made their living from the land they owned: farmers, who made up 70 percent of the Massachusetts population. And the farmers were the least well-prepared to absorb that blow because few of them dealt in cash.

➢ The new taxes set off two chains of reaction. First, the requirement of paying in specie set off a desperate search for hard coin, which usually meant calling in any IOUs or promissory notes a farmer, store owner, or artisan might have accepted from others. Second, farmers who failed to find enough specie to pay their property and poll taxes found themselves in court, faced with the auction of their farms to satisfy the taxes.

- The General Court and Governor James Bowdoin might have seen what was coming. In 1782, an earlier tax hike payable in specie had triggered an outburst in western Massachusetts' Hampshire County, led by an itinerant preacher named Samuel Ely. Ely was promptly arrested. But furious farmers under a former revolutionary captain descended with 600 men and released Ely from jail. Now, four years later, an even larger outburst was about to occur.

SHAYS'S REBELLION

- The outburst began, as before, in Hampshire County at the end of August 1786. When the court's three judges arrived to open the county court of general sessions, they were stopped by an angry crowd of several hundred men who sought to prevent the court from sitting. The judges tried opening the court session at an inn but ultimately announced that all cases would be continued to the next session in November.

- The next week, the county court in Worcester, less than 50 miles from Boston, was closed down by another angry, armed crowd and announced that it, too, would remain closed until November. From there, the trouble threatened to snowball.

  - The Middlesex County court was prevented from opening on September 11, 1786. The judges called for the assistance of the local militia, but the militia balked, and the judges were eventually advised to leave town for their own good.

  - Two weeks later, when the Supreme Judicial Court of Massachusetts tried to open its session in Springfield, Massachusetts, it took the precaution of having the Hampshire County militia turn out in force under its commander, General William Shepard. Although the militiamen numbered 1,000 or more, their opponents had acquired still greater numbers and a leader in the form of Captain Daniel Shays.

ror either.   JAMES BRYSON.

Pennsylvania, ff.

By the *Prefident* and the *Supreme Ex
ecutive Council* of the Common-
wealth of *Pennfylvania,*
A *PROCLAMATION.*

WHEREAS the General Affembly of this Common-
wealth, by a law entituled 'An act for co-operating with
" the ftate of Maffachufetts bay, agreeable to the articles of
" confederation, in the apprehending of the proclaimed rebels
" DANIEL SHAYS, LUKE DAY, ADAM WHEELER
" and ELI PARSONS," have enacted, " that rewards ad-
" ditional to thofe offered and promifed to be paid by the ftate
" of Maffachufetts Bay, for the apprehending the aforefaid
" rebels, be offered by this ftate ;" WE do hereby offer the
following rewards to any perfon or perfons who fhall, within
the limits of this ftate, apprehend the rebels aforefaid, and
ecure them in the gaol of the city and county of Philadelphia,
---- viz. For the apprehending of the faid Daniel Shays, and
fecuring him as aforefaid, the reward of *One hundred and Fifty
Pounds* lawful money of the ftate of Maffachufetts Bay, and
One Hundred Pounds lawful money of this ftate ; and for the
apprehending the faid Luke Day, Adam Wheeler and Eli
Parfons, and fecuring them as aforefaid, the reward (refpec-
tively) of *One Hundred Pounds* lawful money of Maffachufetts
Bay and *Fifty Pounds* lawful money of this ftate : And all
judges, juftices, fheriffs and conftables are hereby ftrictly en-
joined and required to make diligent fearch and enquiry after,
and to ufe their utmoft endeavours to apprehend and fecure the
faid Daniel Shays, Luke Day, Adam Wheeler and Eli Parfons, their aiders, abettors and comforters, and every of them,
fo that they may be dealt with according to law.

GIVEN in Council, under the hand of the Prefident, and
the Seal of the State, at Philadelphia, this tenth
day of March, in the year of our Lord one thoufand
feven hundred and eighty-feven.

BENJAMIN FRANKLIN.

Attest
JOHN ARMSTRONG, jun. Secretary.

Fox. Sale or Charter

> Born in 1747 in Hopkinton, Massachusetts, Shays had served in
> the Massachusetts militia at Bunker Hill and Ticonderoga in 1775;
> he was then commissioned as a captain in the Fifth Massachusetts
> Regiment and fought at the Battle of Saratoga.

    ◆ Like many of his fellow officers, Shays was paid only fitfully,
       and in 1780, he was forced to resign his commission; he
       simply lacked the money to keep up appearances as an
       officer and a gentleman.

- Shays moved to Pelham, Massachusetts, where he managed to eke out a living as a small farmer. By 1785, he was in debt to 10 different lenders; by 1786, he was already under threat of suit for taxes. But he evidently did not think of himself as an insurgent and turned down an appeal from his Pelham neighbors to join in the closure of the Northampton court.

- By the end of September, however, Shays found himself at the head of "great numbers of people" descending on Springfield. "Finding that the government party were acting on the defensive," Shays sent "an insolent demand" to Shepard's militiamen "that no civil cases should be tried except where both parties were willing." Shepard refused, and Shays had some difficulty restraining his men from attacking the courthouse directly. Because Shays's rebels prevented anyone from entering the courthouse, at length, the court adjourned, and Shepard irritably dismissed the militia.

- Alarmed, Governor Bowdoin called the Massachusetts legislature into special session on September 27 in Boston, and the General Court responded by passing "three different laws for easing the burdens of the people." But it was too little too late. When the Worcester County court attempted to reopen its sessions on November 21, another mob of Shaysites closed them down again.

- By now, Governor Bowdoin was in a panic, as was the Confederation Congress. Not only had the Massachusetts militia proven a weak reed, but the Congress maintained an arsenal at Springfield. If Shays got his hands on those weapons, the rebellion might begin to assume much larger proportions. They would "march directly to Boston," Shays promised, "burn [the courthouse] and lay the town of Boston in ashes."

- The recruitment of 1,340 troops was hastily authorized, but Bowdoin could not wait for the Confederation Congress to come to his rescue. On November 28, he issued arrest warrants for five of the Shaysite leaders closest to Boston. On January 4, he called for the recruitment of 4,400 volunteers to put down the insurrection, privately funded by 153 wealthy Bostonians and commanded by the Revolutionary War hero General Benjamin Lincoln. In two weeks, Lincoln managed to whip his little army into presentable shape and, on January 19, set out to secure the Springfield arsenal and bring Shays to bay.

➢ Shays acted at once to beat Lincoln to the punch, but when he arrived at Springfield with between 1,500 and 2,000 men, he discovered that General Shepard had been faster still and occupied the arsenal with approximately 1,200 militiamen. On January 25, Shays and his officers planned a three-pronged assault on the arsenal, which they hoped would bluff Shepard's militiamen into surrender.

➢ But Shepard was in no mood to be bluffed: He drew up his militia in line of battle in front of the arsenal, planting two artillery pieces along the line. "Shays immediately put his troops in motion & marched on rapidly near one hundred yards," Shepard reported. He tried to stop them by ordering the artillery gunners to fire two warning shots over the Shaysites' heads, "but it had no effect on them."

➢ With the next discharge, Shepard's artillerymen fired "through the centre of [Shays'] column," and the next after that "put the whole column into the utmost confusion." Shays struggled to rally them "but in vain." Shepard was ready to charge "upon their rear and flanks with my infantry and the two field pieces, and could have killed the greater part of the whole army within five minutes." But he had done enough already. Four of Shays's men were dead.

➢ Shays and the remnants of his army retreated northward to Petersham, and there, on February 3, they were surprised by the appearance of Benjamin Lincoln and Governor Bowdoin's private militia. Lincoln captured 150 of them, but most of the others, including Shays, melted into the woods, heading for sanctuary elsewhere. A few made it to Canada, where they appealed to the governor-general, Lord Dorchester, for arms and supplies, but the Foreign Office in London refused, and Shays's Rebellion was over.

THE AFTERMATH

> ➢ Shays's Rebellion touched a deep sense of unease about the stability, not only of Massachusetts but the entire Confederation. "Not only this Commonwealth but the Union at large are in the most confused and confounded condition," wrote Samuel Lyman of Springfield, "We do not yet feel that sameness or unity of interest which is the only cement of any nation, and which is absolutely necessary to be felt in order to make us respectable & important."

> ➢ Still, for all the terror Shays's Rebellion had inspired, Massachusetts proved singularly cautious about turning any of the rebels into martyrs. Two rebels, John Bly and Charles Rose, were hanged on December 6, 1787. Sixteen more were condemned to death but pardoned, while 4,000 of the insurgents signed confessions and took an oath of allegiance to the Commonwealth. Shays himself petitioned successfully for a pardon from Vermont, but he never returned to Massachusetts and died in 1825 in New York.

> ➢ Interestingly, the impact of Shays's Rebellion was more profound the further one moved from its epicenter in Massachusetts. Henry Knox, Washington's former artillery chief and now the Confederation's secretary of war, complained that Shays had sparked "a pretty formidable rebellion" which had determined "to overturn, not only the forms, but the principles of the present constitutions."

>> ◆ Washington's former cavalry general, Henry "Light-Horse Harry" Lee, was convinced that some of their leaders avowed the "subversion" of the Confederation "to be their object together with the abolition of debts, the division of property and re-union with G. Britain." And what was worse, "In all the eastern states the same temper prevails more or less, and

will certainly break forth whenever the opportune moment may arrive."

*   The one silver lining, said Knox, was that Shays's near success had "wrought prodigious changes in the minds of men in that state respecting the powers of government—everybody says they must be strengthened, and that unless this shall be effected, there is no security for liberty and property."

SUGGESTED READING

Richards, *Shays's Rebellion*, chap. 1.
Szatmary, *Shays' Rebellion*, chap. 6.

QUESTIONS TO CONSIDER

1. How did the new Massachusetts taxes create a crisis for farmers such as Daniel Shays?

2. Why did Shays's Rebellion unsettle Washington?

Lecture 7

ALEXANDER HAMILTON'S REPUBLIC

As much as Jefferson, Alexander Hamilton believed that the most natural form of government was a republic in which everyone would have the freedom to exercise his natural rights. Hamilton wrote, "I am affectionately attached to the republican theory. I desire above all things to see the equality of political rights, exclusive of all hereditary distinction, firmly established by a practical demonstration of its being consistent with the order and happiness of society." From that point onward, however, no two individuals among the Founders could have appeared so utterly different than Hamilton and Jefferson. In this lecture, we'll look at Hamilton's view of a republic, as opposed to Jefferson's.

HAMILTON'S EARLY LIFE

> Hamilton was born around 1757 on the island of Nevis in the British West Indies. His father was James Hamilton, and his mother was Rachel Faucett Lavien. Unhappily for Alexander, Rachel not was married to James Hamilton but to Johan Michael Lavien, a planter on the island of St. Croix.

- Rachel eventually succeeded in getting a divorce from her husband but not for the purpose of marrying James Hamilton. Hamilton set up a lackadaisical business on St. Croix,

ALEXANDER HAMILTON
(1755/57–1804)

and then, with the excuse of business matters on St. Kitts, disappeared.

- ❖ Undismayed, Rachel set up her own retail business and farmed 12-year-old Alexander out to a merchant firm, where he flourished. By the time he was 14, his employer was leaving orders and sales in his hands. But he was also bored; life in the British West Indies was a dead-end street for a young man with ambitions.

BY 1770, THE BRITISH SUGAR ISLANDS WERE EXPORTING 132,000 TONS OF SUGAR, 11 MILLION GALLONS OF MOLASSES, AND 41 MILLION LITERS OF RUM—ALL ON THE BACKS OF SLAVE LABOR.

- ➢ The islands of the West Indies were a cockpit of political rivalries between the great European powers, especially the British and the French. Their value lay in the commodity the West Indies grew better than anywhere else in the world: sugar. As early as the 1660s, the West Indian sugar crop was yielding more than three times the value of tobacco cultivation in the Chesapeake Bay. Compared to the North American colonies, per capita wealth for whites on a sugar island, such as Jamaica, was £1,196, while in New England, it was £32.

> The riches from the sugar trade created greater concentrations of land and wealth in fewer hands, and all of it was produced by the labor of black slaves. By the 1750s, slave imports in Jamaica reached 6,000 a year, and by 1780, 91 percent of the population of the entire British West Indies were black slaves. In that world, the future for fatherless working boys was decidedly bleak.

> But in 1772, Hugh Knox, a Scots-Irish Presbyterian missionary, arrived in St. Croix. He took the 15-year-old Hamilton under his wing and ultimately sent him to King's College (now Columbia University). But Hamilton never actually took his degree, because by 1775, the American Revolution had begun, and Hamilton was already in the thick of revolutionary activities.

THE WAR YEARS

> Hamilton made his first mark as early as the summer of 1774, speaking at anti-British rallies for the Sons of Liberty and publishing his first revolutionary tract in December. His message was simple, blunt, and straight out of the playbook of Enlightenment politics: "That Americans are entitled to freedom is incontestable on every rational principle." Hierarchy and aristocracy were fictions created by the powerful, not the arrangement sanctioned by nature.

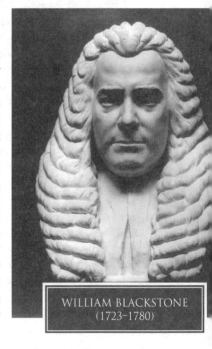

WILLIAM BLACKSTONE
(1723–1780)

> Three months later, Hamilton was further refining his notions of the politics of nature. He did not, however, begin with Locke but with

William Blackstone's description of human nature. This natural law undergirded all human society, and "all civil government" had to be constructed in harmony with it.

♦ This precluded any idea that kings had some God-given sanction to impose their rule on people. To the contrary, "The origin of all civil government," Hamilton argued, "must be a voluntary compact between the rulers and the ruled." In the case of the king of England, therefore, "He is king of America" only by "virtue of a compact between us and the kings of Great Britain," and if that compact had become corrupted, it was time to terminate it.

♦ In an unusually sophisticated insight, Hamilton went on to observe that kings are not the only ones liable to become drunk with power. Parliament, fully as much as George III, was culpable in the oppression of America, and merely the fact that it was an elected legislature would do nothing to restrain it from being "a more intolerable and excessive species of despotism than an absolute monarchy." There was nothing inherently just, wise, virtuous or fair in legislative assemblies.

♦ Power must be dissipated, divided, and distributed in small enough packets to prevent its mutating into the monstrous shapes Hamilton had seen it take in the islands of his birth. It was not that Hamilton was contemptuous of commerce, but he had also seen that the great sugar planters, left to themselves, had warped and twisted commerce into a human catastrophe.

➤ By the summer of 1775, Hamilton had formed his own ad hoc artillery company. He commanded them through the disheartening campaigns of 1776 and, in February 1777, was promoted to lieutenant colonel and a place on the staff of George Washington. Hamilton was the ideal aide-de-camp for Washington, handling Washington's correspondence and carrying out special assignments. Washington became a sort of surrogate father to Hamilton.

REQUIREMENTS OF A REPUBLIC

➢ With the end of the Revolution, Hamilton married into the influential Schuyler family of New York and began practicing law. In 1782, he was designated as a member of New York's delegation in the Confederation Congress. He had never ceased reading, nor had he ceased thinking in terms that moved in different directions than the man who would become his archrival, Thomas Jefferson.

➢ Americans now had themselves a republic, which was, in short, any form of government in which sovereignty resided in the people, not in a separate ruling class or king. But republics varied along a wide spectrum, from oligarchies to true democracies. Unhappily, there had been only a few examples of successful republics in human history—particularly, Rome and Athens—and they offered only a handful of useful rules for guidance:

  ◆ First, a republic must be harmonious. It cannot be divided in purpose; it must be guided by a common vision of the public good.

  ◆ Second, it must be homogeneous—composed of citizens who are ethnically, economically, and socially more or less equal in wealth and status.

  ◆ Third, a republic must be small, if only because harmony and homogeneity break down whenever the boundaries of a republic are drawn to include too many different kinds of people or so much territory that people cannot keep vigil over their fellow citizens.

  ◆ Fourth, every citizen of a republic must be independent and self-sufficient enough to be able to occupy a public office.

➢ These were certainly the rules that guided Thomas Jefferson's notion of a republic. But Hamilton had learned from two very different sources that these rules—and Jefferson's satisfaction with them—might not be quite so admirable as they sounded.

➢ One of those sources was his reading of David Hume. What he learned from Hume was that governments—including republican governments—cannot be invented out of thin air or pressed into an iron maiden of theory. Hume had no particular love for monarchy, but he did not believe that the British monarchy had been bad in all cases or that it merited being thrown out entirely. Politics should rest on experience, not theory; on practical realities, not ideology.

  ♦ Such considerations rendered Hamilton suspicious of reliance on the rule of virtue, much less on reliance of economies limited to agriculture or expectations that keeping republics small would keep them pure. The West Indies, on that logic, should have been showcases for republicanism, which they were decidedly not.

  ♦ Hamilton also felt with personal keenness that Jeffersonian rules about homogeneity and harmony were most likely to operate to the exclusion, not of the corrupt, but of honest outsiders like himself, who had no land, no inheritance, nothing but talent and ambition to offer the new republic. "There is a bigotry in politics, as well as in religions," Hamilton wrote, "equally pernicious in both."

➢ The other source that fed Hamilton's skepticism about elegant but rigid concepts of republicanism was the behavior of the Confederation Congress. Even during the Revolution, he had been sickened by the "folly, caprice [and] want of foresight" which "characterize the general tenor of their actions."

  ♦ What had been folly in war turned out to be folly in peace, as the states asserted their veto over the impost proposal, all the while spewing out unsecured paper money and claiming sovereignty over their own portions of the U.S. war debt.

+ "Our prospects are not flattering," Hamilton sighed to John Jay in 1783, "Every day proves the inefficacy of the present confederation, yet ... we are receding instead of advancing in a disposition to amend its effects."

+ The cherry on top was the New York legislature's move, early in 1786, to begin buying up the Confederation Congress's bonds and notes with $500,000 of paper money. Ostensibly, this was done as an act of charity toward New Yorkers, who had been waiting since the Revolution for Congress to redeem the IOUs and securities it had issued for goods and supplies. What it really did was make Congress a creditor of New York, so that the state legislature had a financial stick with which to beat Congress.

+ Worse still, in another gesture of phony charity, the New York legislature offered to allow the Confederation Congress to collect the long-desired impost on New York commerce— but only if Congress agreed to dedicate the revenue from the impost to servicing its debt, which of course, meant that the impost would end up in the pockets of the New York legislature.

+ From his seat in the state legislature, Hamilton protested, "The United States are intrusted with the management of the general concerns and interests of the community— they have the power of war and peace, they have the power of treaty. ... Let us not endeavour still more to weaken and degrade the federal government, by heaping fresh marks of contempt on its authority." It did no good.

SUGGESTED READING

McDonald, *Alexander Hamilton*, chaps. 1–4.
Wood, *The Radicalism of the American Revolution*, chap. 13.

QUESTIONS TO CONSIDER

1. What was a republic, according to most Americans' understanding?

2. Why was Hamilton suspicious of relying on legislatures, commerce, or virtue?

Lecture 8

JAMES MADISON'S CONFERENCE

On the day he finally returned to Mount Vernon, George Washington had been absent for a decade, and in the meantime, much had gone by the wayside. At the time of his retirement, Washington wondered whether he even had the stamina necessary to bring Mount Vernon back to productivity. He was also involved in efforts to establish the Potowmack Navigation Company, which aimed to develop the Potomac River as a major artery of commerce. In this lecture, we'll see how those efforts highlighted the ineffectiveness of the Continental Congress and resulted in the call for a constitutional convention in Philadelphia.

THE POTOWMACK COMPANY

- ➢ The American colonies had always been blessed with one great asset and two great debits. The asset was land; the debits were the shortage of labor to work the land and the lack of capital to buy more. As long as the colonies were colonies, Americans had ready access to British capital and to politicians who could smooth the way for land acquisitions. But now, the British politicians were gone, as was access to British capital.

- ➢ Before the Revolution, Washington and his brothers had made substantial investments in land development schemes, and he later became deeply involved in plans for the Potowmack Navigation Company, which aimed to develop the Potomac River as a major artery of commerce, linking it with the Ohio River.

- A survey of the headwaters of the Potomac cost Washington the equivalent of $1 million in modern currency, but the company would need to attract the equivalent of $40 million from investors if it were to succeed. And that capital was not going to be forthcoming so long as foreign investors feared that reckless state legislatures would allow American borrowers easy relief from their obligations.

- Investment capital would also not be forthcoming so long as jurisdiction over the Potomac River itself lay between the two states that shared it as a boundary, Virginia and Maryland. Maryland's 17th-century charter set its southern boundary as the far bank of the Potomac, effectively giving Maryland legal jurisdiction over the entire river. But Washington was able to arrange a meeting between representatives of Maryland and Virginia to iron out the legal difficulties concerning jurisdiction of the river.

- Two of the Virginia commissioners, James Madison and Edmund Randolph, never received word of the meeting and missed it entirely. When the others met in March 1785, the Marylanders balked: They wanted Virginia to eliminate the tolls it charged on shipping at the mouth of the Chesapeake Bay, renegotiate fishing rights, and share costs for lighthouses. The commissioners deadlocked.

- Finally, on March 24, Washington himself intervened: Both delegations were invited to Mount Vernon and, once there, agreed that the Potomac should be declared a "common highway," with remission of the Virginia tolls and a variety of other concessions "very important to the commerce of the two states."

- More important, however, was the recommendation Mason made to the Virginia legislature in his report of March 28, 1785: that "it may be proper for the two legislatures, at their annual meeting in the autumn to appoint commissioners to meet, and communicate the regulations of commerce and duties proposed by each State, and to confer on such subjects as may concern the commercial interests of both States."

➢ The Maryland legislature was only too happy to agree and proposed inviting two other parties, Pennsylvania and Delaware. The Virginia Assembly went one step further by proposing that the next meeting of the commissioners "take into consideration the trade of the United States."

MADISON'S EARLY CAREER

➢ The man who offered that resolution to the Virginia Assembly was James Madison, who was supposed to be present at the earlier conferences but didn't receive word of his nomination in time. He was now prepared to make up for that guiltless oversight, because he was about to become the prime mover, not only of the next Potomac River conference but of an entirely new governing document for the United States.

➢ By the time Madison was born in March 1751, his family was the largest landowner in King George County. In 1769, "Jemmy" was sent to Princeton, where he managed to complete his courses in two years and spent a third year under the personal tutelage of Princeton's president, John Witherspoon. Though Witherspoon might have been Presbyterian, his reading lists for students embraced all the great names of the Enlightenment, including Locke, Montesquieu, and Hume.

JAMES MADISON
(1751–1836)

➢ After college, Madison went through the motions of reading law, although it seemed clear that this would never serve as more than a personal adjunct to the far larger responsibility he would one day inherit from his father as a Virginia grandee. He was commissioned in 1775 as a colonel in the county militia, but his ill health probably prevented him from serving. It actually came as something of a surprise when he was elected to the convention of Virginia in 1776, which was charged with proposing a declaration of independence.

➢ He served four years in the Virginia legislature, where he met and formed a lifelong friendship with Thomas Jefferson. In December 1779, just after Jefferson's election as governor of Virginia, Madison was appointed a member of Virginia's delegation to the Continental Congress.

MADISON IN POLITICS

➢ Madison was primarily appointed to Congress to defend Virginia's interests, and he did so on three vital points. The first concerned the Mississippi River: Assuming that the United States would prevail in its Revolution, Congress wanted it clearly understood that the country's western boundary would inevitably have to be fixed at the Mississippi River.

♦ It was another question, however, whether Spain, which still ruled the Louisiana territory and most of the western banks of the Mississippi, would open the river to American trade. Congress hesitated: The revolutionaries needed Spain as an ally, and some of the delegates were willing to trade navigation rights on the river for Spanish assistance against the British.

♦ Madison disagreed. If the American boundary reached the Mississippi, so would Virginia's, and Madison stubbornly insisted that Congress had no business giving away Virginia's claims on the river's commerce.

➢ Madison was just as stubborn on a second issue: the call by Congress for Virginia to cede all its claims to western territory in order to induce small states, such as Maryland, to ratify the Articles of Confederation.

➤ Third, he resisted Congress's decision to recognize Vermont as an independent state because Vermont had been carved out from lands originally claimed by New York. "If the district in Question was comprehended within the Jurisdiction of one or more of the United States," Madison insisted, "it must necessarily follow, that the Inhabitants could have no Right to set up an independent State."

➤ But Madison soon enough learned, as many others did in the 1780s, that a Congress powerless to control the states made for a nation in which no one abroad had confidence. This lesson was brought home to Madison when he made his first big investment in 900 acres of land in upstate New York.

♦ He would have purchased more, but he had not been able to find lenders willing to finance his investment. He turned to Jefferson, who by then was serving as American representative in Paris, to see if French financiers could lend him some money. But Jefferson told him frankly that not even Washington had been able to find lenders for the Potowmack Company in Paris, because of to the "habitual protection of the debtor" by state legislatures.

♦ Congress would have to take the lead by demonstrating that it had the power to pay off its existing wartime loans and by showing that it could control the waywardness of the state legislatures in tax and money matters.

➤ Madison's solution was to support granting Congress the power to levy tariffs, such as the 5 percent impost proposed in 1781. But his pleading on this issue was to no avail, and it left Madison covered with embarrassment when Virginia, which had originally ratified the impost, rescinded the ratification.

JAMES MADISON

> Madison gave up the struggle in December 1783 and took a seat in the Virginia legislature, fighting off proposals to pay state debts in paper money. He missed the Mount Vernon conference, but he persuaded the assembly to endorse George Mason's call for a larger conference and got himself appointed as one of the commissioners. A letter was sent to the other states, inviting them to appoint their own commissioners and to meet in Annapolis, Maryland, in September 1786.

THE POTOWMACK CONFERENCE

> Madison was not exactly giddy with anticipation or optimism before the conference. He feared that "the expedient is no doubt liable to objections and will probably miscarry." His real hope,

as he told Jefferson, was that the Annapolis Convention would pave the way "to a Plenipotentiary Convention for amending the Confederation" as a whole, but he also wrote that he "despaired" of its accomplishment.

➤ At first, Annapolis seemed to confirm Madison's direst fears. Eight states had pledged to send delegates, but only five delegations actually appeared, comprising only 12 commissioners, and Madison was almost prompted to postpone the meeting to another time and place.

➤ But among those commissioners were precisely the individuals most capable of carrying the convention forward, including Madison, Alexander Hamilton, and John Dickinson of Delaware, the architect of the original Articles of Confederation. Once they began deliberating, matters moved ahead handsomely, shifting swiftly from problems in regulating interstate commerce to "the fundamental and essential principles of the Union."

➤ On the fourth day of the convention, the delegates adopted an "Address" to their respective state legislatures. Given the importance of regulating trade, the "Address" called for an "adjustment of other parts of the Federal System." Without pausing, it went on to specify just what mechanism the confederation should adopt for this adjustment:

> a Convention of Deputies from the different States ... to take into consideration the situation of the United States, to devise such further provisions as shall appear to them necessary to render the constitution of the Federal Government adequate to the exigencies of the Union; and to report such an Act for that purpose to the United States in Congress assembled, as when agreed to, by them, and afterwards confirmed by the Legislatures of every State, will effectually provide for the same.

➢ There had been motions in the Confederation Congress for convening a national assembly to reconstruct the articles as early as 1784, but it would take pressure of a kind no one in the Confederation Congress had yet experienced to make a national convention possible. On this occasion, however, the pressure appeared. By the time the Annapolis commissioners had returned home, they were greeted by the news of Daniel Shays's assault on the courthouse in Springfield, Massachusetts.

SUGGESTED READING

Ketchum, *James Madison*, chaps. 7–8.
Randall, *George Washington*, chap. 18.

QUESTIONS TO CONSIDER

1. Why was investment (such as the Potowmack Company) at the mercy of state squabbling?

2. What role was played by the Annapolis Convention in calling for an overhaul of the Articles of Confederation?

Lecture 9

PATRICK HENRY'S RELIGION

*H*e is immortalized for Americans by one phrase; unfortunately, that phrase occurs in a speech whose only printed version first appeared 40 years after the event. He is the subject of Peter Rothermel's greatest painting, although again, the painting was finished 70 years after the event it depicts. He was a man of the most devout personal Christianity, yet he took the lead in stripping the largest church in his state of its tax revenues. His name was Patrick Henry, and he is, above all of the other Founders, the most self-contradictory, the most contrarian, and—sadly—one of the most consistent losers.

THE COUNTER-ENLIGHTENMENT

➤ Patrick Henry's father, a Scot named John Henry, arrived in Virginia in 1727, with a letter of introduction to his half-brother, John Syme, a minor landowner in the Virginia Piedmont. When Syme died four years later, John Henry married his widow, and Patrick, their second son, was born in 1736. John Henry now had more than 7,000 acres and access to an ever-escalating series of civil offices, including vestry of his local Church of England parish, chief justice of the county court, and colonel of the county militia.

➤ These were still small holdings compared to the great Tidewater planters, but they gave the Henry family enough leisure that young Patrick could spend his time fishing and roaming in the woods. There was in him "no hint or token … of the possession of any intellectual gift." That is, until he encountered the formidable Reverend Samuel Davies.

➤ Davies arrived in Hanover County in 1747 and brought with him an alternative universe to the one Patrick Henry had thus far enjoyed. It was especially an alternative universe to that of the 18th-century Enlightenment.

◆ The Enlightenment loved reason because reason, untrammeled by authority, was understood to have the power to peer into the mysteries of human life, discern their true and natural patterns, and present them whole and complete to reshape the world.

◆ But lives lived strictly according to reason had two great defects: First, they became stale, chilly, and unexciting; second, no single human reason was capable of comprehending, sorting, and retaining all the data that the world offered. Every mystery reason solved opened up two more, and reason fell far short of offering an ultimate answer to the most fundamental question of all: How did everything come into being in the first place?

- Blaise Pascal, the French Catholic and mathematical genius, put his finger squarely on reason's limitations when he wrote that "Reason's last step is the recognition that there are an infinite number of things which are beyond it."

- Pascal was only one of several starting points of a vast religious reaction known as the Counter-Enlightenment that was embraced in diverse European Christian movements. But they all had in common a profound conviction that reason told you only so much about life, that religion and the heart had to be an important, even controlling, aspect of human personality and society.

THE GREAT AWAKENING

> In some respects, the preachers of Counter-Enlightenment Christianity remained very much in the spirit of the Enlightenment, because they, too, sought to throw off the restraints of authority and find in experience the genuine springs of religious life. And some of them turned out to be quite formidable reasoners on their own. But the religion of the heart remained the central guide of their lives.

> This evangelical experience made its transit to the British colonies of North America primarily through the agency of George Whitefield. Whitefield was one of the greatest preaching talents of the 18th century.

- Like John Wesley, he was ordained in the established Church of England and his preaching of the strangely warmed heart often made him persona non grata among the more sedate neighborhoods of the Church of England; his solution was to strike out on his own.

- In 1739, Whitefield proposed founding an orphanage in the British colony of Georgia; he embarked on a fundraising campaign through the colonies that featured himself as the principal attraction. The movement he sparked became known as the Great Awakening.

GEORGE WHITEFIELD
(1714–1770)

> One of the pupils being trained for the ministry at the time was Samuel Davies. He arrived in Virginia in 1747 on what was supposed to be a missionary tour of the scattered Presbyterian congregations of the Piedmont, but he was so well received th at he decided to settle in Virginia.

> By 1752, however, the commissary in Williamsburg complained to the bishop of London that Davies was causing "a great defection from our religious assemblies." But Davies proved to be as savvy politically as he was religiously, and a direct appeal to the governor's council in Williamsburg and the king's attorney-general in England "put the affair at rest."

PATRICK HENRY'S AWAKENING

> Patrick Henry thought that Davies was "the greatest orator he ever heard," and even though Henry remained technically a member of the established church, he became attached to the religion of the heart. But the religion made little impression on his father, who was determined to apprentice his son to a merchant.

➢ Soon thereafter, Henry met Thomas Jefferson, who suggested that he begin reading law. He could have devoted little more than six weeks before showing up in Williamsburg to request a law license, which the colony's four law examiners seem to have granted with understandable reluctance.

➢ Henry adapted the oratorical brilliance of the Awakeners to the practice of Virginia law, and between 1760 and 1763, he was attorney of record in 1,185 cases in Hanover and neighboring counties. In an age when law was a genteel side pursuit of the great landowners, Henry took law as his life; even more, he took to the drama of courtroom trials.

◆ In December 1763, Henry was hired to serve as defense lawyer for the parish vestry of Fredericksville, in Louisa County, in a case involving the so-called Two-Penny Act of 1758. The act stipulated that Church of England clergy in Virginia be paid in paper money rather than in tobacco. The Reverend James Maury sued to recover the real value he thought he had been deprived of and appealed to the king's Privy Council, which supported Maury.

◆ But Henry defended the Two-Penny Act on the grounds that neither the king nor the Privy Council had the authority to annul laws duly and properly passed by a legislature of the people. In his defense, Henry said, "The King, from being the father of his people, had degenerated into a tyrant, and forfeited all right to his subjects' obedience to his order regarding it."

◆ This was an extraordinary raising of the stakes in what was otherwise a simple civil suit, but Henry was accustomed to seeing great consequences in small decisions, and the "excited people … seized their champion and bore him on their shoulders in triumph around the court-yard." A year and a half later, they elected him to the House of Burgesses.

> The Awakeners also imparted to Patrick Henry a suspicion of authority, whether it was the Church of England in Virginia or more distant versions. And that suspicion blossomed in the 1760s, as Parliament began reaching ever-deeper into the colonies to control and regulate the colonial economy for Britain's benefit.

  ♦ In May 1765, the House of Burgesses adopted a series of resolutions Henry had composed protesting the Stamp Act, and Henry strode to the floor in their defense with a blistering eloquence. The Stamp Act, Henry declared, was tyranny, and tyranny would meet with only one end.

  ♦ 1n 1774, when he called on the House to begin arming Virginians for resistance to the Crown, Henry spoke his most famous words: "Is life so dear, or peace so sweet, as to be purchased at the price of chains and slavery? Forbid it, Almighty God! I know not what course others may take; but as for me … give me liberty, or give me death!"

HENRY IN POLITICS

> But the man known as the "Demosthenes of America" did not prove terribly successful beyond oratory. He was elected governor of Virginia in 1776, but in general, his accomplishments were few and unremarkable—something for which Henry unhesitatingly blamed his fellow Virginians' lack of virtue.

> Henry was not any more enamored of the Confederation Congress. When he left office, he declined election to the Congress, and to the surprise of George Mason, used his seat in the Virginia Assembly to begin promoting a variety of debt-relief measures, including delaying tax payments, prohibiting British merchants from doing business in Virginia, and permitting Virginia debtors to pay off prewar debts to those merchants in depreciated Virginia paper money.

- An effort to impose new taxes, Massachusetts-style, was met by Henry's argument "that this was a premature attempt; that policy required that the people should have some repose after the fatigues and privations to which they had been subjected, during a long and arduous struggle for independence."

- Mason, however, sternly reminded Henry in 1783 that the Revolution had not been waged "to avoid our just debts, or cheat our creditors; but to rescue our country from the oppression and tyranny of the British government, and to secure the rights and liberty of ourselves, and our posterity."

➤ Oddly, however, Henry believed that the one mechanism for restoring virtue to Virginia and preserving liberty to America was in public funding for religion, not a state-established church but support for "teachers of the Christian religion," regardless of denomination. In 1784, he proposed a general assessment on Virginia taxpayers that would support the teachers of any denomination.

- Henry's bill left the jaws of Madison and Jefferson hanging open. The whole "project" was, as Madison wrote to Jefferson, "extraordinary," and would probably have expired quietly in committee had it not been "preserved from a dishonorable death by the talents of Mr. Henry."

- But not even Henry's fabled eloquence was a match for Madison's relentless logic or for his sharp hand at political maneuvering in the assembly. When the bill came up for debate in December 1784, Madison skewered it by asking a series of embarrassing questions. In the end, the bill died in committee.

SUGGESTED READING

Kidd, *The Great Awakening*, chap. 5.
———, *Patrick Henry*, chap. 2.

QUESTIONS TO CONSIDER

1. How did Patrick Henry establish his reputation for oratorical brilliance?

2. Why did Henry favor public financial support for religion?

Lecture 10

JAMES MADISON'S VICES

*I*t is somewhat curious that the most important figures in moving the republic from under the shadow of the Articles of Confederation were men with tenuous connections to family and place. George Washington, for example, compensated for his lack of a large family by creating a "military family" around Alexander Hamilton, the marquis de Lafayette, John Laurens, and others. Such men as Madison and Washington came out of the Revolution unencumbered by vast family responsibilities and, thus, were free to think in broad, national terms. As one observer wrote of Madison, because he was "unencumbered with the cares of a family," he was free to do a substantial amount of homework before leaving for Philadelphia and the Confederation Congress.

JAMES MADISON

LEAD-UP TO THE CONFEDERATION CONGRESS

> ➤ It seems as though, at almost the last minute, the Confederation Congress realized how long things had been let slide and how needy the Articles of Confederation were for amendment or more. At the end of Lecture 8, we mentioned that in the spring of 1786, Charles Pinckney of South Carolina had upbraided the Confederation Congress about the need to put its house in order, only to run hard into the refusal of New York, Pennsylvania, Rhode Island, and other states.

> ➤ In August of 1786, a Grand Committee that included Pinckney proposed a series of amendments to the Articles of Confederation that added seven new articles and amended the others to give Congress "the sole and exclusive power of regulating the trade

of the States as well as foreign nations ... with each other, and of laying such prohibitions and Imposts and duties ... as may be Necessary for the purpose" and to levy a 10 percent fine on states that failed to submit their financial quotas.

➤ But this was all too little, too late, especially after the eruption of Shays's Rebellion that fall and the paralyzed indecision with which Congress greeted it. Instead, on February 21, 1787, the Confederation Congress meekly approved the proposal of the Annapolis Convention for "a convention of representatives ... for the purpose of revising the Articles of Confederation" to render "the federal constitution adequate to the exigencies of the Government & the preservation of the Union."

➤ James Madison, meanwhile, had already embarked on his own private study of "ancient and modern Confederacies," surveying the classical confederations and trolling through Montesquieu, Polybius, Plutarch's *Lives*, Sir Walter Raleigh's *History of the World*, and other sources. Alongside this compendium of examples, Madison then composed a summary of what he called the "vices of the political system of the U. States," from which he would survey the failures of the Articles of Confederation in a fashion so unsparing that any thought of mere amendment would be worthless. Madison listed 11 such vices:

- ◆ "Failure of the States to comply with the Constitutional requisitions"—in other words, to pay up their portion of the federal budget.

- ◆ "Encroachments by the States on the federal authority," which Madison saw particularly in "the troops raised and to be kept up by Massachusetts" during Shays's Rebellion.

- ◆ "Violations of the law of nations and of treaties." Madison had seen how individual states, including his own Virginia, interpreted the treaty of peace with Great Britain, France, and Holland to suit themselves, either by refusing to return confiscated Loyalist property or to satisfy prewar debts to British subjects.

- "Trespasses of the States on the rights of each other," particularly with regard to the flood of state paper money.

- "Want of concert in matters where common interest requires it."

- "Want of Guaranty to the States of their Constitutions and laws against internal violence." Customary as it was to regard the chief threat to a republic as coming from power imposed from the top down by a conqueror, Madison had seen in Pennsylvania, Rhode Island, and western Massachusetts that a few unscrupulous demagogues can whip up the body politic, seize power, and make themselves fully as dictatorial a tyranny as any king's.

- Madison's seventh "vice" flowed directly out of the sixth: "Want of sanction to the laws, and of coercion in the Government of the Confederacy." Time and experience had shown that "it is no longer doubted that a unanimous and punctual obedience of 13 independent bodies to the acts of the federal Government ought not to be calculated on." The national government had the responsibility to ensure that the nation remained a republic, not only as a nation but in its component parts, too.

- "Want of ratification by the people of the articles of Confederation." Madison had noticed that recognition of the Confederation's authority had never been incorporated into several of the state constitutions and "has received no other sanction than that of the legislative authority."

- "Multiplicity of laws in the several states."

- "Mutability of the laws of the states."

- Finally, in the 11th point, Madison unleashed his most personal arrow, for not only were the state laws as changeable as the weather, but their very instability suggested something ominous about republican government itself. Madison wrote, in terms as stinging as they were accurate:

> Individuals of extended views and of national pride may bring the public proceedings to this standard, but the example will never be followed by the multitude. Is it to be imagined that an ordinary citizen or even Assemblyman of R. Island, in estimating the policy of paper money, ever considered or cared in what light the measure would be viewed in France or Holland, or even in Massachusetts or Connecticut? It was a sufficient temptation to both that it was for their interest; it was a sufficient sanction to the latter that it was popular in the State; to the former, that it was so in the neighbourhood.

> The state legislatures, to be blunt, are filled with greedy, small-minded, provincial types who are incapable of rising above the narrow horizons of self-interest—an attitude not only fatal to the articles, but a contradiction of the self-denial and civic virtue that was supposed to suffuse a republic and one that made the world wonder, as Washington had feared, that a republic might be beyond the capacity of ordinary people.

MADISON'S PROPOSALS

- In mid-April 1787, Madison laid his ideas for an entirely new frame of government before the one man who, more than any other, could make it happen: George Washington. In fact, Washington told Madison that "a thorough reform of the present system is indispensable." That was enough of an opening for Madison, who submitted some of his ideas for a new system.

➤ First, wrote Madison, there is no need to believe that the "individual independence of the States is utterly irreconcileable with their aggregate sovereignty." The solution was not to abolish the states and consolidate them into a whole. Instead, what Madison had in mind was "some middle ground, which may at once support a due supremacy of the national authority" yet "not exclude the local authorities wherever they can be subordinately useful."

   ◆ The way to this, Madison recommended, was through "a change … in the principle of representation" in Congress. Representatives in Congress should be elected directly by the people of the states in proportion to each state's population.

   ◆ The Congress would then become the representatives of the people, not the states, and "the lesser States [for example, Rhode Island] must in every event yield to the predominant will."

➤ In contrast, Madison wanted none of the unicameral Pennsylvania nonsense when it came to the structure of Congress. "The Legislative department might be divided into two branches; one

of them chosen every years by the people at large, or by the legislatures; the other to consist of fewer members, to hold their places for a longer term, and to go out in such a rotation as always to leave in office a large majority of old members."

➤ Next, Madison proceeded, give "the national Government … positive and compleat authority in all cases which require uniformity; such as the regulation of trade, including the right of taxing both exports & imports, the fixing the terms and forms of naturalization, &c."

➤ In order to prevent the states from passing the multitude of laws they would pass to obstruct this "compleat authority," Congress should be given "over and above this positive power, a negative"—a veto—"in all cases whatsoever on the legislative acts of the States."

➤ Finally, Madison added, "a national Executive must also be provided" and not just a chairman or president of Congress. For this executive, Madison already had in mind Washington himself.

➤ Washington took careful notes on Madison's letter and filed them away with correspondence he had been conducting with John Jay and Henry Knox on the same subject. But would he do anything about it? Madison had made sure that Washington's name, along with his own, appeared on the list of Virginia's delegates to Philadelphia. But Washington was feeling his years that winter. Even though Shays's Rebellion had quickened his fury and frustration, he was not exaggerating when he told Henry Knox that he was finished with public life and wanted only to retire.

➤ As opening day for the convention arrived, Madison was disheartened that "the number as yet assembled is but small." But he had despaired too quickly. On Sunday, May 13, the chiming of bells, the noise of crowds thronging the streets, and the clatter of the First City Troop of Cavalry announced the arrival of

Washington. The first man of the republic had come to bless the convention with his participation.

SUGGESTED READING

Glover, *Founders as Fathers*, chap. 1.
Ketcham, *James Madison*, chap. 9.

QUESTIONS TO CONSIDER

1. What were the 11 vices Madison detected in the Articles of Confederation?

2. What recommendations for reform did Madison make to Washington?

Lecture 11

EDMUND RANDOLPH'S PLAN

*I*f Washington's arrival gladdened James Madison's heart and reassured him that the greatest man in America would be at the convention to add the *imprimatur* of his presence, then he was only slightly less happy when, on May 15, Edmund Randolph arrived in Philadelphia. In this lecture, we'll explore the opening of the convention in May of 1787; the characteristics of the delegates; the selection of the president and secretary; and Randolph's plan for revising the Articles of Confederation.

BACKGROUND ON RANDOLPH

> The ancestry of the Randolphs, like so many of the Tidewater aristocracy, stretched back to 1643. They had intermarried with the Jeffersons, founded the College of William and Mary, and generated various governors, members of the Governors' Council, and members of the House of Burgesses. Edmund Randolph's father, John Randolph, was "a man of literary tastes, a skeptic in religion, and not much inclined to politics"; he was also the king's attorney.

> Edmund was born in 1753, and at his father's Williamsburg home, he was introduced to everyone in Virginia society worth being introduced to, including Washington, Jefferson, Richard Henry Lee, and George Wythe. He went to William and Mary and read law with his father to become an attorney himself.

> The Revolution, however, was a bolt of destruction to the Randolphs. John left for England in 1775, never to return. Edmund felt keenly the shadow of suspicion that fell over him, and in August, he volunteered himself to Washington as a staffer. But Edmund had more than enough redeeming qualities to make up for the deficits of his father's Toryism.

EDMUND RANDOLPH
(1753–1813)

> He was soon recalled to Virginia to serve as a delegate to the Virginia Convention of 1776, and he was elected attorney-general under the new state constitution; he was

then elected to the Continental and Confederation Congresses, where he formed a close attachment to Madison. Like Madison, he was convinced that the inability of the Confederation to fund itself would sooner or later undermine the advantages of the Revolution.

➤ But Randolph would soon be in a position to do something about it. On January 21, 1786, he was appointed by the Virginia Assembly to head the Virginia delegation to the Annapolis Conference, and the following November, he was elected governor of Virginia. Washington was delighted at his old staffer's elevation to the governor's mansion. In December, Randolph was one of the five Virginians dispatched to Philadelphia.

➤ Like Madison, Randolph had already been thinking ahead toward the likeliest results of the convention. He feared that resistance to any substantial change from Patrick Henry and others would mean that "the alterations should be grafted on[to]" the Articles of Confederation; the proposals he eventually wrote out were anything but mere band-aids.

- ◆ Randolph had had enough of a confederation where the states behaved as though they were independent powers. There must be a new "compact in which the people themselves are the sole parties, and which they alone can abrogate." It should have, Randolph wrote, a preamble and a declaration to establish a "supreme legislative, executive, and judiciary." He also specified that the supreme legislative body "shall consist of two branches: viz. (a) a House of Delegates; and (b) a Senate."

- ◆ At the end, Randolph added what turned out to be a highly perceptive requirement: "The ratification of the reform is ... to be made by a special convention in each State— ... to be chosen for the express purpose of considering and approving, or repealing it in toto."

- Whatever came out of the convention, Randolph wanted to take no chances that a jealous Congress or truculent state legislatures would strangle it in its cradle. The new frame of government would go before special conventions in each of the states, outflanking both the Confederation Congress and the state legislatures, and it would have to be taken as a single piece, not picked to death by special interests.

INDEPENDENCE HALL, PHILADELPHIA, PA

CONSTITUTIONAL CONVENTION

➤ This was all music to Madison's ears, and when the last member of the Virginia delegation, George Mason, arrived on May 17, it began caucusing with the Pennsylvania delegation on the direction they wanted the convention to take once a quorum was reached. And to Madison's relief, that quorum was finally achieved on May 25. Delegates included those from Pennsylvania, Virginia, North Carolina, South Carolina, New York, New Jersey, Delaware, Massachusetts, Connecticut, and Georgia. Rhode Island refused to participate.

➤ There was no sense in which these men were intended to be representative of the people of the United States. They were, for one thing, there to represent the interests of the states that had sent them, not the people at large or on average.

➤ New York had sent a surprisingly feeble delegation, and two of its delegates departed the convention in protest after little more than a month. The joint letter they wrote to New York Governor George Clinton announced, "A general government, however guarded by declarations of rights, or cautionary provisions, must unavoidably, in a short time, be productive of the destruction of the civil liberty of such citizens who could be effectually coerced by it."

➤ That left the representation of New York in the hands of one man: Hamilton, who arrived in Philadelphia on May 25. As a general rule, people either adored or hated Hamilton, and those who hated him did so with a perfect passion. Another colorful—and rakish—figure at the convention was Gouverneur Morris. He became Robert Morris's assistant and protégé as the confederation's financial officer. (Although they shared the same last name, they were not related.) Gouverneur Morris was impatient with the financial weakness of the confederation and was unguarded in his expressions of contempt for it.

> Thus, the members of the Constitutional Convention represented a different stratum of American society than the one they could see around them in Philadelphia. Even the numbers of the convention's delegates effectively meant that there would be only 1 delegate in the convention for every 71,000 Americans; even worse, counting only those delegates who sat consistently throughout the whole convention, the number would be 1 for every 118,000 Americans. Still, when the delegates finally convened for their first working session on May 25, 1787, no one expressed any hesitation about the authority with which they proposed to act.

GOUVERNEUR MORRIS
(1752–1816)

> The issue of the presidency of the convention was taken up by Robert Morris and the Pennsylvanians as the first trick, and they were determined to win it. Morris nominated Washington, who was unanimously elected. William Jackson, one of the inner ring of Washington's old staff, was chosen as secretary. In the end, Jackson's election didn't matter, because James Madison pulled up a chair at the secretary's table. There, in no capacity except his own self-appointed one, Madison proceeded to take meticulous notes on the convention's proceedings.

> The next item of business was to create a Rules Committee, which fell into the hands of Hamilton, the South Carolinian Charles Pinckney, and the Virginian George Wythe. In fact, there was only one sour note to disturb the first day's proceedings: As

the credentials of each of the state delegations were read into the record, George Read of Delaware added the proviso the Delaware legislature had tacked on: "that those from Delaware were prohibited from changing the article in the Confederation establishing an equality of votes among the States."

- ◆ Read did not mind revising the Articles to award stronger powers to Congress, but he did not want his little state, with only 60,000 people, to lose the equal standing it had with every other state in the Confederation Congress.

- ◆ Madison, Morris, and Washington might have won the brief first round of the Convention, but Read's words were an ominous reminder that the way ahead was liable to be filled with longer and more difficult rounds. And they all agreed: The man to take the point was Edmund Randolph.

SUGGESTED READING

Beeman, *Plain, Honest Men*, chap. 5.
Stewart, *The Summer of 1787*, chap. 5.

QUESTIONS TO CONSIDER

1. What did Edmund Randolph believe were three indispensable reforms of the Articles of Confederation?

2. Which of the following delegates to the Philadelphia Convention would you most like to meet: Gouverneur Morris, Alexander Hamilton, or Edmund Randolph?

Lecture 12

WILLIAM PATERSON'S DISSENT

*T*he Rules Committee of the Constitutional Convention reported on Monday, May 28: A quorum of seven states was necessary to do business, all speakers were to address the president, all deliberations would take place behind closed doors, and motions to reconsider items would always considered. These might seem to be mere procedural matters, but in fact, they turned out to be important. Closing the proceedings allowed members of the convention to speak their minds freely. And keeping all subjects open for reconsideration allowed the delegates to keep their minds open and malleable as the scaffolding of a new instrument of government emerged.

RANDOLPH'S RESOLUTIONS

➢ The main business of the convention opened on May 29, initiated by Edmund Randolph of Virginia. Randolph respectfully ticked off a list of "defects" in the articles that had emerged in the course of their implementation, including commercial discord among the states, foreign debts, the havoc of paper money, and the violations of treaties. Randolph then laid 15 resolutions before the convention as Virginia's plan for a new national government:

- Congress should be restructured "to consist of two branches."

- Representation "in the National Legislature ought to be proportioned ... to the number of free inhabitants" in each state.

- "The first branch of the National Legislature ought to be elected by the people of the several States," and the "members of the second branch of the National Legislature ought to be elected by" the "individual Legislatures" of the states.

- This "National Legislature ... [should] be impowered to ... legislate in all cases to which the separate States are incompetent, or in which the harmony of the United States may be interrupted by the exercise of individual Legislation; to negative all laws passed by the several States, contravening in the opinion of the National Legislature the articles of Union; and to call forth the force of the Union agst. any member of the Union failing to fulfill its duty under the articles thereof."

- Almost as radical was Randolph's resolution that "a National Executive be instituted" with "a general authority to execute the National laws." This executive would represent a second, independent department of the government.

- There was also to be a third department, "a National Judiciary" to hear "cases in which foreigners or citizens of other States applying to such jurisdictions may be interested, or which respect the collection of the National revenue."

- ◆ Just to make it clear that political power was now shifting decisively from the state to the national level, Randolph added a penultimate resolution: "that the Legislative, Executive, and Judiciary powers within the several States ought to be bound by oath to support the articles of Union."

- ➤ Although Randolph may have had a hand in drafting these resolutions, the voice was clearly that of Madison, which made all the more surprising the proposal by the next speaker of the day: Charles Pinckney.

PINCKNEY'S PLAN

- ➤ The South Carolina delegation was composed of two men with the name Pinckney; the first was the influential Charles Cotesworth Pinckney, who had led South Carolina into the Revolution. His younger cousin, Charles Pinckney, had also fought in the Revolution, but he was discounted by many as an empty-headed fop.

- ➤ It was entirely outside of Madison's careful planning to have the younger Pinckney announce that he had his own "draught of a federal government." What was even more galling was that Pinckney's plan was not a bad one; in fact, it was not dissimilar to what Madison and the Virginia delegation had worked on so carefully. The plan included the following:

  - ◆ There should be a bicameral national Congress (consisting of the Senate and the "House of Delegates").

  - ◆ The House of Delegates was to be elected by the citizens of the United States as a whole, with "one Member for every thousand Inhabitants," while the Senate was "to be elected from four Districts," either by the House of Delegates or directly by "the People at large."

- Together, the House of Delegates and the Senate "shall by joint Ballot annually chuse" a "President" in whom "the executive authority of the U. S. shall be vested."

- Every state would retain "its Rights," but like Randolph's plan, state laws and legislation would be subject to review by the Congress.

➤ In fact, Pinckney's plan was actually slightly more radical than Randolph's, and it is peculiar that Madison's otherwise exquisitely detailed notes make no mention of any of the Pinckney plan's provisions. Whether Pinckney really drafted a viable forerunner of the Constitution on his own or (as Madison believed) confected such a plan after the fact to boost his own self-importance remains a mystery.

PATERSON'S OBJECTIONS

➤ The most vocal opponent of any plan to change the voting rules was William Paterson of New Jersey. Irish by birth, Paterson had been brought to New Jersey by his immigrant parents and graduated from Princeton in 1763. He became a lawyer, had been the first attorney-general of

WILLIAM PATERSON
(1745–1806)

revolutionary New Jersey, and represented Somerset County in the New Jersey legislature.

- ➤ Like Patrick Henry, Paterson was unreconciled to the idea of rewriting the articles. For all the years of the Continental Congress and the Confederation Congress, small states, such as New Jersey, had enjoyed the same vote in Congress that large states, such as Virginia, had—that is, one apiece.

  - ◆ In the minds of Randolph and Madison, this was absurd. A state with only 1/10 the population of Virginia was accorded equal say in national policy and, in the case of Rhode Island, could obstruct, defy, and even veto legislation as though it had the same heft as Virginia.

  - ◆ But to Paterson, this was the only safeguard small states would have against being ground up as bait by the Virginians or the Pennsylvanians. This was not because Paterson had any personal sympathy with the fast-and-loose money policies of state legislatures. But as he listened to Randolph's presentation on May 29, he began scribbling extensive notes, punctuated by expressions of dismay.

- ➤ Even as Paterson scribbled, Randolph was planning to keep the initiative firmly in the hands of the Virginians by moving that the convention "resolve itself into a Committee of the Whole" to discuss his plan. A *committee of the whole* is a parliamentary device that allows a deliberative or legislative body to convert itself into a committee; as such, the usual procedural rules can be relaxed, proposals made or withdrawn, and ideas batted around informally—all without any sense of final decisions being irretrievably made.

- ➤ For the next nine days (May 30–June 8), the initiative stayed firmly in the hands of the Virginians, and the ebb-and-flow of discussion centered entirely on the Randolph proposals. In case there was any doubt what the ultimate result of the Randolph Plan might be,

Gouverneur Morris took the opportunity to make the proposals clear on May 30:

- "That a Union of the States merely federal will not accomplish the objects proposed by the articles of Confederation."

- "That no treaty or treaties among the whole or part of the States, as individual Sovereignties, would be sufficient."

- "That a national Government ought to be established consisting of a supreme Legislative, Executive & Judiciary."

➤ In other words, the Virginians sought to discard the Articles of Confederation and invent a new document. There was a good deal of disagreement, but the momentum was irresistible: A vote on Morris's three guidelines passed with the support of six of the eight state delegations.

➤ For the next several days, the business of the Committee of the Whole was taken up with questions of how to adopt the Randolph Plan. One by one, Randolph's proposals were relentlessly pushed toward the committee's vote:

- The "equality of suffrage" for each state mandated by the articles would yield to representation based on size of population.

- The national legislature would have two branches, the first elected generally by the people.

- The first branch would be the place where all legislation would originate.

- The national legislature would have authority to "negative all state laws contravening in the opinion of the Nat. Leg. the articles of union."

- A national executive would "consist of a single person" and be elected by the national legislature.

> But Randolph could not quite erase muttered suspicions and dissents over several annoying details, and that muttering finally found a voice on June 9, when William Paterson spoke.

  - He believed that the whole proposal for a new national legislature based on proportional representation rather than an equal number of votes per state struck at the very "existence of the lesser States." He went on: "The articles of the Confederation were therefore the proper basis of all the proceedings of the Convention," and "we ought to keep within its limits." Even if everyone in the assembly room agreed with Edmund Randolph's plan, that was not what the American people had called them to Philadelphia to do.

  - Paterson continued: "Give the large States an influence in proportion to their magnitude, and what will be the consequence? Their ambition will be proportionally increased, and the small States will have every thing to fear." The idea that Virginia or Pennsylvania should have more representation in Congress simply because they had greater populations was like saying "that a rich individual citizen should have more votes than an indigent one." Eventually, Paterson warned, "If we are to be considered as a nation, all State distinctions must be abolished."

  - What, Paterson asked, was so wrong with the current system of equal representation for each state in Congress? "It has been said that if a Natl. Govt. is to be formed … the representatives ought to be drawn from the people." Was that goal less well served when Congress is supplied by delegates chosen by the states? Aren't the state legislatures that choose these delegates "filled … by the people who chuse the State Legislatures?" With a flourish of defiance, Paterson announced that "N. Jersey will never confederate on the plan before the Committee. She would be swallowed up."

➢ It had seemed until that moment that the Randolph Plan was sailing to adoption by the Committee of the Whole. But the waters Paterson had roiled were too disturbed to be pacified, just as the momentum Randolph and Madison had built behind the Randolph Plan was too great to be stopped by Paterson's speech alone.

➢ Starting on June 11, the Committee of the Whole began voting on the Randolph resolutions, with the New Jersey and Delaware delegations almost always voting no, and enough of the others voting yes to carry them all through, now in the form of 19 resolutions to be presented to the convention.

SUGGESTED READING

Collier and Collier, *Decision in Philadelphia*, chap. 13.
Stewart, *The Summer of 1787*, chap. 8.

QUESTIONS TO CONSIDER

1. What were the main elements of the Randolph Plan?

2. Why did William Paterson's June 9th speech threaten to derail the goal of the convention?

Lecture 13

ROGER SHERMAN'S COMPROMISE

William Paterson had prepared his attack on the Randolph Plan and the ease with which he believed the Virginians intended to force into place an arrangement that would guarantee their dominance of any new modeled Congress. He needed one more day after the report of the Committee of the Whole to complete an alternative "purely federal" plan. With the opening of the convention's session—now as a convention again—Paterson was ready to lay before "the Convention the plan which ... several of the deputations wished to be substituted in place of that proposed by Mr. Randolph." Paterson's plan resulted in weeks of deadlock, but Roger Sherman would respond with a compromise formula of his own.

THE NEW JERSEY PLAN

- ➢ As the Committee of the Whole proceeded, Paterson had circulated among the other small-state delegations, confecting a plan of his own, cementing alliances, and lining up individuals to speak to any objections from the Madison-Randolph quarter. In the words of Madison, Paterson's efforts "began now to produce serious anxiety for the result of the Convention."

- ➢ John Dickinson had, in passing, remarked to Madison in a patronizing tone that the Virginians had wanted too much, too fast in creating a single, powerful national government. It may well be that the delegations would embrace a bicameral national legislature, but the representation in both houses had to be as it was in the Confederation Congress: each state, one vote.

- ➢ Of course, to Madison, this was no improvement on the Articles of Confederation; single states would continue to carry an outsize weight in any new Congress, and the results would always be the same: paralysis at the national level and reckless abandon at the state level. After enough recklessness, the whole Union would come tumbling down.

- ➢ But not even Madison dared deny the degree to which equal representation of states in the new government was a fetish for the small states. Just how alluring that fetish would be became apparent as Paterson took the floor at the beginning of the June 15 session. He had nine resolutions to submit, making up what would be called the New Jersey Plan.

  - ♦ First, in the spirit of reasonableness, Paterson allowed that "the articles of Confederation ought to be so revised, corrected & enlarged, as to render the federal Constitution adequate to the exigencies of Government, & the preservation of the Union."

- ◆ He was even willing to admit that Congress should "be authorized to pass acts for raising a revenue" and "to pass Acts for the regulation of trade & commerce"—provided that all "punishments, fines, forfeitures & penalties to be incurred for contravening such acts rules and regulations shall be adjudged by the Common law Judiciaries of the State in which any offence ... shall have been committed or perpetrated." That meant the delivery of a veto power over the operation of "trade & commerce" to state courts. Under the veneer of reasonableness, Paterson was already ensuring more of the status quo.

- ➢ Paterson next turned to the kind of taxation that would be necessary to support a new national government. He said that Congress should levy taxes on the states "in proportion to the whole number of white & other free citizens & inhabitants of every age sex and condition including those bound to servitude for a term of years & three-fifths of all other persons not comprehended in the foregoing description." Here was a scheme for proportionate representation that even Madison could applaud—except that it was about taxation, not representation.

- ➢ Fourth, Paterson conceded that it would be a good idea to elect "a federal Executive" with "general authority to execute the federal acts." But Paterson left unstated whether this executive should be one person or a committee. Further, Paterson wanted this executive to be "removeable by Congs. on application by a majority of the Executives of the several States."

- ➢ Finally, Paterson was willing to see "a federal Judiciary ... established to consist of a supreme Tribunal, the Judges of which" would be "appointed by the Executive." But its powers would be limited to strictly federal matters. Nothing was said about the federal judiciary having any restraining power on the actions of the states.

> The New Jersey Plan created the semblance of a new national government but granted it hardly any new powers and certainly none that might seriously threaten the free hand of each state to do what it wanted.

HAMILTON: A RETURN TO MONARCHY?

> Nothing, Madison later wrote, "created more embarrassment, and a greater alarm for the issue of the Convention" than Paterson's plan. "The little states insisted on retaining their equality," while "the large States ... urged that as the new Government was to be drawn from the people immediately and was to operate directly on them ... it was necessary that the representation ... should be in proportion to their size."

> The situation was not helped by the confused response of the delegates who rose to defend the Virginia Plan. James Wilson, a Pennsylvania legal scholar, offered a patient, logical contrast of Randolph's and Paterson's plans, pointing out that people looked to "Natl. Councils" when they expected relief. He further noted that smaller governments are notoriously the most corrupt, primarily because corruption is easier to achieve in smaller groups.

  ♦ The same principle applied to the kind of unicameral legislature Paterson was advocating. "If the Legislative authority be not restrained, there can be neither liberty nor stability. ... It can only be restrained by dividing it within itself, into distinct and independent branches. In a single House there is no check."

  ♦ But the same principle worked in reverse when it came to an executive. "In order to controul the Legislative authority, you must divide it," but "in order to controul the Executive you must unite it. ... Three will contend among themselves till one becomes the master of his colleagues."

> When Alexander Hamilton followed Wilson on June 18, he nearly threw the game away entirely. Hamilton, of course, had no use for

Paterson's New Jersey Plan, but he had little more for Randolph's. He was "fully convinced, that no amendment of the Confederation, leaving the States in possession of their Sovereignty could possibly answer the purpose" of the convention. Only by lodging "a compleat sovereignty in the general Governmt" would the American experiment in republicanism survive.

> Then, Hamilton committed the unthinkable: He proposed as a serious alternative to both plans the model of the British monarchy. He was willing to allow a bicameral legislature if Randolph insisted, but "Let one branch of the Legislature hold their places for life." And "let the Executive also be for life." Was this a republican government? Yes, Hamilton answered confidently, "if all the Magistrates are appointed, and vacancies are filled, by the people, or a process of election originating with the people."

> With this speech, Hamilton handed Paterson, Luther Martin, and Gunning Bedford a stick with which to beat the Virginia Plan on the grounds that anything that pointed toward a strong national government was tantamount to monarchy. No one spoke in reply or seconded Hamilton's plan. When Madison took the floor the next day to assail the New Jersey Plan, he never even referred to Hamilton.

ROGER SHERMAN'S PROPOSALS

> Now began nearly three weeks of deadlocked misery in the convention, as the partisans of the Virginia Plan—Madison, Randolph, James Wilson, and Gouverneur Morris—traded fruitless, wearying blows with the partisans of the New Jersey Plan—Paterson, John Lansing, Robert Yates, and Luther Martin. At one point, Franklin felt desperate enough that he urged the convention to get down on its knees and pray for guidance. But even this plea fell short.

> By June 30, tempers in the convention had grown so short that James Wilson actually told the small-state opposition that they

might as well go form their own confederation. Gunning Bedford retorted that if the small states really had no choice but the Virginia Plan, they "will find some foreign ally of more honor and good faith, who will take them by the hand and do them justice." Drearily, the convention voted on July 2 to take an extended adjournment "to attend to the celebrations on the anniversary of Independence."

➤ Despite the deadlock, though, the means for resolving the standoff already lay at hand, and in two forms. The first was a seemingly innocuous proposal by Connecticut's Roger Sherman, submitted back on June 11: "that the proportion of suffrage in the 1st. branch should be according to the respective numbers of free inhabitants; and that in the second branch or Senate, each State should have one vote and no more."

➤ Sympathetic as he was in many ways to Paterson, Sherman understood that "the national debt & the want of power somewhere to draw forth the National resources, are the great matters that press." On June 20, he agreed to have two legislative branches, with a proportional representation in one of them, "provided each State had an equal voice in the other." This time, more of the delegates were listening.

➤ But Madison was unyielding. "The History & fate of the several confederacies modern as well as Antient" proved to Madison's satisfaction that nothing less than a legislature with proportional representation by population would serve American interests. James Wilson likewise dug in even deeper: "Can we forget for whom we are forming a Government?" he bellowed angrily on June 30. "Is it for men, or for the imaginary beings called States?"

➤ Not even Madison and Wilson could persuade the convention that they were not on the brink of breaking up. When they forced a vote "for allowing each State one vote in the second branch," the convention split straight down the middle. "We are now at full stop," Roger Sherman warned.

CHARLES COTESWORTH PINCKNEY'S SOLUTION

> The solution came in the form of a proposal by Charles Cotesworth Pinckney. He had voted against the New Jersey Plan, but he conceded that "some compromise seemed to be necessary." To that end, he suggested the creation of a Grand Committee, "consisting of a member from each State," which should take the opportunity of the Fourth of July adjournment "to devise & report some compromise."

> Thus, in addition to Sherman's compromise proposal, the convention appointed a committee to consider compromise. Madison fought it to the last minute, but the vote to create the Grand Committee was lopsidedly in favor, nine to two. Still, nobody

was celebrating as the convention broke up for the adjournment. Even Washington wrote, "I almost dispair of seeing a favorable issue to the proceedings of our convention, and do therefore repent having had any agency in the business."

SUGGESTED READING

Beeman, *Plain, Honest Men*, chap. 8.
Hall, *Roger Sherman and the Creation of the American Republic*, chap. 5.

QUESTIONS TO CONSIDER

1. Give a summary of Paterson's New Jersey Plan of June 15th.

2. Why was Hamilton's speech of June 18th a blunder?

Lecture 14

ELBRIDGE GERRY'S COMMITTEE

*T*he composition of the Grand Committee to resolve the deadlock between the Virginia and New Jersey plans for a national government could not have offered much consolation to either James Madison or James Wilson, fixed as they were on the proposal for a two-house Congress, both popularly elected by the people at large rather than chosen by the state legislatures. Each state delegation was to contribute one member to the Grand Committee, and it all leaned in the opposite direction from Madison and Wilson. The committee's chairman was Elbridge Gerry of Massachusetts, who hadn't said a word in support of Madison and Wilson.

THE GRAND COMMITTEE

➢ The Grand Committee set to work as soon as the convention adjourned on July 2. The atmosphere was tense. Elbridge Gerry, the chair of the Grand Committee, thought the moment was "so serious as to threaten a dissolution of the Convention." But Franklin pressed on the committee a series of formulas that he believed would placate both Madisonian big-staters and Patersonian small-staters.

➢ According to Franklin's formula, there would be two houses to the national Congress. The lower house—the House of Representatives—would be elected by the population at large, so that the large states would have a disproportionately large representation over the small states, and one representative would be elected to the House for every 40,000 inhabitants. The upper house—the Senate—would be the place where each state, regardless of size, would be represented equally. Finally, all legislation concerning money and taxation would be the domain of the House and all bills for apportioning and spending money would originate there.

➢ Gerry, as the chair of the Grand Committee, would make the report when the convention reassembled on July 5. A spare, thin, sunken-cheeked merchant, Gerry graduated from Harvard in 1762, went into the family business, went into politics, and was elected to the Second Continental Congress. He was, by temperament, suspicious; he also had limitations as a speaker. Gerry was clear enough, though, when he made the report of the Grand Committee:

1. That in the 1st. branch of the Legislature [the House of Representatives] each of the States now in the Union shall be allowed 1 member for every 40,000 inhabitants. ... [and] that each State not containing that number shall be allowed 1 member: that all bills for raising or appropriating money,

and for fixing the Salaries of the officers of the Governt. of the U. States shall originate in the 1st. branch of the Legislature, and shall not be altered or amended by the 2d. branch: and that no money shall be drawn from the public Treasury but in pursuance of appropriations to be originated in the 1st. branch

2. That in the 2d. branch [the Senate] each State shall have an equal vote.

➤ The report set off Wilson and Madison. Wilson accused the Grand Committee of having "exceeded their powers." Madison was furious. Making concessions to the small-staters would merely perpetuate the problems that had brought them all to the convention in the first place. Madison also warned that the delegates should not be deceived "by threats from the small-staters to break up the Union."

ELBRIDGE GERRY
(1744–1814)

➤ But Gerry, in fact, defended the bargain precisely because it was the only one that would keep all the states together. If no compromise took place, some states might secede, and the American republic would fall apart and become easy prey to the empires all around them. George Mason chimed in weightily: "There must be some accommodation on this point."

- ➤ If there was any one moment in the Constitutional Convention's proceedings when it felt that something tectonic was shifting under the feet of the delegates, it surely came with Mason's declaration. Whatever disappointment it spelled for Madison, from this moment on, there was no more serious debate on whether there should be one or two houses or whether they should be elected by the general population or by the states.

ELECTION DETAILS

- ➤ The next order of business was to arrange the details of how the House of Representatives and the Senate were to be elected. Franklin's idea had fixed on having one representative in the lower house for every 40,000 inhabitants.

- ➤ But Gouverneur Morris was ready with an objection: Any states with populations below 40,000 would still be entitled to at least one representative. This cheated the larger states, because 3,000 or 4,000 people in a smaller state would get more of a say in Congress than the same number of people in the larger states.

- ➤ Other objections crowded in. How, exactly, should the states be represented in the Senate—with one vote for both senators or with each senator voting as he saw fit? Eventually, the convention settled on allowing each state two senators, each of whom would be permitted to vote independently.

THE ISSUE OF SLAVERY

- ➤ What proved infinitely more contentious was the idea of reckoning property into the formula for determining representation in the lower house. Any discussion of property led ineluctably to a subject almost everyone in the convention would sooner have ignored: slavery.

- ➤ By the best calculations we have, the United States was home in 1787 to about 800,000 Africans—most of them enslaved as

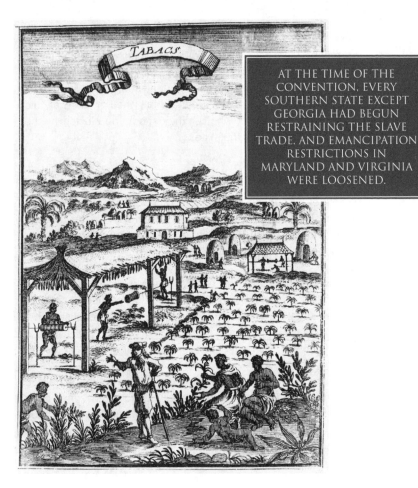

AT THE TIME OF THE CONVENTION, EVERY SOUTHERN STATE EXCEPT GEORGIA HAD BEGUN RESTRAINING THE SLAVE TRADE. AND EMANCIPATION RESTRICTIONS IN MARYLAND AND VIRGINIA WERE LOOSENED.

the human property of their owners. This population was heavily skewed toward the Southern states; almost half of South Carolina's population was black, and so was 40 percent of Virginia's.

➤ Yet slavery was by no means a robust institution, in part because it squarely cut across the political philosophy of the Enlightenment. "All men are originally equal," wrote the Scottish philosopher Francis Hutcheson, because every human being is born with the same set of natural rights. Hence, Hutcheson concluded, "Nature makes none masters, none slaves."

> Another issue stemmed from pure economics: Slave labor was introduced into the Chesapeake in the 17th century largely for growing tobacco, and many were the Virginia and Maryland fortunes that had been built on the back of it. But tobacco as a cash crop had been in trouble for a long time. Another slave-grown crop, rice, flourished in the Carolina lowlands in the 1700s, but the price had gone flat in the 1770s.

> - Meanwhile, ordinary grain crops that did not require the labor-intensity of tobacco or rice were taking off. "As population increases," observed Oliver Ellsworth at the convention, "poor laborers will be so plenty as to render slaves useless. Slavery in time will not be a speck in our Country."

> - But that would not be the case if slaves were going to be counted among the population that determined each state's number of representatives; for small states, such as New Jersey and Delaware, adding slaves would create even more of an imbalance in the lower house.

> On July 6, a five-member panel was created to specify how many representatives each state would receive based on the 40,000 per representative rule. On July 9, the panel reported that the House of Representatives would have 56 representatives: Virginia, 9; Pennsylvania, 8; Massachusetts, 7; New York, North Carolina, and South Carolina, 5; Connecticut and Maryland, 4; New Hampshire and Georgia, 2; and Rhode Island and Delaware 1.

> This struck Roger Sherman as odd: "It did not appear to correspond with any rule of numbers," and he quizzed them for the basis of their calculations. Nathaniel Gorham vaguely replied,

"The number of blacks & whites with some regard to supposed wealth was the general guide."

- ◆ But that set Paterson off, who could only imagine the Virginians stacking their representation in Congress on the basis of counting black slaves and free whites equally—this, despite the fact that black slaves had no say in the politics of Virginia.

- ◆ No one counted slaves as the basis for representation in the Virginia legislature. Why here? What this really meant was "an indirect encouragemt. of the slave trade."

➢ Paterson's assault on including slaves in the formula for determining representation stung the slaveholders in the convention, especially those from the South, and on July 12, William Davie of North Carolina had had enough. He assured the convention that North Carolina "would never confederate on any terms that did not rate them [slaves] at least as three-fifths. If the Eastern States meant therefore to exclude them altogether the business was at an end."

➢ Three-fifths was the formula that had been used under the Articles of Confederation for assessing contributions from the states, and no one less than Edmund Randolph rose to support Davie. He was not pleased at this prospect, but given that slavery existed, any "design" to ignore it would be construed as a plan "by some of excluding slaves altogether."

➢ Again, tempers mounted, and Gouverneur Morris frankly declared that "the people of Pena. will never agree to a representation of Negroes as slaves, by any fifths." Just as vehemently, Pierce Butler of South Carolina responded that a three-fifths representation of slaves was necessary as "security" against the possibility that "their negroes may not be taken from them."

➤ When the entire report of Gerry's Grand Committee finally came to a vote on July 16, it still embodied the fundamental proposition that there would be "an equality of votes in the 2^d branch." The number of representatives in the lower house was now set at 65, based strictly on population, with a census to be taken every 10 years to provide data for adjustments.

◆ The vote was far from unanimous, and the next morning, the nay-voting delegations caucused ominously on their own. "No good Governnt. could or would be built on" the notion of equal state representation, even when it was limited to just one house of Congress," and maybe, some of the wondered, they should simply walk out of the convention.

◆ But, as Madison recorded in his notes, this was mostly "vague conversation … without any specific proposition or agreement." And for now, any determination of what fraction of the slave population—if any—would be used for calculating representation in the future was left unresolved.

SUGGESTED READING

Berkin, *A Brilliant Solution*, chap. 4.
Collier and Collier, *Decision in Philadelphia*, chap. 13.

QUESTIONS TO CONSIDER

1. What formulas did the Grand Committee develop to defuse the standoff between the Randolph Plan and the New Jersey Plan?

2. How did the question of slavery encroach on the debate over representation?

Lecture 15

JAMES WILSON'S EXECUTIVE

*F*or all practical purposes, the vote that took place on the Grand Committee's report on July 16 settled the question of what the new Congress would look like: two houses, the lower house to be elected broadly by the people as a whole, the upper house to elected by the state legislatures, and the authority for originating all revenue matters lodged with the lower house. This was a compromise, and neither James Madison, who wanted everything elected broadly, nor William Paterson, who wanted everything in the new Congress to represent state interests, was entirely happy with the result. But that result yielded at once to the next great subject before the convention: the shape of a new national executive.

COLONIAL GOVERNORS

> The question of the national executive promised to be no less thorny than the issue of representation in Congress, primarily because the colonial governors presented such an unappealing executive example. Before the revolution, every colony had a legislative assembly elected by the people and a governor and a governor's council appointed by the Crown (only Connecticut and Rhode Island elected their own governors).

◆ The lot of the colonial governors was not a happy one. Because their appointment came from the Crown, they were expected to represent the Crown's interests; they had the power to make land grants and appointments to public office to their friends, but their salaries were provided by the legislatures, and the legislatures never hesitated to use salaries as leverage to counteract the authority of the Crown.

◆ In 1754, the royal Committee of Council for Plantations complained to New York's colonial legislature that it had apparently taken over the responsibilities of the governor, including the use of public money, the regulation of the military, and more. No wonder so many of the Crown's governors actually stayed in England and delegated authority to some hapless appointee who was really the lieutenant-governor.

> The governors who did stay in America only made the reputation of governors worse in the 1770s by stubbornly resisting the movement toward independence. By the end of the Revolution, Americans wanted as little to do with high-and-mighty executives as they could.

> The American political climate had not been much better for governors under the Confederation, either. "The temper of the people," wrote the Revolution's first historian, David Ramsay, "would not permit that any one man, however exalted by office, or

distinguished by abilities, should have a negative on the declared sense of a majority of their representatives."

➢ The state constitutions that emerged from the Revolution, when they provided for a governor at all, ensured that they were kept on short leashes, with one-year terms, limitations on reelection, and election by the legislature. In several states, an executive council created by the legislature further limited the governors' authority.

➢ As we saw earlier, the Articles of Confederation were no more eager to authorize any form of free-wheeling executive. The Confederation Congress reserved virtually all government powers, legislative and executive, to itself, and only provided for a standing committee to manage affairs during Congress's adjournment and "to appoint one of their number to preside, provided that no person be allowed to serve in the office of president more than one year in any term of three years."

➢ But a Congress that could only haphazardly summon a quorum could not begin to handle both the legislative and executive business of the United States. Thus, because the Articles of Confederation had also provided Congress with the authority "to appoint such other committees and civil officers as may be necessary," it created superintendents for the treasury, foreign affairs, and war. But even then, Congress struggled to keep as many of the reins of government in its hands as possible, appointing a confusing plethora of temporary committees.

➢ As James Madison explained to Jefferson, any talk about a national executive would sharpen the old fear of power jeopardizing liberty. "Wherever the real power in a Government lies, there is the danger of oppression." But there was no refuge from oppression in merely emasculating the executive power and handing it all to the legislatures. As Madison said, "There is a tendency in all Governments to an augmentation of power at the expence of liberty."

THE EXECUTIVE

➢ The seventh of Edmund Randolph's original Virginia Plan resolutions had called for the creation of "a National Executive ... to be chosen by the National Legislature" with "a general authority to execute the National laws." The first debate on the subject followed almost immediately, on June 1, as the convention went into a Committee of the Whole; four days were spent in what amounted to preliminary skirmishing around the idea of the "National Executive."

➢ Madison was not, as he admitted to Washington, prepared to enter a discussion of the executive. Others were, however, and on both sides. The primary advocate for a chief executive was a legal scholar from Pennsylvania, James Wilson.

  ◆ Wilson was as fully prepared as Madison to raise "the federal pyramid to a considerable altitude" and, together with Madison, fought a doomed rearguard action against the concessions made by the Grand Committee to William Paterson's objections.

  ◆ Like so many of the confederation's critics, Wilson had been stymied by the states' erratic fiscal policies in his investments in western lands, yet he was no elitist aristocrat and denied that "property was the sole or primary object of government and society. The cultivation and improvement of the human mind was the most noble object."

➢ Wilson snatched the lead on the executive debate almost at once, seconding Pinckney's motion for a "vigorous Executive" and adding that it should be filled by "a single person," preferably "a single magistrate." But Edmund Randolph's notion of an executive had not been that of a quasi-king. Madison intervened at this moment and diverted the subject: "It would be proper before a choice shd. be made between a unity and a plurality in the Executive, to fix the extent of the Executive authority" and let that determine whether the executive should be a single person or, as Randolph preferred, a committee of three.

> But Wilson was ready to continue the fight, arguing that the executive should be elected at large by the people, that the term of office should be three years, and that an option for reelection should be allowed. Especially, Wilson was determined that the executive should be filled by a national election, not by the new Congress or by the state legislatures.

> The direct election idea horrified Roger Sherman even more than a single executive had disturbed Edmund Randolph, and Sherman retorted that he "was for the appointment by the Legislature, and for making him absolutely dependent on that body. ... An independence of the Executive on the supreme Legislature was ... the very essence of tyranny if there was any such thing."

> But Wilson had his eye not on the past, where all the examples from British rule had underscored the corruption that flowed from kings, but on the future. An executive appointed by the state legislatures would always be beholden to them; an executive appointed by either house of the new Congress would likewise be beholden to them. Only "Appointment by the people," Wilson argued, would guarantee a national executive free of such dependence, and fully in a position to check the Congress and the states from careening off the republican track. This was consistent with the overall desire of the Virginia Plan.

> Wilson "repeated his arguments in favor of an election without the intervention of the States" over the following week, and just as tenaciously, critics of such an executive waved the bloody shirt of kings. Wilson won at least a partial victory: The Committee of the Whole voted in favor of "a single Executive" but also in favor of electing "the Executive by the national Legislature for the term of seven years." After that, the more contentious matter of Congress and representation took over, and Wilson had to wait.

➢ From the moment the Committee of the Whole committed itself to "a single executive," Pierce Butler noticed that "many of the members cast their eyes towards General Washington as President; and shaped their Ideas of the Powers to be given to a President, by their opinions of his Virtue."

➢ By the time the convention was ready to deal with the committee's conclusions on the executive on July 17, the likelihood that Washington would be the first occupant of the "single executive" became an increasingly powerful persuasive in favor of a nationally elected president, with a full array of executive powers that ranged from a veto over congressional legislation to commander-in-chief of the armed forces.

➢ This time, Wilson did not have to fight alone; James Madison had finally made up his mind that Wilson's notion of the executive was the best way forward, and Gouverneur Morris now became Wilson's pit bull. The "one great object of the Executive is to controul the Legislature," Morris frankly announced. Continuing, he said, "The Executive … ought to be so constituted as to be the great protector of the Mass of the people."

➢ But not even Morris could overcome the resistance of Roger Sherman, who insisted that "the sense of the Nation would be better expressed by the Legislature, than by the people at large," or of George Mason. According to Mason, the people at large were

uneven in their capacity to estimate the worth of an individual for this office, in part because of the sheer size of the country.

> When the question was called on direct election "by the people instead of the Legislature," the vote was nine to one against. Wilson then proposed a compromise: Let the people at large vote, not for a national executive but for a group of electors, who would, in turn, do the voting for the executive. At first, the resolution passed, but it was reversed on July 24.

> Elbridge Gerry, who had chaired the Grand Committee, proposed resorting to the same strategy: the formation of a Committee of Detail, which would take up all of the issues before the convention and provide a set of recommendations. At the end of the day on July 26, the convention wearily voted to create a Committee of Detail and refer to it all the resolutions it had adopted thus far. Then, having sat for two months in the heat of a Philadelphia summer, the convention adjourned for a week's recess, hoping that the Committee of Detail could resolve what the convention had not.

SUGGESTED READING

Stewart, *The Summer of 1787*, chap. 13.
Thach, *The Creation of the Presidency*, chap. 5.

QUESTIONS TO CONSIDER

1. What were James Wilson's arguments in favor of a single-person executive?

2. What arguments were put forward for direct election of the executive?

Lecture 16

JOHN RUTLEDGE'S COMMITTEE

*T*he convention had been sitting for two months when the members agreed to adjourn, partly to let the Committee of Detail do its work and partly to take a break. On Monday, Washington rode to Moore Hall, an estate near Valley Forge; his mind turned back to the sufferings of that winter. On Friday, he traveled to Trenton, the site of his greatest victory. In August, he paid a visit to Whitemarsh "and contemplated on the dangers which threatened the American Army at that place." At least then, the enemy had been identifiable, and one dealt with him in simple terms of winning or losing. The wranglings in the convention were a different matter, where nothing ever seemed decisive.

THE CONVENTION'S RECESS

➤ During the adjournment, James Madison received nagging letters from his father and an uncle, begging for news of the convention, but Madison stood behind the rule of silence that governed the convention. The problem was that silence was creating a vacuum, and into the vacuum rushed imagination.

- ◆ A rumor was circulating in New England that the convention was near collapse and was about to invite Frederick Augustus, the duke of York (and the second son of George III) to be "crowned King over this continent" as a solution to "the inefficacy of our Government & the tumults which prevailed in Massachusetts during the last winter."

- ◆ The newspapers veered in the other direction: *The Pennsylvania Packet* rejoiced to hear that "so great is the unanimity, we hear, that prevails in the Convention upon all great federal subjects that it has been proposed to call the room in which they assemble Unanimity Hall."

➤ For a few members of the convention, the recess was an excuse to leave Philadelphia for good. George Wythe of the Virginia delegation had already bolted home before the recess because his wife was in ill health. James McClurg of Richmond, one of Madison's strongest supporters, left for the recess and informed Madison that he had no plans to return. Hamilton had to keep another member, William Pierce of Georgia, from being sent indefinitely beyond recall, when one of Hamilton's clients challenged Pierce to a duel. William Paterson, having gotten the equal representation he wanted in the Senate, left on July 23 and didn't put in a further appearance at the convention until it was ready to close.

JOHN RUTLEDGE

> Meanwhile, the Committee of Detail pitched at once into its work. The committee was constructed to represent each region of the republic and included precisely the people best situated to get things done, especially on the unresolved question of the national executive: James Wilson, Edmund Randolph, Nathaniel Gorham, Oliver Ellsworth, and John Rutledge. Unlike the Grand Committee, which had to address only the question of representation, the Committee of Detail had been assigned to resolve the logjam over the executive and gather up all the resolutions the convention had adopted thus far and work them into a single document.

> Up to this point in the convention, Rutledge, an attorney, had had comparatively little to say. He had followed the family profession by studying law in Britain. He returned to the colonies in 1761 to begin a practice that, over 26 years, was reputed never to have sustained a loss in court. By 1764, he was state attorney-general; in 1765, he represented South Carolina in the Stamp Act Congress, then in the Continental Congress in 1774 and 1775. The South Carolina legislature elected him as its president in 1776. He was closely allied to Madison from the start and had urged that representation in the new Congress be based "in proportion to their wealth" rather than with the Paterson Plan's scheme for equal state voting.

> The convention had, up to this point, adopted 23 "resolutions," based on the original Randolph Plan and subsequently debated, teased, reworked, reconsidered, and sometimes left unfinished. Given that Randolph had submitted the original plan, it only made sense for him to take the lead in pulling the results together in a coherent format, and he took as his guide two markers: "to insert essential principle only" and "to use simple and precise language."

> ◆ Working from a copy of the resolutions prepared by Wilson, Randolph then set out "the legislative, judiciary and executive in their order," followed by "miscellaneous subjects as they occur." The legislature would consist of a "house of delegates"

and "a senate," and its responsibilities would be "to raise money by taxation, unlimited as to sum, and to establish rules for collection."

+ Voting for the lower house would be regulated by the rules prevailing "in the particular states," rather than spelled out nationally by the legislature. It would "regulate commerce both foreign and domestic" but lay no tax on exports nor pass "a navigation act," regulating foreign trade. And it would be limited by a strict enumeration of powers, rather than a general grant; this was an important distinction, because enumerated powers would limit the legislature to only those powers specified, while a general grant of authority would give the legislature a freer rein to claim new powers.

+ Randolph had reconciled himself to the idea that the executive would be a "single person," elected by Congress, with a veto on legislation and a term of seven years. The judiciary would consist of "one supreme tribunal" whose members would be appointed by the Senate.

➢ Wilson took over from Randolph and inserted a preamble. In it, the states were given their due, but the primary authority would be that of the "We the people." Wilson also changed the title of the lower house from *delegates* to House of Representatives. He was originally inclined to insert a requirement that only freeholders— owners of property—be allowed to vote, but in his final version, the freehold requirement was dropped; Wilson acquiesced in Randolph's formula for letting the states decide who did or didn't qualify as a voter. Like Randolph, Wilson proposed a specific list of enumerated powers: to collect taxes, regulate commerce, coin money, and so on.

➢ Wilson was even more specific about the executive, substituting the title *president* for governor, in whom a broad "Ex. Authority of the U.S. shall be vested," and adding Randolph's requirement that this be "a single person ... elected by Ballot by the Legislature."

The president was to "attend to the Execution of the Laws of the U.S.," "be Commander in Chief of the Land Forces of U.S. and Admiral of their Navy," and have a veto over congressional legislation that could only be overridden by a two-thirds vote of the "House in which it shall have originated."

➤ Wilson also substituted a new title for Randolph's "supreme tribunal," which now became a Supreme Court. And he extended Randolph's ban on "a navigation act" to forbid any "Tax or Duty … on Articles exported from any State; nor on the Emigration or Importation of such Persons as the several States shall think proper to admit; nor shall such Emigration or Importation be prohibited"—an innocuous-sounding proposition that would soon come back to haunt the committee.

➤ We can only trace Rutledge's contribution to the committee's work in marginalia he scrawled on Randolph's proposals. But he must have ruled from the chair fairly vigorously, because in its 11 days of work, the Committee of Detail produced an expansive document of 23 articles. In so doing, the Committee of Detail took a long step toward producing a working constitution that contained a number of features not included in the resolutions but now seen as cornerstones of American constitutionalism:

- The limitation of the powers given to Congress by explicitly enumerating them

- A similar list of powers prohibited to the states

- The basic wording for several of the key terms and clauses that eventually found their way into the final version (e.g., *president, the necessary-and-proper clause*)

- A clear commitment to a single executive, the president.

REVIEWING THE COMMITTEE'S DOCUMENT

➤ The committee printed copies of its draft constitution, with wide margins for notes, ready to distribute when the convention reassembled on August 6. Rutledge, as the committee's chair, introduced the document. When discussion began, Rutledge, Wilson, Ellsworth, and Gorham were ready to act as the document's guardians. The preamble and the first two articles sailed past without a single dissent; some heavy going began on the third article, describing the two houses of the legislature. But Gorham, Wilson, and Randolph shouldered aside everything but the most minor amendments.

➤ The first subsection of Article IV brought the most heated debate, because its provisions for electing members of the House of Representatives left the qualifications for voting to the states; Gouverneur Morris at once objected that this would let down the bar to anyone who wanted to vote if their states permitted it. And he was not entirely wrong to see where this would lead; already voting-rights restrictions had fallen in many of the states.

   ◆ But Morris's objection had more to it than social snobbery. In the first place, he objected to what amounted to a concession to the states to determine who could vote. "The clause as it stands ... makes the qualifications of the Nat^l Legislature depend on the will of the States," which he thought "not proper."

   ◆ He was also motivated by a fear that failing to limit voting rights to "freeholders" would be not the way to prevent aristocracy, but the fastest method to ensure it. "Give votes to the people who have no property," Morris declaimed, "and they will sell them to the rich who will be able to buy them."

   ◆ Look to the future, he urged: "The time is not distant when this Country will abound with mechanics & manufacturers," and when that time arrives, the people who work for the manufacturers will also be the people "who receive their bread from their employers." Did anyone suppose they would be immune to bribery or threat? "The ignorant & the dependent can be ... little trusted with the public interest." But Ellsworth, Rutledge, and Wilson leapt to the defense of the section on voting as written, and Morris's motion was defeated.

- After that, the balance of Article IV was approved in swift fashion—until the convention hit the fourth subsection, where the Committee of Detail had set the "number of representatives ... at the rate of one for every forty thousand." The section, in fact, had only just been introduced when Rufus King of Massachusetts threw a lighted bomb into the debate by asking, "what influence the vote just passed was meant to have on ... the admission of slaves into the rule of Representation." Slavery had returned, unheralded, as the ghost at the constitutional banquet.

SUGGESTED READING

Beeman, *Plain, Honest Men*, chap. 14.
Wood, *The Idea of America*, chap. 8.

QUESTIONS TO CONSIDER

1. Who wrote the preamble of the Constitution, and why was it so remarkable?

2. What fundamental cornerstones of American constitutionalism were developed by the Committee of Detail?

Lecture 17

RUFUS KING'S SLAVES

*R*ufus King's family had owned slaves, but the Revolution had painted the Massachusetts lawyer into a tight ideological spot: It was difficult to reconcile owning slaves with protests against a British monarch for treating Americans like slaves. King served in the Revolution before hanging out his shingle in 1780. He was elected to the Massachusetts state legislature in 1783 and to the Confederation Congress in 1784. But he continued to be nagged by the incongruity of slave owning in the midst of a revolution for liberty. In 1785, it was King's motion in the Confederation Congress that required "that there shall be neither slavery nor involuntary servitude in any of the States" to be formed from the Northwest Territories.

SLAVE OWNING AMONG THE FOUNDERS

> Slavery was legal in all the states but Massachusetts in the 1780s, and a rough count of the number of slaves in the entire republic would have yielded approximately 650,000. Although much of this slave owning was concentrated in the South, even Pennsylvania, which had begun a gradual emancipation plan in 1780, still had a slave population of 3,700 at the time of the Constitutional Convention. Of the 55 delegates selected for the convention, just under half of them were slave owners, and 19 of those relied heavily on their slaves to provide their livelihood and leisure.

> This was all despite the fact that Americans understood clearly that slavery was a horror—the diametric opposite of the liberty they so cherished. There was no sentimental romanticization of happy slaves, dancing away the hours to the pluck of the banjo. Slavery meant, in the words of a famous sermon by the South Carolinian Hugh Alison in 1769, "to live at the mere mercy and caprice of another," and was laden "with ignorance, wickedness and misery." Slavery was "a continual state of uncertainty and wretchedness;

THE SLAVE, WROTE SOUTH CAROLINA DELEGATE HENRY LAURENS, HAVING NO "FUTURE PROSPECTS" WAS "THE MOST MISERABLE OF ALL MEN, DOOM'D TO LABOUR IN THE PLANTING & WATERING, WITHOUT HOPES OF REAPING THE HARVEST."

often an apprehension of violence; often the lingering dread of a premature death."

➤ There were other signs, too, that the dissonance between liberty and slavery was taking its toll on American patience. Just after independence, all but three of the states began to enact bans on the importation of slaves. In Massachusetts, a proposed state constitution in 1778 would have explicitly legalized slavery; it was, however, rejected, and a rewritten constitution in 1780 began with the declaration: "All men are born free and equal, and have certain natural, essential and inalienable rights; among which may be reckoned the right of enjoying and defending their lives and liberties." In 1780, the Pennsylvania Assembly passed a gradual emancipation bill.

DEBATES AT THE CONSTITUTIONAL CONVENTION

➤ No state legislature gave any of its delegations to the Constitutional Convention any directives on what to do about slavery, and indeed, the issue seemed to have been peripheral to what the delegates thought they were doing.

- ◆ The Articles of Confederation were originally supposed to levy assessments on the states based on wealth, but in 1783, the difficulties in making this sort of determination moved the Confederation Congress to switch the assessment basis to population, taking care to count slaves as only three-fifths of a person.

- ◆ This three-fifths stipulation had nothing to do with representation, because the Articles of Confederation had fixed representation in Congress at one vote for each state.

➤ The convention did not spend much time on the subject of slavery for the first two months of its sittings. When the subject of proportional representation had surfaced, there was serious grumbling about whether slaves should be included in the base population used for determining each state's number of representatives, and the three-fifths formula from the Articles of Confederation was trotted out as a pacifier. The Committee of Detail hoped it could be made to work again. But they had not reckoned with Rufus King.

➤ King did not particularly like slavery, but his primary concern was whether counting slaves to determine representation gave an incentive to slave owners to import more slaves. King was sure that "the people of the Northern States could never be reconciled to it," at least not without some national prohibition in the new Constitution on "the importation of slaves." He never could agree "to let them be imported without limitation & then be represented in the Natl. Legislature."

➤ The guardians of the Committee of Detail swung into action to snuff out objections. Roger Sherman assured King that he, too, regarded "the slave trade as iniquitous; but the point of representation having been settled after much difficulty & deliberation," it was not a good idea to rock the boat. However, Gouverneur Morris then moved to insert *free* before the word *inhabitants*. In other words, *no-fifths* of the slaves would be counted. Unlike King, Morris's rationale for such an amendment rasped directly across the dissonance of slavery and liberty.

RUFUS KING
(1755–1827)

➤ Needless to say, Morris's motion went down to a resounding defeat (only New Jersey's delegates voted in favor). But if the slave owners in the convention hoped that Morris's eruption was going to be only an isolated moment, they reckoned without the formidable Luther Martin.

- ♦ Although Martin was himself the owner of six slaves, he saw better than most in the convention that, without some alteration, the Committee of Detail's report would end up granting the larger slave states an untoward edge in the deliberations of the new Congress.

- ♦ Because "five slaves are to be counted as 3 free men in the apportionment of Representatives," and because "such a clause wd. leave an encouragement to" the importation of more slaves, the solution, Martin announced, was "to allow a prohibition or tax on the importation of slaves." To let things stand "was inconsistent with the principles of the revolution and dishonorable to the American character."

➤ Up until this moment, the Southern state delegations had been remarkably restrained in the face of this criticism; they could afford to be, because they were winning most of the points. But tempers were now fraying dangerously, and South Carolina's John Rutledge, the chair of the Committee of Detail, was on his feet at once with a violent riposte to Martin.

- ♦ Rutledge "did not see how the importation of slaves could be encouraged by" the three-fifths rule. But what galled him were the top-lofty moralisms he had heard from the other critics.

- ♦ "Religion & humanity had nothing to do with this question," Rutledge warned. "Interest alone is the governing principle with nations." If the convention wanted to consider prohibiting slave imports or taxing them, then the question would become "whether the Southn. States shall or shall not be parties to the Union."

> Once again, the guardians swung into action, with Roger Sherman assuring Rutledge that he "disapproved of the slave trade; yet as the States were now possessed of the right to import slaves, as the public good did not require it to be taken from them, & as it was expedient to have as few objections as possible to the proposed scheme of Government, he thought it best to leave the matter as we find it." After all, slavery was dying out on its own.

> But Gouverneur Morris's denunciation of slavery on principle could not be stuffed back into the genie's bottle. Now it fell to one of the greatest slave owners in the convention, George Mason, to wield the antislavery sledge hammer: "This infernal traffic originated in the avarice of British Merchants" and "the British Govt." It was time now for the slave "to be properly given up," and the way to do it was "that the Genl. Govt. should have power to prevent the increase of slavery."

> It was one thing for a New Yorker, such as Gouverneur Morris, to attack slavery; it was quite another for one of the most prominent slave owners in the convention to do so, and Mason's fellow Southerners turned on him in a paroxysm of rage. Charles Pinckney resented the implication that there was something wrong with slavery, and his older cousin, Charles Cotesworth Pinckney, insisted that slavery was actually good for the republic. But the Pinckneys got nowhere; too many members of the convention agreed in whole or in part with Morris, Mason, and King about the embarrassment slavery posed to the public reputation of the United States.

> The way out of this corner was proposed by Edmund Randolph: a committee. And with only a few dissenting votes, the convention gratefully handed the future of slavery to 11 of the delegates.

CONTEMPORARY HISTORIANS' VIEWS

> In the years to come, people would debate—often angrily—whether the convention had managed to encourage or discourage

slavery and whether its Constitution was a proslavery or an antislavery document.

➤ The optimists in the historical profession understand slavery in the new republic as a contradiction of the fundamentals of American independence, which the Constitutional Convention set about undermining—but slowly and subtly. No effort was made to convert slavery into a nationally legalized institution, holding off what could have been a fatal slide toward enshrining a race barrier in American life. The national government was given power to regulate slave imports and abolish the Atlantic slave trade. Even the concession of a provision authorizing the rendition of fugitive slaves across state boundaries was so vaguely worded that no one knew quite how to enforce it.

➤ For centuries, almost all Europeans and Americans had to labor from first light to dusk just to keep the wolf from the door, and for many of them, it seemed that labor under the duress of circumstances was little different from labor under the duress of bondage.

◆ But the American environment had changed the nature of labor simply because labor was no longer doomed to produce a subsistence living; in America, labor was the path to unprecedented prosperity and wealth.

◆ Slavery, instead of appearing merely as part of labor's spectrum of drudgery, now began to appear as an aberration, and people who tried to defend it would be forced into increasingly bizarre arguments, until they finally decided that the new American experiment itself, including both the Declaration and the Constitution, had been a mistake.

➤ Progressive historians are more pessimistic. They see a society, for all its love of liberty, palsied with racism and perfectly willing to limit liberty to white people, and from this, they conclude that the Founders' failure to demolish slavery in 1787 suggests that the Constitution actually entrenched slavery more deeply. The progressives are a useful reminder that the Founders were not prophets, only men, and it was not given them as a group to see the tiger slavery would grow into. But Rufus King would.

SUGGESTED READING

Collier and Collier, *Decision in Philadelphia,* chap. 16.
Stewart, *The Summer of 1787*, chaps. 10 and 16.

QUESTIONS TO CONSIDER

1. Which states had banned slavery by the time of the Philadelphia Convention?

2. Why did the arguments for banning slavery in the Constitution fail to win support?

Lecture 18

DAVID BREARLEY'S POSTPONED PARTS

*A*ppointed on August 22, the committee formed to produce a compromise on the issue of slavery was ready with a report on August 24. Despite the high words spoken on the floor of the convention, the climate of the committee meeting was substantially lower. "Notwithstanding their aversion to slavery," recalled Luther Martin, the delegates from the Northern states proved "very willing to indulge the Southern States," especially if the Southern delegates were willing to allow the federal government to tax slave imports. Thus, "after a very little time the committee, by a very great majority, agreed on a report by which the general government was to be prohibited from preventing the importation of slaves for a limited time."

DEBATING THE IMPORTATION ISSUE

- The report of the committee appointed to produce a compromise on slavery called for a prohibition on government actions preventing the importation of slaves for 13 years. When the committee report came up for a vote on August 25, Charles Cotesworth Pinckney demanded that the limited time be extended to a full 20 years.

- This provoked James Madison. Although the Madisons were themselves slave owners, Madison also loathed slavery as an institution, and Pinckney's amendment brought Madison to his feet: "Twenty years will produce all the mischief that can be apprehended from the liberty to import slaves. So long a term will be more dishonorable to the National character than to say nothing about it in the Constitution."

- Madison's objection did no good. Pinckney's amendment passed, although at least Madison's own Virginia delegation voted against it. In response, Gouverneur Morris savagely proposed that the convention drop all pretense to embarrassment over slavery and simply rewrite the entire clause to call it "the importation of slaves." But the South Carolina delegation was not finished.

- On August 29, Pierce Butler proposed yet another amendment, making the extradition of fugitive slaves a matter of federal responsibility, which in effect, forced the Northern states into legal cooperation with Southern slaveholders in hunting down runaway slaves. This time, no one even bothered to object.

- The South Carolinians had held the entire Constitution hostage. "Great as the evil is," Madison sighed, "a dismemberment of the union would be worse," and he would not have put it past South Carolina to "disunite from the other states" and "solicit and obtain aid from foreign powers."

BREARLEY AND THE COMMITTEE
ON POSTPONED PARTS

➤ The fact that a single objection to the Committee of Detail's work had almost derailed the entire convention was not a good sign. It is easy to become weary in doing good, and with the end of August looming and no conclusion to the wrangling over the Committee of Detail in sight, John Rutledge began complaining about "the length of the Session, the probable impatience of the public and the extreme anxiety of many members of the Convention to bring the business to an end."

➤ It is also easy, though, to lose sight of how great a service the Committee of Detail performed. The 23 articles that the committee drafted contained almost all of the Constitution as we know it today. But by August 27, the convention still had not finished its deliberations over 12 of the 23 articles. On August 31, the 12 articles that had failed to generate a consensus were referred to a Committee on Postponed Parts.

➤ This was the fourth committee the convention had created, and at first, its prospects did not look encouraging, largely because the convention handed the chairmanship to William Paterson's friend David Brearley.

◆ A lawyer, Brearley had served as a lieutenant-colonel in the Continental Army. In 1779, he was named chief justice of the New Jersey Supreme Court and attached himself politically to William Paterson, the architect of the one-state-one-vote New Jersey Plan.

◆ Brearley inspired respect but not enthusiasm or loyalty. William Pierce described him as "a man of good, rather than of brilliant parts." Others were more blunt: "Although hardly a brilliant figure, he was capable and respected."

- Brearley owned neither land nor investments and was not the man to carry the New Jersey Plan forward on his own; after Paterson quit the convention in July, Brearley begged him to return, but Paterson refused.

➤ Despite having Brearley in charge, in many respects, the Committee on Postponed Parts turned out to be the most effective committee the convention created. Its principal business was to reconcile the competing demands about the shape of the new national president, and they did so in unusually direct ways, ultimately settling on election by a "college of Electors ... chosen by those of the people in each State."

- The committee also ironed out the issues of the qualifications for office, the term of office, and the foreign and domestic powers the president should exercise.

- In addition, the committee added provisions requiring the states to grant "Full faith and credit ... to the public acts, records, and Judicial proceedings of every other State" and granted to Congress the power "to raise and support armies."

➤ The Committee on Postponed Parts made its report over several days, and after a flurry of proposed amendments, Roger Sherman navigated the report, piece by piece, to approval. A fifth committee—the Committee on Style—was then formed "to revise the stile of and arrange the articles which had been agreed to by the House."

THE COMMITTEE ON STYLE

➤ Strictly speaking, the sole task of the Committee on Style was that of smoothing everything that had been agreed to in the convention into a single flowing document. But neither Madison nor Morris could quite let go of one last opportunity to push the Constitution in the directions they had always favored.

- Morris, in particular, had the itch and the talent to make words work; he would, years later, actually claim that he had written the Constitution. He initially wrote the states out of the Committee of Detail's preamble. The preamble now read, as Madison and Morris had both wanted it, as the action not of the states but of the American people as a whole.

- In four days, Morris trimmed the 23 articles of the Committee of Detail's report down to just 7. One article each dealt with the presidency, the national legislature, and the judiciary; another regulated the interaction of federal and state governments; a fifth described a process for amending the Constitution; and the sixth dealt with national indebtedness, the prohibition of any "religious Test" as a qualification for public office, and Morris's federal supremacy clause. The last article simply stated, "Ratification of the Conventions of nine States, shall be sufficient for the Establishment of this Constitution between the States so ratifying the Same." Ratification would be the job of special-purpose state conventions.

DEBATING THE CONSTITUTION

- On September 12, committee chair William Samuel Johnson had the full text of the new document ready for distribution. Yet even at this last hour, there were surprises, the first of which came from Elbridge Gerry. He now decided to make an issue of the provision that delegated to Congress the power to "make war; to raise armies; to build and equip fleets." On the last day of debate, Gerry promised not to sign the Constitution if Congress retained authority to "raise armies and money without limit."

- Gerry found a surprisingly sympathetic spirit in George Mason, who had come to the convention in May fully prepared to endorse a replacement for the Articles of Confederation, but who had been gradually hemorrhaging enthusiasm for the new Constitution as the weeks dragged by.

- Three months before, Mason was convinced that "the present confederation was not only deficient in not providing for coercion & punishment agst. delinquent states; but argued very cogently that punishment could not in the nature of things be executed on the States collectively, and therefore that such a Government, was necessary as could operate directly on individuals."

- But Mason was uneasy over the creation of a single national president and over the powers awarded to the Senate, and he was genuinely alarmed at the 20-year allowance granted to slave imports.

- By the time the Committee on Style submitted its draft of the Constitution to the convention, Mason had convinced himself that the real threat was posed, not by too feeble a government but by a too-powerful government, and at that point, he took the floor to ask that the Constitution be "prefaced with a Bill of Rights."

➢ By itself, no one who had endured the storm of the American Revolution would have any resistance to a bill of rights. But Madison was incredulous at Mason's motion for a number of reasons.

- First, the Constitution did little else other than set limits on the power of government.

- Second, the Constitution in fact contained a number of specific protections for rights.

- Third, Mason, by insisting on the need for one, was suggesting that the new Constitution was endangering the rights that all previous bills of rights had been created to protect. That, Madison perceived as a subtle attempt at sabotage, especially when the Constitution was submitted for ratification to the states' conventions.

> More alarming was the dissent from the man who had introduced the first plan of the Constitution at the end of May, Edmund Randolph. Like Mason, Randolph had grown more uneasy over the powers being ceded to the new national government. By September, he was no happier with the finished Constitution, and on September 10, he warned that "if no change should be made in this part of the plan, he should be obliged to dissent from the whole of it."

- Randolph had come to the convention with "a set of republican propositions as the basis and outline of a reform" of the Articles of Confederation. But these "Republican propositions had ... been widely, and ... irreconcilably departed from." His best hope was that the state ratifying conventions would offer "amendments to the plan" and that these amendments should be incorporated into a second constitution, drafted by a second convention.

- When this warning was ignored, Randolph repeated it on September 15, adding that "Should this proposition be

THE OFFICIAL SIGNING CEREMONY OF THE U.S. CONSTITUTION WAS HELD ON SEPTEMBER 17, 1787; 39 OF 55 DELEGATES AFFIXED THEIR SIGNATURES TO THE PARCHMENT.

disregarded, it would … be impossible for him to put his name to the instrument." Mason joined him, prophesying that the "dangerous power and structure" of the new national government "would end either in monarchy, or a tyrannical aristocracy," and he, too, called for a second convention. Gerry, of course, followed suit.

➤ But to Madison's relief, the convention turned a deaf ear to these complaints. The motion to provide for a second convention was unanimously voted down; on "the question to agree to the Constitution as amended," every state delegation voted aye. The convention adjourned.

SUGGESTED READING

Brookhiser, *Gentleman Revolutionary*, chap. 7.
McDonald, *We the People*, chap. 8.

QUESTIONS TO CONSIDER

1. How did the Committee on Postponed Parts define the presidency?

2. What was the significance of the ratification process prescribed by the Committee on Style?

Lecture 19

JOHN DUNLAP AND DAVID CLAYPOOLE'S BROADSIDE

One day after the Constitutional Convention adjourned, 500 copies of the new Constitution were printed in *The Pennsylvania Packet and Daily Advertiser*, published by David Claypoole and John Dunlap. William Jackson, the convention's secretary, took some of the copies to New York City for the Confederation Congress; Washington and other delegates picked up copies before leaving Philadelphia for home. The publication of the Constitution must have come as a surprise to anyone outside the circle of the convention's delegates. The delegates had, after all, been given the mandate of rewriting the Articles of Confederation, not creating an entirely new instrument of government, and there was no telling what the response was likely to be, starting with Congress itself.

THE NEW CONSTITUTION

> The first emotion felt at the end of the convention was not relief but anxiety. A cover letter, signed by Washington and added as an addendum to the first printing, tried to smooth the shock of the new Constitution. Preemptively, the letter conceded that the convention did not expect that the new Constitution "will meet the full and entire approbation of every state." But "it is liable to as few exceptions as could reasonably have been expected" and will "promote the lasting welfare of that country so dear to us all, and secure her freedom and happiness." The letter was, of course, whistling in the dark.

> What was it about the new Constitution that generated so much uneasiness in the minds of those who had written it? The obvious answer was that they had not been commissioned to write a new Constitution; consequently, Congress had every right to reject it and call a new convention. Nor would Congress show any greater appreciation when it discovered that the ratification process proposed by the convention—using popularly called state conventions—bypassed it completely. Yet 18 of the 33 members of the Confederation Congress had been in the convention and were not likely to vote against their own handiwork.

> After only two days of debate, Congress obligingly referred the new Constitution "to the several legislatures in Order to be submitted to a convention of delegates chosen in each state by the people thereof in conformity to the resolves of the Convention." It was in those state conventions that Madison, Washington, and the other promoters of the new Constitution had reason for worry, because it was the authority of the states that took the most severe beating.

> The preamble announced that the purpose of the Constitution would be "to form a more perfect Union, establish Justice, insure domestic Tranquility, provide for the common defence, promote the general Welfare, and secure the Blessings of Liberty." The implication from the outset, therefore, was that the states had

failed in doing these things. To correct that, the Constitution would give five new powers to the new federal Congress and impose five restrictions on the states' powers.

> The first new congressional power was taxation, allowing Congress to levy taxes for its needs: national tariffs on imports, excises (or user fees), and direct assessments. Of the three, tariffs would be the most important, partly because they would generate a substantial volume of revenue and partly because the revenue would come from commercial sources, not farmers.

> The second new power, linked to the taxing authority, was the authority Congress would have to "regulate Commerce with foreign Nations, and among the several States." There would be no more need for clumsy interstate commercial conventions, such as the one at Annapolis. Further, a gigantic free-trade zone would be created in place of the welter of state tariffs and duties that had prevailed under the Articles of Confederation.

> As the third new power, Congress could now preempt the states' control of their own armed forces by "calling forth the Militia to execute the Laws of the Union, suppress Insurrections and repel Invasions."

> Congress was also authorized to use the militia of the states "to protect each of them against Invasion; and on Application of the Legislature, or of the Executive … against domestic Violence." This was clearly intended as an insurance policy against further Shays-style rebellions.

> The most sweeping new power was the provision that authorized Congress "To make all Laws which shall be necessary and proper for carrying into Execution the foregoing Powers, and all other Powers vested by this Constitution in the Government of the United States, or in any Department or Officer thereof." Ostensibly, the necessary-and-proper clause was only intended to ensure, according to James Wilson, that Congress "shall have

The Pennſylvania Packet, *and* Daily Advertiſer.

[Price Four-Pence.]   WEDNESDAY, September 19, 1787.   [No. 2690.]

W E, the People of the United States, in order to form a more perfect Union, eſtabliſh Juſtice, inſure domeſtic Tranquility, provide for the common Defence, promote the General Welfare, and ſecure the Bleſſings of Liberty to Ourſelves and our Poſterity. do ordain and eſtabliſh this Conſtitution for the United States of America.

ARTICLE I.

Sect. 1. ALL legiſlative powers herein granted ſhall be veſted in a Congreſs of the United States, which ſhall conſiſt of a Senate and Houſe of Repreſentatives.

Sect. 2. The Houſe of Repreſentatives ſhall be compoſed of members choſen every ſecond year by the people of the ſeveral ſtates, and the electors in each ſtate ſhall have the qualifications requiſite for electors of the moſt numerous branch of the ſtate legiſlature.

No perſon ſhall be a repreſentative who ſhall not have attained to the age of twenty-five years, and been ſeven years a citizen of the United States, and who ſhall not, when elected, be an inhabitant of that ſtate in which he ſhall be choſen.

Repreſentatives and direct taxes ſhall be apportioned among the ſeveral ſtates which may be included within this Union, according to their reſpective numbers, which ſhall be determined by adding to the whole number of free perſons, including thoſe bound to ſervice for a term of years, and excluding Indians not taxed, three-fifths of all other perſons. The actual enumeration ſhall be made within three years after the firſt meeting of the Congreſs of the United States, and within every ſubſequent term of ten years, in ſuch manner as they ſhall by law direct. The number of repreſentatives ſhall not exceed one for every thirty thouſand, but each ſtate ſhall have at leaſt one repreſentative; and until ſuch enumeration ſhall be made, the ſtate of New-Hampſhire ſhall be entitled to chuſe three, Maſſachuſetts eight, Rhode-Iſland and Providence Plantations one, Connecticut five, New-York ſix, New-Jerſey four, Pennſylvania eight, Delaware one, Maryland ſix, Virginia ten, North-Carolina five, South-Carolina five, and Georgia three.

When vacancies happen in the repreſentation from any ſtate, the Executive authority thereof ſhall iſſue writs of election to fill ſuch vacancies.

The Houſe of Repreſentatives ſhall chuſe their Speaker and other officers; and ſhall have the ſole power of impeachment.

Sect. 3. The Senate of the United States ſhall be compoſed of two ſenators from each ſtate, choſen by the legiſlature thereof, for ſix years; and each ſenator ſhall have one vote.

Immediately after they ſhall be aſſembled in conſequence of the firſt election, they ſhall be divided as equally as may be into three claſſes. The ſeats of the ſenators of the firſt claſs ſhall be vacated at the expiration of the ſecond year, of the ſecond claſs at the expiration of the fourth year, and of the third claſs at the expiration of the ſixth year, ſo that one-third may be choſen every ſecond year; and if vacancies happen by reſignation, or otherwiſe, during the receſs of the Legiſlature of any ſtate, the Executive thereof may make temporary appointments until the next meeting of the Legiſlature, which ſhall then fill ſuch vacancies.

No perſon ſhall be a ſenator who ſhall not have attained to the age of thirty years, and been nine years a citizen of the United States, and who ſhall not, when elected, be an inhabitant of that ſtate for which he ſhall be choſen.

The Vice-Preſident of the United States ſhall be Preſident of the ſenate, but ſhall have no vote, unleſs they be equally divided.

The Senate ſhall chuſe their other officers, and alſo a Preſident pro tempore, in the abſence of the Vice-Preſident, or when he ſhall exerciſe the office of Preſident of the United States.

The Senate ſhall have the ſole power to try all impeachments. When ſitting for that purpoſe, they ſhall be on oath or affirmation. When the Preſident of the United States is tried, the Chief Juſtice ſhall preſide: And no perſon ſhall be convicted without the concurrence of two-thirds of the members preſent.

Judgment in caſes of impeachment ſhall not extend further than to removal from office, and diſqualification to hold and enjoy any office of honor, truſt or profit under the United States; but the party convicted ſhall neverthelſs be liable and ſubject to indictment, trial, judgment and puniſhment, according to law.

Sect. 4. The times, places and manner of holding elections for ſenators and repreſentatives, ſhall be preſcribed in each ſtate by the legiſlature thereof; but the Congreſs may at any time by law make or alter ſuch regulations, except as to the places of chuſing Senators.

The Congreſs ſhall aſſemble at leaſt once in every year, and ſuch meeting ſhall be on the firſt Monday in December, unleſs they ſhall by law appoint a different day.

Sect. 5. Each houſe ſhall be the judge of the elections, returns and qualifications of its own members, and a majority of each ſhall conſtitute a quorum to do buſineſs; but a ſmaller number may adjourn from day to day, and may be authoriſed to compel the attendance of abſent members, in ſuch manner, and under ſuch penalties as each houſe may provide.

Each houſe may determine the rules of its proceedings, puniſh its members for diſorderly behaviour, and, with the concurrence of two-thirds, expel a member.

Each houſe ſhall keep a journal of its proceedings, and from time to time publiſh the ſame, excepting ſuch parts as may in their judgment require ſecrecy; and the yeas and nays of the members of either houſe on any queſtion ſhall, at the deſire of one-fifth of thoſe preſent, be entered on the journal.

Neither houſe, during the ſeſſion of Congreſs, ſhall, without the conſent of the other, adjourn for more than three days, nor to any other place than that in which the two houſes ſhall be ſitting.

Sect. 6. The ſenators and repreſentatives ſhall receive a compenſation for their ſervices, to be aſcertained by law, and paid out of the treaſury of the United States. They ſhall in all caſes, except treaſon, felony and breach of the peace, be privileged from arreſt during their attendance at the ſeſſion of their reſpective houſes, and in going to and returning from the ſame; and for any ſpeech or debate in either houſe, they ſhall not be queſtioned in any other place.

No ſenator or repreſentative ſhall, during the time for which he was elected, be appointed to any civil office under the authority of the United States, which ſhall have been created, or the emoluments whereof ſhall have been increaſed during ſuch time; and no perſon holding any office under the United States, ſhall be a member of either houſe during his continuance in office.

Sect. 7. All bills for raiſing revenue ſhall originate in the houſe of repreſentatives; but the ſenate may propoſe or concur with amendments as on other bills.

Every bill which ſhall have paſſed the houſe of repreſentatives and the ſenate, ſhall, before it become a law, be preſented to the preſident of the United States; if he approve he ſhall ſign it, but if not he ſhall return it, with his objections to that houſe in which it ſhall have originated, who ſhall enter the objections at large on their journal, and proceed to reconſider it. If after ſuch reconſideration two-thirds of that houſe ſhall agree to paſs the bill, it ſhall be ſent, together with the objections, to the other houſe, by which it ſhall likewiſe be reconſidered, and if approved by two-thirds of that houſe, it ſhall become a law. But in all ſuch caſes the votes of both houſes ſhall the power of carrying into effect the laws which they shall make under the powers vested in them by this Constitution," not a grant of "general legislative power."

- ♦ After all, Rutledge's Committee on Detail had clearly decided that the federal government's powers were to be enumerated, rather than providing a general grant of powers; in other words, those powers were to be identified one by one, so that it was clear that the new government would be exercising only those powers and none other. Madison concluded, "whatever meaning this clause may have, none can be admitted that would give an unlimited discretion to Congress." A law must be necessary, not merely convenient.

- ♦ But Edmund Randolph had made the "general clause concerning necessary and proper laws" one of his chief objections to signing the Constitution, precisely because he feared it would give Congress power to enact any law it pleased under the guise of it being necessary and proper. Elbridge Gerry had also objected on the same grounds.

- ➢ The Constitution put no restrictions on the internal powers the states could exercise, but anything beyond internal powers now became vastly curtailed. Article I, Section 10, set out a lengthy list of powers the states were forbidden to exercise, including no "Treaty, Alliance, or Confederation … no Letters of Marque and Reprisal … no Bills of Credit," and so on.

- ♦ No longer would the states be the tail that wagged the American dog. In particular, the free-wheeling fiscal carnivals in the state legislatures would stop: Under these terms, states could not issue paper currency or even mint their own specie.

- ♦ Further, they could not threaten to strike up alliances with suspiciously friendly foreign nations. And debtors could not hide behind state boundaries and courts to evade payment of their debts. No wonder North Carolina delegate William

Davie thought Section 10 was "the best in the Constitution" and "founded on the strongest principles of justice." Charles Pinckney thought it was "the soul of the Constitution."

➢ Of course, this was not entirely a one-way street. Article I, Section 9, had limitations for Congress, as well: No export taxes could be levied, no money could be spent without explicit legislative authorization, and no titles of nobility could be given. States could not be subdivided against their will by Congress, and Congress could not use the *bill of attainder*, which had allowed Parliament to function as a court in determining the guilt of high crimes.

➢ There were also powers that some members of the convention had wanted for Congress, but in the end, the Constitution failed to include. Madison had hoped for a direct congressional veto power over state legislation but had to settle for a blander statement. George Mason had wanted Congress to have the power to pass laws to forbid the import of luxuries and to restrict voting rights based on property ownership; he got neither.

ANALYZING THE CONSTITUTION

➢ In many ways, the Constitution continues to harbor surprises. For one thing, the American Constitution was, and is, remarkable just for being written. In English jurisprudence, there is a British Constitution, but it is actually an accumulation of parliamentary statute, judicial decisions, and the common law. Because the American Constitution was ratified through state conventions rather than by an act of the Confederation Congress, it is superior even to statute law. The American Constitution sits above and outside the government, drawing circles of containment around it.

➢ The American Constitution is also unique for the way it divides sovereignty. We sometimes call this the *separation of powers*, and by that, we usually refer either to the division of political powers between the states and the federal government or among the three branches: the executive, Congress, and the federal courts.

- In most contexts in 1787, the idea of dividing sovereignty was thought to be delusionary; what a nation wanted to do was to concentrate sovereignty, to mass its power behind a king or a representative institution, such as Parliament.

- The American Constitution does the exact opposite: It permits the states to enjoy some exercises of sovereignty over their internal affairs but places other exercises of sovereignty with the federal government; it does the same thing with the branches. In the eyes of Europeans, such separation looked suicidally clumsy; however, Americans were not concerned in the Constitution with efficiency but with liberty.

> The Constitution is a document of mixtures. It created neither a classical republic nor an outright democracy. It makes no assumptions about the virtue of the citizenry and imposes no requirements for civic virtue. Unlike the Articles of Confederation, it made no statement about being a permanent arrangement, yet it also made no reference to its dissolution and contained no instruction for withdrawal from its rule.

- It provided for a federal judiciary but only specified the creation of a Supreme Court and left it to Congress to create "inferior Courts." It winked at slavery, gave no countenance to women's rights, and failed to specify the qualifications for national citizenship—or even what citizenship was.

- The Constitution was a statement of what political theorist Isaiah Berlin once described as "negative liberty"; it was meant to free citizens from molestation by power, not to empower or require them to behave in certain ways. It was designed, as historian John Patrick Diggins once wrote, to prevent evil, not to realize some virtuous good; to control the abuse of power, not to shape beliefs and values.

- The Constitution did not so much attempt to resolve American conflicts as to detach conflict from authority. In the view of the Founders, it was only men of sinister motives who hoped to link their fortunes to authority; the free citizen pursued his own ends and interests apart from government, and the Constitution was designed to secure that pursuit.

> In this way, the Constitution decisively addressed the critical issues of the 1780s—of who should and should not hold power, of the disjointed animosity of the states, of the peril of drifting alone in a sea of aristocratic and monarchical sharks. And for every selfish privilege it cancelled, it managed to hold out a compensating advantage. It would need to. Even before leaving Philadelphia, George Mason had prepared the first round of attacks on it.

SUGGESTED READING

Maier, *Ratification*, chap. 3.
McDonald, *Novus Ordo Seclorum*, chap. 8.

QUESTIONS TO CONSIDER

1. Why did the delegates sign the Constitution as states rather than individuals?

2. What were the new powers granted by the Constitution to Congress?

3. What restrictions were placed on the powers of the states?

4. What is meant by the *separation of powers?*

Lecture 20

ALEXANDER HAMILTON'S PAPERS

George Mason left Philadelphia in what James Madison called "an exceeding ill humor." He had agreed to give a lift to Baltimore to delegate James McHenry, who (like Mason) had reservations about the Constitution but who (unlike Mason) had signed it anyway. The two argued for most of the trip between Philadelphia and Baltimore, before Mason's carriage overturned outside the city. Both Mason and McHenry were injured, and a month later, Mason was still complaining about head and neck pains. His injuries, however, did nothing to alter his "fixed disposition to prevent the adoption of the plan if possible" by the state ratifying conventions.

MASON'S "OBJECTIONS"

➤ On their return from the convention, neither Madison nor Mason let any grass grow under their feet. Writing on the reverse of the printed copy of the Constitution provided by the Committee of Style, Mason began drafting what he shortly published in pamphlet form as the text of resistance to the Constitution, his "Objections to This Constitution of Government."

➤ The "Objections" repeated much of what Mason had already said during the convention. The House of Representatives is too small, which means that each representative will have to represent a district so large that he will never be able to speak for everyone in it. By the same token, in such large districts, the only names likely to gain any recognition (and votes) would be the wealthy and famous.

➤ The vagueness of the commerce clause would allow the House of Representatives to "grant monopolies in trade and commerce, constitute new crimes, inflict unusual and severe punishments, and extend their powers as far as they shall think proper." Not that it would matter, because the Senate was too big; it would "destroy any balance in the government, and enable them to accomplish what usurpations they please upon the rights and liberties of the people."

➤ The judicial branch was just as bad. It would "absorb and destroy the judiciaries of the several States; thereby rendering law as tedious, intricate and expensive, and justice as unattainable … as in England, and enabling the rich to oppress and ruin the poor." But the president was even worse. "The President of the United States" will become a tool to the Senate, and together, "by declaring all treaties supreme laws of the land, the Executive and the Senate have, in many cases, an exclusive power of legislation."

> What troubled Mason most was the absence of a bill of rights. "There is no Declaration of Rights," he objected, "and the laws of the general government being paramount to the laws and constitution of the several States, the Declarations of Rights in the separate States are no security."

OTHER ANTICONSTITUTIONALISTS

> Madison expected to hear from New York's George Clinton, who had stymied the confederation's attempt to levy the impost of 1785 because it threatened to dry up New York's tariff revenues. Sure enough, the first volley from the Clinton faction appeared in the *New York Journal* only a week after the printing of the Constitution, from someone writing under the classical pseudonym Cato.

> Cato was brief but cleverly indirect: "If you find that the influence of a powerful few, or the exercise of a standing army, will always be directed and exerted for your welfare alone, and not to the aggrandizement of themselves, and that it will secure to you and your posterity happiness … adopt it; if it will not, reject it with indignation."

> Cato was followed on October 5 in Philadelphia by an author calling himself Centinel, probably the work of George Bryan, a former president of Pennsylvania under its 1776 constitution, or his son Samuel Bryan.

  ♦ The Constitution, argued Centinel, concentrated "all the great executive powers of a confederation." It allowed for "a Standing Army in time of peace," imposed "absolute control over the commerce of the United States," and through the necessary-and-proper clause, "may construe every purpose for which the State legislatures now lay taxes, to be for the general welfare, and thereby seize upon every object of revenue."

  ♦ Like Mason, Centinel was convinced that the congressional districts were too large. The real moving power would be in the Senate, which would be composed of an aristocracy and would reduce the president to "a mere pageant of State." And like Mason again, Centinel objected that the Constitution made "no provision for the liberty of the press ... [and] no declaration of personal rights."

➢ The damning chorus of Cato and Centinel was joined on October 8 by the Federal Farmer and on October 18 by Brutus, both probably New Yorkers, writing at George Clinton's direction. Indeed, for the next six months, the newspapers would teem with a mounting crescendo of denunciation, coalescing around six principal objections:

♦ The Constitution had not created a reformed federal government to replace the Articles of Confederation but an entirely new monstrosity of a single, consolidated government.

♦ The size of the United States would force this consolidated government to rule with a heavy hand.

♦ The powers awarded to the consolidated government were put in such vague terms that no one could find ground on which to stand against them.

♦ The president and the Senate had too much power and were the seeds of a monarchy.

♦ The new Congress should not be given the power to maintain a national professional army.

♦ There was no bill of rights.

RESPONSES TO THE ANTICONSTITUTIONALISTS

➢ The first freestanding counterattack on the Anticonstitutionalists came in Philadelphia on October 6, when James Wilson addressed "a very great concourse of people" outside the State

House "to explain and elucidate the principles and arrangements of the constitution that has been submitted to the consideration of the United States." He did not actually spend much time explaining but moved right away to punch back at the Anticonstitutionalists' arguments.

- Wilson argued that there should be no bill of rights in the Constitution; the document gave the national government only limited and enumerated powers, and restrictions of basic rights—especially ones already secured by state constitutions—were not among them.

- On the issue of the standing army, Wilson asked, what nation in the world "has not found it necessary and useful to maintain the appearance of strength in a season of the most profound tranquility"?

- Would the Constitution "reduce the State governments to mere corporations and eventually … annihilate them"? Wilson claimed that couldn't happen when the Senate is elected by the state legislatures, and the president is chosen by an electoral college whose members are "nominated in such manner as the legislature of each State may direct."

- If there are errors in the Constitution, "it should be remembered that the seeds of reformation are sown in the work itself" by the procedures it specifies for amending it.

➤ Wilson's speech was met with "loud and unanimous testimonies of approbation, but he was at once drowned out by a cascade of refutations, including one from Centinel. Something more thorough and analytic than a speech would have to be mustered in support of the Constitution before the ratifying conventions began to meet.

THE FEDERALIST

> ➤ Alexander Hamilton, Washington's one-time aide, had left Philadelphia confident that the Constitution had everything it needed to carry it through ratification. He was jolted when he returned to New York City in early October to find "the full flood of official influence is let loose against" ratifying the Constitution. He began laying plans for a series of newspaper articles that would "explain and elucidate" the Constitution in far greater depth than Wilson had been able to do. The partners Hamilton recruited for this endeavor included John Jay (the confederation's secretary of state) and Madison.

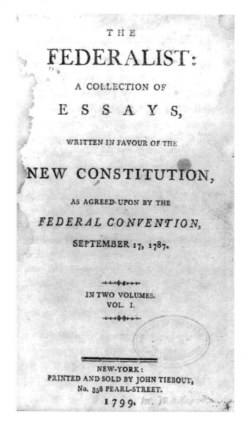

THE

FEDERALIST:

A COLLECTION OF

E S S A Y S,

WRITTEN IN FAVOUR OF THE

NEW CONSTITUTION,

AS AGREED UPON BY THE

FEDERAL CONVENTION,

SEPTEMBER 17, 1787.

IN TWO VOLUMES.
VOL. I.

NEW-YORK:
PRINTED AND SOLD BY JOHN TIEBOUT,
No. 358 PEARL-STREET.
1799.

➢ Hamilton chose the title of his series, *The Federalist*, which was at that moment a daring act of aggression, because it was the Anticonstitutionalists who saw themselves as the defenders of federalism and a confederation. With this title, Hamilton would gain the high ground by asserting that the Constitution represented a better version of federalism than the Articles of Confederation. He also gave a collective pseudonym to his authors: Publius.

➢ Overall, the series had 85 articles, 51 written by Hamilton, 29 by Madison, and 5 by Jay. Hamilton and Madison were not content merely to offer rebuttals to the Anticonstitutionalists— who now, by default, became the Antifederalists. In the very first Federalist, Hamilton laid down six themes by which Publius would demonstrate the indispensability of the new Constitution:

1. The utility of the Union to your political prosperity

2. The insufficiency of the present confederation to preserve that Union

3. The necessity of a government, at least equally energetic with the one proposed, to the attainment of this object

4. The conformity of the proposed constitution to the true principles of republican government

5. Its analogy to your own State constitution

6. The additional security, which its adoption will afford to the preservation of that species of government, to liberty and to property.

➢ It was a remarkable collaboration, and all the more remarkable for the flashes of ingenuity *The Federalist Papers* demonstrated in handling the Antifederalists' objections.

- In *Federalist* 10, Madison confronted the argument that the United States was too large to sustain a single national government without resorting to tyranny by replying that the size of the United States was exactly what would cause tyranny to fizzle away. Conflict would not have to be stamped out by the national government because it "will be unable to spread to a general conflagration through the other states."

- In *Federalist* 23, Hamilton defended the necessary-and-proper clause with an argument that "carries its own evidence along with it," that "the means ought to be proportioned to the ends." How can we confide "to a government the direction of our most essential national concerns, without daring to trust it with the authorities which are indispensable to their proper and efficient management"?

- Above all, Madison, in *Federalist* 51, turned the necessity of separating the powers of the executive, legislative, and judicial branches in the Constitution into a positive by arguing that the three branches, precisely by being separate, would be too occupied with minding each other's boundaries to have time to plot against the liberties of the people.

> In 1821, looking back on the achievement of the Founders, Chief Justice John Marshall would call *The Federalist Papers* the "complete commentary on our constitution," and Jefferson would describe them as the "best commentary on the principles of government which ever was written." It would not, however, be the decisive word on the fate of the Constitution. That would depend on what was said in the state ratifying conventions.

SUGGESTED READING

Broadwater, *George Mason*, chap. 9.
Maier, *Ratification*, chap. 11.

QUESTIONS TO CONSIDER

1. Who were the principal critics of the Constitution once it was published?

2. What were the objections registered by the opponents of ratification?

3. What six themes did Hamilton, Madison, and Jay develop in defense of the Constitution?

Lecture 21

PATRICK HENRY'S CONVENTION

As we saw earlier, Patrick Henry was unenthused about the calling of the Philadelphia Convention in the first place; he was not any more enthused when he saw what it produced. "I have to lament that I cannot bring my mind to accord with the proposed Constitution," he told Washington, who personally appealed to Henry to swing his considerable influence and talents behind it. Henry protested that he had only the "highest reverence" for Washington's opinion, but "The concern I feel on this account, is really greater than I am able to express." That concern meant that Henry would mobilize every political resource and employ every political strategy at his command to stop the new Constitution in its tracks.

THE RATIFYING CONVENTIONS

➤ As the Constitution prepared to make its passage through the state ratifying conventions, it had four elements working in its favor: prestige, surprise, organization, and momentum. Franklin and the Pennsylvania delegation moved at once to lay the Constitution before the Pennsylvania Assembly and ask for a state convention.

➤ Franklin, in his role as president of the assembly, wanted quick action, largely because he also wanted Pennsylvania to be the first to offer the 10-mile square district that would become the national capital. He would not get his wish, though, because the assembly was scheduled to adjourn from September 29 to October 9 for elections; not even Franklin could ask for the calling of a convention until word had been received from New York that Congress was actually sending the Constitution to the states.

➤ When that word finally arrived on September 28, George Clymer (one of the Pennsylvania delegates) moved to call a state ratifying convention, which would hold elections on the first Tuesday in November and meet on the last day of November. That slight delay gave the Delaware legislature the chance to jump ahead and call a convention, with elections to be held on November 9 and 10.

◆ When the Delaware convention met on December 4, the 30 members had but one thing in mind: The new Constitution would unshackle the tiny state from paying tariffs to Pennsylvania for goods shipped through the port of Philadelphia. The move to ratify on December 7 was swift and unanimous.

◆ In short order, Connecticut and Massachusetts called their town meetings to choose delegates to a state convention to meet in November and January; New Jersey called a convention that ratified the Constitution on December 18, followed by Georgia, whose convention was called on October 26.

➢ From that point, however, the momentum began to slow. The Pennsylvania ratifying convention met in Philadelphia on November 20, but its members showed no sense of urgency in their deliberations. Just as he had done in October, James Wilson leapt forward with a lengthy speech in support of ratification and supporting the call of Thomas McKean, the chief justice of the Pennsylvania Supreme Court, for a single vote on the whole Constitution.

- ◆ Taking his cue from *The Federalist Papers*, Wilson insisted that the new Constitution was a genuinely federal document that struck the middle-of-the-road note between a disconnected shambles and a centralized despotism. It would "admit all the advantages, and ... exclude all the disadvantages which are incidental to the known and established constitutions of government."

- ◆ But Wilson was just as promptly brushed back by a vicious attack by John Smilie, a small farmer from Fayette County, who demanded that the convention begin "to alter or amend" the Constitution piece by piece. Thus, the Pennsylvania convention commenced plowing doggedly through each article. Again, the absence of a bill of rights was cited as a "radical wrong," and the nightmare of a consolidated government was conjured.

- ◆ On November 26, Wilson and McKean won a test vote and, on December 12, managed to force a vote on ratification and won. But the dissenting delegates were so unreconciled to the ratification that they refused to sign the resolution.

➢ The Pennsylvania ratification was not a good sign, apart from the single fact that it added a fourth state to the required nine. The Connecticut convention, which had been called in mid-October, did not assemble in Hartford until January 3, and several of the town meetings instructed their delegates to bring up proposed amendments. Once assembled, the convention then moved tediously through a review of each article, and not until January 9 did Connecticut finally vote to ratify. That made five states, but the issue was clearly losing its headway.

- Because New Hampshire's legislature was not scheduled to meet until January 1788, John Sullivan, the state president, called a special session of the legislature for December 14; a ratifying convention was duly authorized, but it would not meet until February 13. After nine days, it voted not to ratify but to adjourn.

- In New York, the unsympathetic governor, George Clinton, waited until the legislature convened in its regular session in January 1788. The legislature then scheduled the ratifying convention for June.

- Maryland ignored Federalist demands for a ratifying convention until November and, even when it authorized the convention, did not schedule it until April. The South Carolina legislature did not take up the Constitution until January and held its own debate before finally authorizing a convention in May.

- More might have been hoped for from Massachusetts, which issued a call for a convention in late October. But the lower house of the legislature refused to schedule a ratifying convention's first meeting in Boston until January 9, and even then, the delegates arrived with instructions from their town meetings to demand a variety of amendments, including a bill of rights and religious tests for federal officeholders.

- The president of the convention was John Hancock, who refused to declare himself for or against ratification; another old revolutionary, Samuel Adams, was chosen as a delegate from Boston and had no hesitation in expressing himself as absolutely against the Constitution.

JOHN HANCOCK
(1737–1793)

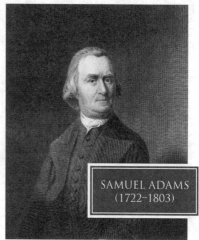

SAMUEL ADAMS
(1722–1803)

- Beginning on January 14, the Massachusetts convention proceeded to pick its way through the Constitution paragraph by paragraph; this went on until January 23, when a Federalist delegate moved to consider the Constitution as a whole. The debates dragged out until February 6, and the final vote to ratify was an uneasy 187 to 168, with 9 absences.

VIRGINIA'S CONVENTION

➢ The Constitution's decaying momentum set an unhappy stage for what everyone understood would be the ultimate test: Virginia. The Virginia General Assembly, meeting in October, set the meeting of the convention in June. Virginians were clearly divided among those who wanted the Constitution as it was, those who were prepared to concede the necessity of amendments, and those, such as Patrick Henry, who refused any part of it.

➢ The long prelude to the Virginia convention was a gift to Virginia's Antifederalists, including Richard Henry Lee, George Mason, and of course, Patrick Henry, to (as Madison put it) "create difficulties." They were joined by Virginians from whom Madison had hoped for more cooperation.

PATRICK HENRY
(1736–1799)

> Richard Henry Lee took the lead as a writer, publishing a 64-page pamphlet of extracts from the Constitution, along with vitriolic attacks on them. But it was Henry who orchestrated "with his usual address, every possible interest into a spirit of opposition." He shrewdly frightened Virginians who had unpaid prewar debts to British merchants or who had occupied confiscated Tory properties with the specter of being dragged into far-away federal courts.

> Elections to the convention became fiercely competitive, but the real test would come in the convention itself, which assembled on June 2, 1788. On a motion from George Mason, the delegates agreed to begin a "full discussion, clause by clause." But they were not really weighing the clauses; they were waiting for Henry, and on June 4, he did not disappoint them. "I conceive the republic to be in extreme danger," he announced solemnly. This anxiety "arises from a proposal to change our government—a proposal

that goes to the utter annihilation of the most solemn engagements of the states."

- ♦ The evidence was to be found at the very beginning, in the first three words of the Constitution: "We the People." Henry said, "Who authorized them to speak the language of *We, the People*, instead of *We, the States*? States are the characteristics, and the soul of a confederation. If the states be not the agents of this compact, it must be one great consolidated national government."

- ♦ George Mason was quick to follow Henry's line of attack. "Whether the constitution be good or bad," Mason claimed, is irrelevant; the power to levy tariffs without the consent of the individual states "clearly discovers, that it is a national government, and no longer a confederation." Mason asked whether a national government could supervise a nation as large as the United States without becoming tyrannical by necessity.

➢ Still, for all the rhetorical fireworks, Henry and Mason would not be allowed to hijack the convention. Speaking briefly at the end of the June 4 session, Madison paved the way for Henry "Light-Horse Harry" Lee to go on the attack. Why, Lee asked, was Patrick Henry resorting to scare tactics? What could be more proper than to begin a constitution by appealing to the people whose sovereignty it embodied?

➢ On June 6, Madison delivered a calm dissection of Henry's alarm. Was Henry fearful for a loss of liberty? "Upon a review of history, he would have found, that the loss of liberty very often resulted from factions and divisions—from local considerations, which eternally lead to quarrels—he would have found internal dissentions to have more frequently demolished civil liberty" than consolidated government. The truth is, Madison continued, that the new Constitution created a middle ground between a disconnected group of states and a single, concentrated government.

> For nine days, the arguments swayed back and forth. On June 25, after three weeks of wrangling, a roll-call vote was demanded by George Mason, and ratification won.

> But the Federalists had not won their victory without conditions. The ratifying resolutions required that "any imperfections" in the Constitution be remedied by amendments, particularly the rights to religious freedom and freedom of the press. In shorter terms, Madison and his fellow Federalists had pledged themselves to concede a bill of rights.

> The irony of the concession was that, technically speaking, Madison need not have made it. Tardily, the Maryland and South Carolina conventions ratified the Constitution in April and May. New Hampshire's convention voted to ratify in June, making it the ninth state and, thus, giving the Constitution legal standing even while the Virginia delegates were still voting. New York, its Antifederalists felled by the news of Virginia's ratification, would narrowly follow suit in July. The Constitution had arrived at last.

SUGGESTED READING

Kidd, *Patrick Henry*, chap. 9.
Labunski, *James Madison and the Struggle for the Bill of Rights*, chaps. 4–5.

QUESTIONS TO CONSIDER

1. What factors were operating in favor of ratification?

2. What made Madison concede the writing of a Bill of Rights?

Lecture 22

GEORGE WASHINGTON'S INAUGURAL

*O*n July 2, 1788, Congress was informed that the ninth state needed to ratify the Constitution had done so. It was typical of the history of the Confederation Congress that it now proceeded to tie itself in knots over where the new Congress should meet. It was not until September 14 that the members set New York as the meeting place; other dates were set for each state to appoint presidential electors and for the electors to cast their votes for the first president. All the operations of the new Congress and government would begin on the first Wednesday in March 1789. But as we'll see in this lecture, the new government was off to an erratic start.

LAUNCHING THE NEW GOVERNMENT

➢ After setting the dates for the new government to begin operations, Congress briefly adjourned on October 2, which seems to have been the signal for almost everyone to leave. By October 14, attendance dwindled to just two states; after November 1, the members met only "occasionally," and after February 19, no one bothered to show up at all except for the ever-faithful secretary, Charles Thomson.

➢ North Carolina and Rhode Island still declined ratification, but few observers expected that they would hold out for long. North Carolina finally ratified in November 1789. The holdouts in the Rhode Island legislature fought the calling of a convention until January. The convention finally met on March 1, 1790, then adjourned. Not until the new Congress voted to embargo all trade with Rhode Island did the convention reassemble and vote—to ratify.

➢ No one was more relieved at the final result than Washington. Madison was able to breathe deeply, too. Writing to Jefferson in Paris, Madison predicted, "Notwithstanding the formidable opposition made to the New federal Government … there is now both a certainty of its peaceable commencement in March next, and a flattering prospect that it will be administered by men who will give it a fair trial."

➢ Madison fully expected to be one of those men, but Patrick Henry, in a spasm of vengeance, secured the election of two Antifederalists—Richard Henry Lee and William Grayson—to be Virginia's first two senators and tried to induce the state legislature to rig the boundaries of Madison's new congressional district to deny him election to the House of Representatives. But when Virginia voters went to the polls on February 2, Madison was easily elected to the new House.

> What was not up for grabs was the presidency. "General Washington will certainly be called to the Executive department," Madison informed Jefferson. Washington, of course, would not campaign for election; he even refused to declare whether he would serve if elected. At one point, Washington suggested that John Adams might be worth considering as an alternative to himself, but nobody was listening. When the state electors met on February 4, 1789, all of them cast their first ballot for Washington; Adams had the second highest number and was "duly elected Vice President."

WASHINGTON'S INAUGURATION

> The new Congress assembled for its first session on March 4, 1789, only to prove shy of a quorum in both houses. Only eight senators were in attendance. When no other senators appeared after a week, they resolved to send "a circular letter ... to the absent members, requesting their immediate attendance." The stragglers finally began to appear on March 19, and finally, on April 6, a quorum was declared—with 12 senators.

> They proceeded at once to draw up an official tally of the electoral votes in the Senate chamber. John Adams took the chair of the Senate on April 21, politely protesting his own inadequacy and praising the election of Washington.

> Word of his election was carried personally to Washington at Mount Vernon on April 14. Washington left Mount Vernon on April 16, and at every stop between Alexandria and New York, he was hailed with crowds, banners, bell-ringing, and cannon salutes.

> Washington took the presidential oath from New York chancellor Robert Livingston on the second-floor balcony of Federal Hall on April 30. To the skeptical eye of one Pennsylvania senator, William Maclay, the 57-year-old general looked as though he would have been more comfortable leading a charge against the British than enduring the inaugural ceremony. In delivering his inaugural

FEDERAL HALL, NEW YORK, NY

address, Washington "trembled, and several times could scarce make out to read, though it must be supposed he had often read it before."

> No one, of course, had ever been inaugurated as president of the United States; thus, there was some buzzing in the Senate about the proper titles to be used. Some suggested "Excellency" or "Elective Highness." It took jockeying from James Madison for Congress finally to agree to address Washington simply as "president of the United States" and "Mr. President."

THE NEW HOUSE AND SENATE

> According to the Constitution's initial apportionment of representation, the House of Representatives was to be composed of 59 representatives and, until North Carolina and Rhode Island ratified the Constitution and chose members of Congress, 22 senators. There were a number of familiar faces, including those

who had been at the Philadelphia Convention the year before, but there were also a number of new faces—not only new to Congress but new to national political life. These included William Maclay from Pennsylvania, James Jackson from Georgia, Judge Aedanus Burke from South Carolina, and Fisher Ames from Massachusetts.

➤ Ames was easily the most interesting of the new Congressmen. Shays's Rebellion had startled him into political action in 1786, and he laid the blame for Shays squarely on the shoulders of the Articles of Confederation. People readily compared Ames to Alexander Hamilton, and indeed, Ames lauded Hamilton for his "integrity and honor." But Ames lauded Washington even more.

➤ Denial of a Senate seat had deeply wounded James Madison, much as he struggled to conceal it. Fisher Ames drew a shrewd bead on Madison when he wrote that Madison was "a man of sense, reading, address, and integrity." But at the same time, Ames observed that Madison was "not a little of a Virginian, and thinks that state the land of promise," and is, therefore, "afraid of their state politics, and of his popularity there, more than I think he should be."

  ◆ Theodore Sedgwick, also from Massachusetts, drew the same conclusion: "No man, in my opinion, in this country has more fair and honorable intentions, or more ardently wishes the prosperity of the public," and yet Madison "is constantly haunted with the ghost of Patrick Henry."

  ◆ Nevertheless, as Cyrus Griffin, the outgoing president of the Confederation Congress, told Madison as he left, "We consider you as the main pillar of the business," and to that business Madison turned.

➤ The first order of business touched on the fundamental reason the new Constitution had been written: revenue. As soon as the House had a quorum and adopted a set of rules, Madison was on his feet to propose the first national import tariffs on rum, wine, coffee, molasses, steel, and more, plus a variety of targeted tariffs that would favor countries willing to sign commercial treaties with the United States.

- That, of course, was a smack in the face of the British, who had still not completely fulfilled their obligations under the Treaty of Paris, much less sought any new agreements with the United States. Still, if that triggered a trade war with Britain, so be it: "I have ... no fears of entering in a commercial warfare with that nation," Madison declared, "if fears are to be entertained, they lay on the other side."

- But he could not easily wish away the ghost of Patrick Henry; thus, Madison "gave notice, that he intended to bring on the subject of amendments to the Constitution"— and by amendments, what he meant was the bill of rights Henry and George Mason had clamored for at the Virginia state convention.

➢ Madison had been suspicious of calls for amendments, fearing that they would chip away the powers the Constitution had won for the national government. He was even less enchanted with the demand for adding a bill of rights. Once it had been agreed that the Constitution would be a grant of enumerated, rather than general, powers, the need for a bill of rights that a general grant of powers could not touch seemed pointless. If the Constitution granted the national government only certain specified powers, there should be no worry about it reaching for powers that the states already secured in their own bills of rights.

➢ But Madison had not been able to convince Virginians of that at the ratifying convention, and their ratification had come with attachments demanding a bill of rights; unless Madison wanted to jeopardize his own political future with Virginia voters, he had every reason for changing his mind. On June 8, 1789, he presented 19 amendments to the House, beginning with a rewriting of the preamble to include an appeal to the natural rights

Jefferson had identified in the Declaration of Independence. The other amendments would guarantee:

- That "the civil rights of none shall be abridged on account of religious belief or worship, nor shall any national religion be established, nor shall the full and equal rights of conscience be in any manner, or on any pretext, infringed."

- That "the people shall not be deprived or abridged of their right to speak, to write, or to publish their sentiments; and the freedom of the press ... shall be inviolable."

- That "the people shall not be restrained from peaceably assembling."

- That "the right of the people to keep and bear arms shall not be infringed."

- In addition, Madison added prohibitions against self-incriminations, against deprivation "of life, liberty, or property, without due process of law," against unreasonable search and seizure, and a promise that "The powers not delegated by this constitution, nor prohibited by it to the States, are reserved to the States respectively."

➢ Oddly, Madison was least successful in persuading his Federalist sympathizers in the House. He wanted the amendments inserted into the body of the Constitution at various relevant places; Roger Sherman objected that this would mutilate the Constitution he had signed in Philadelphia and proposed to attach them at the end.

➢ After wrangling in committee, finally, on August 24, the House forwarded Madison's bill of rights, now recast as 17 amendments, to the Senate. The Senate did its own wrangling until September 14, condensing the list to 12, and on September 24, the House approved the Senate's changes. The whole document then had to go out to the states, and they took until March 1, 1792, to finish their ratifications.

SUGGESTED READING

Elkins and McKitrick, *The Age of Federalism*, chap. 1.
Randall, *George Washington*, chap. 19.

QUESTIONS TO CONSIDER

1. Why were people worried about how Washington should be addressed?

2. What was at the top of the to-do list of the first Congress?

ALEXANDER HAMILTON'S REPORTS

Article II of the Constitution stipulates that "the executive power shall be vested in a President of the United States of America." Apart from creating an office of vice president and a vague reference to certain "executive departments" and their "principal officer," the Constitution said nothing more about what should compose the executive branch. Thus, it was not clear what these executive departments should be or what should be the roles of the people who filled them. There was, however, the precedent set under the Articles of Confederation for departments of finance, state affairs, and war, and in fact, the holders of those offices under the Confederation would continue to act in those capacities until something different emerged.

EXECUTIVE DEPARTMENTS

➢ On May 19, 1789, New Jersey representative Elias Boudinot introduced the subject of "departments of an executive nature in aid of the President," calling for the formation of offices to handle the "finances of the United States," as well as a war department and a department of foreign affairs. When Boudinot's motion looked like it would lose, Madison stepped forward and offered a sweeping motion that at once established the three offices and the secretaries to fill them.

➢ But who would Washington appoint to fill these secretaryships? For the War Department, it would be Washington's old artillery chief, Henry Knox. For the new Department of State, Washington invited Thomas Jefferson, and for the Department of the Treasury, Washington nominated Alexander Hamilton, who set to work in September 1789.

AMERICA'S DEBT

➢ The task confronting Hamilton was daunting. The new Constitution gave the national government a dependable source of revenue, but that revenue would probably meet only the government's current operating costs. It would not do much to deal with the vast debts the United States had incurred during and after the Revolution.

➢ In compiling his initial report on the credit status of the United States, Hamilton found that the overall position of the country broke down in this fashion:

- ◆ Foreign debt: The United States owed $10 million in direct foreign loans. Annual interest on these loans amounted to approximately $1 million a year, but already, the United States was $1.6 million in arrears on interest payments and $1.4 million behind on repayment of principal.

U.S. DEPARTMENT
OF THE TREASURY,
WASHINGTON, DC

- Domestic debt: The Confederation had financed the war by issuing a dismaying variety of bonds, notes, warrants, and certificates for the pay and supply of the Continental Army. Overall, the United States was obligated to repay $16 million just in principal; together with the unpaid interest, the total came to $40 million.

- State debt: Under the loose reins of the Confederation, individual states had accumulated their own indebtedness, which tacked another $25 million onto the bill.

➢ Against this, Hamilton could expect an overall income from federal tariffs and excise taxes of a little more than $4.4 million, and most of that would go to fund current operations. The possibilities for dealing with this situation were not appetizing. The national government might:

- Repudiate the debt as a responsibility of the confederation, which no longer existed or, at least, repudiate the unpaid interest and pay off the principal at the current depreciated market value.

- ♦ Discriminate, that is, pay interest and principal only on notes and debts still held by the original owners, not by second buyers.

- ♦ Pay off the entire national debt by imposing enormous taxes and by selling public land in the west.

➤ Repudiation was the simple solution, but it meant that no lenders in either Europe or America would ever agree to loan money to Americans. For the indefinite future, the American economy would be cash-poor, American enterprises would be capital-poor, and the whole country would remain what it had been under British rule: an agricultural appendage of Europe.

➤ Discrimination satisfied the moralizers, who didn't mind paying off what they deemed to be honest debts but who condemned rewarding speculators. The problem was that not everyone who had bought up discounted government securities and notes was a speculator.

➤ Paying off the debt entirely also had the appeal of being simple, but the kind of taxes necessary to do so were precisely what had sparked Shays's Rebellion. Further, any expectation that the sale of western lands would bring in sufficient cash to pay off the debt collided with the need to clear those lands of the Indian tribes who occupied them.

➤ None of these solutions did anything toward extinguishing the state debts, and as long as those debts remained outstanding, foreign investors would shy away from lending to Americans.

HAMILTON'S SOLUTION

➤ Despite all the complexities, Hamilton was ready, once Congress reassembled on January 4, 1790, with the *Report Relative to a Provision for the Support of Public Credit*. What he proposed was to look at the debt, not as a problem but as an asset.

➤ Borrowing, after all, is what makes possible "trade … agriculture and manufactures." Rather than treat the debt as an illness to be cured, treat it as a plant to be cultivated "by being well-funded." Payoff, repudiation, and discrimination would all scare off further investment; instead, let the federal government pledge, through its tax revenues, to fund the debt on a gradual but dependable schedule, with regular interest payments coming from specifically dedicated tax resources. Moreover, Hamilton recommended, let the U.S. government assume the indebtedness of the states.

➤ Of course, funding the debt would require new revenue, even if it was not in the quantities that a complete pay-down would require,

ALEXANDER HAMILTON

and Hamilton proposed to find that new revenue in western land sales and taxes on luxuries, such as alcohol. To manage the funding of the debt, Hamilton also proposed "the medium of a National bank."

➤ The fury that Hamilton's report let loose exceeded all but the most acrimonious debates in the Constitutional Convention. Fisher Ames, however, vigorously defended the report: "What, let me inquire, will be the pernicious consequences" of not funding the debt as Hamilton recommended? "No individual would be found willing to trust the Government, if he supposed the Government had the inclination and power, by virtue of a mere major vote, to set aside the terms of the engagement."

➤ What was surprising, though, was Madison's contribution to the debate. Madison moved to defuse the issue of discrimination by suggesting that the current owners of notes and warrants be issued new ones based on the highest price the original securities had fetched on the open market. This was not Madison's brightest moment; any effort to re-rig the price of redeeming securities would have driven foreign investment out of America, and Madison's proposal was defeated on February 22.

➤ The back-and-forth raged with few intermissions in the House until June, when the House passed a funding bill incorporating Hamilton's recommendations; it took another month for the Senate to agree. But the effects of the Report on Public Credit were immediate. U.S. government securities tripled in value, thus handing Americans $30 million in capitalization that had not existed before.

THE NATIONAL BANK

➤ But Hamilton was not through with generating political explosions. The next arrived on December 13, 1790, when he submitted a report to implement his proposal for creating a national bank.

> If the funding report was intended to stabilize the republic's credit status, the report on a national bank would take that one step further toward the creation of an active economy. Banks, after all, are the legal means whereby groups of individuals pool their private wealth, make it available for entrepreneurs to borrow, and in the end, receive profits in the form of interest or dividends. They are the pumping-stations of capitalism.

> What Hamilton now proposed to Congress was the creation of a joint public-/private-sector venture, a bank of the United States, in which both the federal government and private investors would pool funds up to $10 million. The federal government would provide one-fifth of the capitalization from its own revenues and, in return, would use the bank as its instrument for receipt and disbursement of funds and use the bank's paper notes as its national currency.

> The federal government's involvement in the bank would guarantee its soundness for private investors, and the remaining four-fifths of the bank's capitalization that they contributed would be available for lending out to businesses to fuel economic development. The profits the bank would earn would not only enrich the private depositors but would also help pay off the remaining federal debt.

> The proposal for a bank of the United States was greeted with a new round of derision and hostility. Once again, Madison parted company with Hamilton in calling for a discussion of the bank as "a constitutional question in the Committee of the whole." The powers of the federal government do not include "a general grant … it is a grant of particular powers only, leaving the general mass in other hands"; among those particular powers, Madison found no trace of authority to create a bank of the United States.

> The bill to incorporate a national bank squeezed through the House after approval by the Senate, but Jefferson intervened with a lengthy letter, at Washington's request. The letter claimed that because "all powers not delegated to the United States by the constitution … are reserved to the States or to the people. …

To take a single step beyond the boundaries ... is to take possession of a boundless field of power, no longer susceptible of any definition." And "the incorporation of a bank, and the powers assumed by this bill," are perfect examples of such constitutional overreach.

➢ Hamilton plied Washington with an equal amount of argument to support his position that a national bank was a necessary-and-proper function of a national government. He understood Jefferson's larger point, that "no government has a right to do merely what it pleases." But in this case, there is a "natural & obvious relation between the institution of a bank, and the objects of several of the enumerated powers of the government." Washington signed the bill on February 5.

➢ It was a political victory for Hamilton, but it came at a cost, first in alienating Madison and Jefferson, then in opening a fissure in Congress that Fisher Ames described as a line between "the two ends of the continent"—north and south. "To the northward, we see how necessary it is to defend property." But in the South, "A debt-compelling government is no remedy to men who have lands and negroes, and debts and luxury, but neither trade nor credit, nor cash, nor the habits of industry, or of submission to a rigid execution of law." They "have assiduously nursed the embryos of faction, which the adoption of the Constitution did not destroy," and it done something none of the Founders anticipated: "made two parties."

SUGGESTED READING

Chernow, *Alexander Hamilton*, chap. 18.
McDonald, *Hamilton*, chaps. 7–9.

QUESTIONS TO CONSIDER

1. How bad was the American debt situation in 1789?

2. What options were open to dealing with the debt crisis?

3. What convinced Washington to sign the bank bill?

Lecture 24

THOMAS JEFFERSON'S PARTY

*T*homas Jefferson may not have met Alexander Hamilton until he arrived in New York City to serve as secretary of state, but it took him no time to conclude that Hamilton was the consummation of every political evil in Jefferson's dictionary. "Hamilton was indeed a singular character," Jefferson wrote years later, "a compromise between the two systems of royalism & republicanism." Washington had hoped that "Hamilton & myself would coalesce in the measures of the govmt," but Jefferson frankly told Washington it was his "wish ... to see both houses of Congr. cleansed of all persons interested in the bank or public stocks," and especially of "a corrupt squadron of voters in Congress at the command of Treasury."

THE FRENCH REVOLUTION

> When Louis XVI became king of France in 1774, his sole qualification for exercising absolute power was his birth. He was utterly unequipped by temperament, training, or intellect to comprehend the seriousness of the problems he had inherited. France was on the edge of bankruptcy and faced population pressure, agricultural failures, the mismanagement of the treasury, and more; all these failures finally came together in a crescendo of crisis in 1789.

> In desperation, the king had called together a national convention, the États-Généraux, in the spring of 1789 to force reforms down the throat of an unwilling aristocracy. The États-Généraux swiftly declared itself a National Assembly with full governing powers for the nation. But the assembly's deliberations were themselves overtaken by bread riots in the streets of Paris in June and July. These climaxed on July 14, when the rioters captured the royal armory in Paris's old Bastille.

> Ten days after the Bastille fell, the assembly began debate on a new constitution for France, beginning with a Declaration of the Rights of Man and Citizen, which distilled into 17 articles the whole of the Enlightenment's notions of human society. In the four months between May and July 1789, France was transformed from an absolute monarchy to a constitutional monarchy, with real political power now belonging to the National Assembly.

> Until 1784, when he was posted to Paris as the chief American diplomatic representative, Jefferson's Enlightenment had been a conventionally English one, dominated by John Locke, and his first impressions of America's principal ally in the Revolution were not positive ones. The events of the spring of 1789 soon changed his opinion, however. "The National Assembly," he wrote Thomas Paine, "having shewn thro' every stage of these transactions a coolness, wisdom, and resolution to set fire to the four corners of the kingdom and to perish with it themselves rather to relinquish an

iota from their plan of a total change in government" had excited his imagination as nothing before.

➤ Jefferson's admiration for the French Revolution seemed to increase in direct proportion to his distance from it, and once he returned to America at the end of 1789, one of his chief motives for taking the post of secretary of state was to observe and encourage the French eruption. When the National Assembly seized and redistributed the lands of the Catholic Church; when the king foolishly attempted to flee France, only to be captured and executed; and when the Reign of Terror began, Jefferson continued to describe the French Revolution as part of "the holy cause of freedom."

HAMILTON'S *REPORT ON MANUFACTURES*

➤ The most obvious question that the creation of a bank of the United States had posed was: In whose interest would a national bank operate? Hamilton's answer to that question was the *Report on Manufactures*, submitted to Congress on December 5, 1791. "The expediency of encouraging manufactures in the United States," Hamilton asserted, "which was not long since deemed very questionable, appears at this time to be pretty generally admitted."

  ◆ The United States could not forever remain an agricultural nation, depending on exporting its surpluses to Europe and using the proceeds to purchase manufactured goods from abroad. Britain's unwillingness to open its ports, especially in the West Indies, to American trade, was proof of the folly of that.

  ◆ To attain real independence, the United States needed to develop its own manufacturing base and let its agricultural profits stay at home to buy American-manufactured goods. Manufacturing would promote foreign emigration, stimulate entrepreneurship, and render the United States "least dependent on the combinations, right or wrong, of foreign

HAMILTON SEIZED ON A NEW DEVELOPMENT AS A PARTICULAR EXAMPLE OF THE PRODUCTIVITY OF MANUFACTURING: THE DEPLOYMENT OF ARTIFICIAL MEANS OF POWER THAT CONCENTRATED THE PRODUCTION OF GOODS IN A MILL OR FACTORY.

policy." Admittedly, it would also produce rivalry and conflict. But Hamilton saw no difficulty in economic rivalries sitting happily beside a national consensus on liberty.

➢ Hamilton proposed to aid manufacturing by "the funded debt." The bank of the United States would become the chief guarantor of investments in manufacturing. Hamilton fully anticipated that this would generate "a question … concerning the constitutional right of the government of the United States to apply this species of encouragement." But Hamilton waved this away as easily as he had waved away the same objection to the bank, this time citing the Constitution's authority to "provide for the common defense and general welfare."

> These proposals maddened Jefferson, who had raised no stop sign to the progress of the first two of Hamilton's reports and had not even succeeded in obstructing Hamilton's establishment of a national mint and a new, heavier coin as the American gold standard. And they raised the hackles of agrarians, such as John Randolph of Roanoke, who believed that American farm interests were now going to be fleeced for the benefit of "speculators," "monarchists," "aristocrats," and "Tories."

JOHN RANDOLPH OF ROANOKE
(1773–1833)

> In the face of such evil, Jefferson saw no "corrective of what is corrupt in our present form of government" except "the augmentation of the numbers in the lower house, so as to get a more agricultural representation, which may put that interest above that of the stock-jobbers."

  ◆ The idea that a republic was composed of "interests" was a fearful one in the minds of the makers of the new government. It wasn't that varieties of special interests didn't exist; it was that, according to the model of virtuous classical republicanism, they shouldn't exist or, if they did, should be deplored, because interests promoted conflict rather than consensus.

  ◆ Madison, in *Federalist* 51, had suggested that although interests would exist in the United States, the sheer number of them would cancel out each other's influence and prevent any one from gaining the upper hand. He was by no means applauding the existence of special interests as a good but, rather, as a manageable evil. In a monarchy, interests ran wild, and the collision of those interests produced corruption, instability, and political factions, or parties.

➤ At best, parties were mere engines of patronage; at worst, they were conspiracies against the common good. Jefferson had been so averse to the notion of parties that in March of 1789, he had written Francis Hopkinson from Paris to denounce them. Now, however, Jefferson began the formation of the first American political party through three distinctive actions: assembling allies, appealing to carefully selected individuals to run for Congress, and playing for control of the media.

HAMILTON'S FIGHT

➤ Just how much heavy political weather Jefferson could generate soon became apparent when Congress took up Hamilton's *Report on Manufactures in February 1792.*

◆ Hamilton began off-balance: His longtime business partner, William Duer, had embarrassed him in December by setting up charters for three new private banks in New York City, all to be capitalized at more than $1 million apiece and seeming as if they wore a Hamiltonian blessing. But the speculation collapsed in March 1792, with prices of shares plummeting, Duer's partners fleeing the city, and Duer himself spending the next seven years in debtors' prison.

◆ Hamilton was also in the grasp of a blackmail scandal involving a flirtatious 23-year-old widow, Maria Reynolds, who turned out not to be a widow at all. When her husband, James Reynolds, reappeared, he tried to get money out of Hamilton and offered to hostile Congressmen to "make disclosures injurious to the character of some head of a department."

➤ Hamilton managed only to get approval for new tariffs before the Jeffersonians rose in the House on March 8, 1792, to blame the New York City bank failures on Hamilton and to demand Hamilton's resignation from the treasury. He was saved by a vote of 31 to 27, with Fisher Ames leading his defense. Later in March, the Jeffersonians demanded an investigation into military procurements; again, Hamilton was exonerated.

➤ Finally, in September, Jefferson launched his ultimate missile at Hamilton: a letter to George Washington, listing Hamilton's crimes against the republic.

THOMAS JEFFERSON

• Jefferson had always planned, as secretary of state, to "intermeddle not at all with the legislature, & as little as possible with my co-departments." But Hamilton had "duped" him in the reports on public credit and the national bank; Jefferson now wanted satisfaction. "His system flowed from principles adverse to liberty, & was calculated to undermine and demolish the republic, by creating an influence of his department over the members of the legislature."

• Especially, the *Report on Manufactures* is a scheme "to draw all the powers of government into the hands of the general legislature, to establish means for corrupting a sufficient corps in that legislature to divide the honest votes & preponderate, by their own, the scale which suited, & to have that corps under the command of the Secretary of the Treasury for the purpose of subverting step by step the principles of the constitution, which he has so often declared to be a thing of nothing which must be changed."

> But Washington had been deeply wounded by the partisan turn of the newspapers, and now, he turned the tables on Jefferson by threatening not to stand for a second presidential term that fall if the bickering went on.

♦ He had known, he told Jefferson, "that there was a marked … difference in our political sentiments, but he had never suspected it had gone so far in producing a personal difference, and he wished he could be the mediator to put an end to it." This, of course, was wishful thinking on Washington's part. But for the moment, Washington held all the cards. In the fall, the state electors once again handed Washington a unanimous ballot, and John Adams, a resounding 77 for vice president.

♦ But the challenge of parties—especially Jefferson's party— would not go away either. Jefferson was convinced that the congressional elections in 1792 "have produced a decided majority in favor of the republican interest." Hamilton's *Report on Manufactures* was never fully adopted, and what's more, Washington and Hamilton were soon to hear another challenge, this time in the echoes of Daniel Shays.

SUGGESTED READING

Elkins and McKitrick, *The Age of Federalism*, chap. 7.
O'Brien, *The Long Affair*, chaps. 4–5.

QUESTIONS TO CONSIDER

1. Why was Jefferson so entranced by the French Revolution?

2. How did Jefferson go about mobilizing an opposition party?

WILLIAM FINDLEY'S WHISKEY

*W*hiskey is a Gaelic word that, roughly translated, means "water of life" or "lively water." It's a surprisingly recent concoction, as the history of fermentation goes, and only made its first appearance in the 15th century as a medicinal prescription. But on the frontier of the early republic, the making and selling of whiskey was a major business, chiefly because it allowed farmers who grew surpluses of wheat to convert them into a liquid and easily storable form. This explains why, when Pennsylvania farmers learned of Hamilton's proposal to fund the national government's debt with an excise tax on whiskey, their first response was wrath as hot and vehement as the whiskey itself.

EXCISE TAX ON WHISKEY

- ➢ Because specie was difficult to find in the Appalachian back country, whiskey became the coin of the realm. This explains why, when western Pennsylvania farmers learned that Hamilton proposed funding the national government's debt with an excise tax on whiskey, the first response was outrage.

- ➢ Unlike tariffs, which are levied on goods imported from abroad and extracted before the goods pass into American hands, an excise tax is domestic and internal. And the levying of internal taxes had been at issue in the 1760s between Britain and America with the Stamp Act.

IN THE WAKE OF THE REVOLUTION, WHISKEY BECAME THE COIN OF THE REALM IN APPALACHIA, WITH A GALLON GOING FOR $0.50 IN THE WEST AND DOUBLE THAT IN THE EAST.

> Thus, it was not any particular fondness for inebriation that set off the second great Shays-like uprising in the life of the new republic in the summer of 1794. Instead, it was, in the words of Joseph Smith, a Presbyterian missionary, "an impression that they were wrongfully and oppressively taxed in the very article which alone they could turn to account in trade and commerce, and thereby secure to themselves and families the very necessaries of life."

REACTION IN PENNSYLVANIA

> The Scots-Irish and German emigrants who came to Pittsburgh imagined that they had found the New Jerusalem. No one, however, anticipates taxes in paradise. Public meetings in Pittsburgh in 1792 adopted defiant resolutions, modeled on the old Stamp Act protests and promising to withhold "all aid, support, or comfort" from excise collectors; representatives in the Pennsylvania Assembly adopted still more resolutions denouncing the excise. Hamilton was flabbergasted, given that the excise could be easily passed on by the producer to consumers.

> Washington, convinced that the opposition was being stirred up by "demagogues," issued a cease-and-desist proclamation against "certain violent and unwarrantable proceedings ... tending to obstruct the operation of the laws of the United States for raising a revenue upon spirits distilled within the same." Congress acted to "obviate causes of objection" by reducing the amount of the tax in May 1792. Washington, who was responsible for appointing the collectors, struggled to appease the back-country opposition by reorganizing the administrative districts.

> Unfortunately, the unrest only spread, from Pennsylvania to western Virginia, the Carolinas, and inland Georgia. And it did not take Washington or Hamilton long to decide where to lay the blame or what to do about it.

REPUBLICAN SOCIETIES

> The elections in the fall of 1792 had not produced any noticeable backlash against Hamilton's policies, but they had not made dissent disappear either. On April 11, 1793, the "Germans" of Philadelphia announced their creation of a political club whose goal would be to lend "advice and watchfulness" to "Republican government ... that its principles may remain incorrupt."

> Six weeks later, an even larger meeting in Philadelphia incorporated itself as the Democratic Society of Pennsylvania. Inspired by "the successive Revolutions of America and France," the Democratic Society promised "to discuss without fear the conduct of the public servants in every department of the government"—clearly, Hamilton—and "to aid and approve those men and measures which have an influence in promoting the prosperity of the Commonwealth."

> The two Philadelphia clubs were followed in short order by the organization of 42 more societies, from Massachusetts to Georgia. The members were largely workingmen, artisans, and anyone who blamed "commerce" for "introducing ... corrupt principles ... injurious to the morals of the state." And they were not shy about the tactics they used. One of Hamilton's allies in Congress was threatened by "15 republicans and boys of Liberty" who were pledged to "exterpate Torys" and, in his case, to "mangle his body."

> The societies were the last stage in the emergence of that bane of all virtuous republicans: a political party. Madison had already bolted in this direction, and Jefferson soon followed. They did not actually join the societies, but they didn't need to, so long as the societies were calling for "a radical change of measures" and denying "the continuance of our confidence to such members of the legislative body as have an interest distinct from that of the people." Just how radical this change might be was indicated by: (1) the repeated assertions of the republican societies that the

interests of the American and French revolutions were bound together and (2) what was happening in the French Revolution.

CITIZEN GENÊT

➤ Once Louis XVI was executed by revolutionaries in January 1793, aristocratic Europe (England, Spain, Prussia, and Austria) declared war on France. The revolutionaries responded with the Reign of Terror.

➤ Americans might have done nothing more than observe these events, until the behavior of the new French emissary to America began to suggest that the French had plans to export their brand of revolutionary fervor to the American Republic.

◆ Edmond-Charles Genêt was the son of a minor diplomatic official in the government of Louis XVI. After the execution of the king, Genêt allied himself with the Girondist faction. In January 1793, while the Girondists still held power, he was dispatched to the United States as the revolution's new minister plenipotentiary. His instructions were peculiar: to recruit any French-speaking inhabitants of North America as volunteers for an expedition against the Spanish along the Mississippi River, commission American merchant vessels as privateers to wage war on British shipping, and if possible, persuade the Washington administration to join France in a "national pact."

EDMOND-CHARLES GENÊT
(1763–1834)

- He arrived in Charleston on April 8, 1793, to a tumultuous reception, which convinced Genêt that he had only to nudge Washington to prod the old gentleman into compliance with the French Republic's wishes. Thus, he issued letters-of-marque for four privateers, dropped hints that he planned to "excite the Canadians to free themselves from the yoke of England," and even paid to outfit a captured British ship as a 14-gun French brig.

- Washington erupted when he learned of Genêt's activities, and Genêt responded, in a breach of diplomatic protocol, by announcing that he would appeal over Washington's head to the American people. It did nothing to endear Genêt to Washington that Genêt allowed himself to be elected president of one of the republican societies or that Jefferson, as secretary of state, had been an audience to Genêt's schemes.

- To Washington, Genêt posed the twin threat of starting wars with both Spain and England at a time when the Americans were barely starting to pay their own bills; to Hamilton, Genêt was the symbol of a revolution gone awry, and he did not hesitate to mimic the organization of the societies by encouraging Rufus King and John Jay to sponsor anti-Genêt rallies in New York and New England.

➢ Jefferson, struggling to disentangle himself from Genêt, announced his resignation at the end of July 1793, but the societies were another matter. Washington saw in the societies only the clubs that had toasted "Citizen" Genêt, and he warned that they desired "nothing short of the subversion of the Government of these states." Thus, when protests over the whiskey excise exploded in violence in the summer of 1794, Washington was prepared to turn his full wrath on the tax protesters as the treasonous offspring of Genêt and "the first formidable fruit of the Democratic Societies."

THE WHISKEY REBELLION

➤ In July 1794, a newly appointed federal marshal, David Lenox, arrived in western Pennsylvania with 39 summonses for defiers of the whiskey excise to appear in federal court in Philadelphia. For aid in serving his writs, Lenox turned to the wealthy Federalist John Neville.

➤ Lenox and Neville were shot at, and on July 16, a band of 50 armed men showed up at Neville's farm, Bower Hill, just southwest of Pittsburgh. Neville barricaded himself in his house, and shooting began, leaving 5 attackers wounded. The next day, the attackers returned, now swollen to between 400 and 800. Neville fled, and Bower Hill burned to the ground.

➤ On August 1, a mass meeting of 7,000 "Whiskey Rebels" was called at Braddock's Field, urging defiance of the excise and promising to march on Pittsburgh. The most hot-headed of the rebels, David Bradford, openly called for "secession from the Union" and praised the French "system of terror" as a means of intimidation.

➤ The connection to the societies explained everything to Washington and Hamilton. The Pennsylvania democratic-republican societies had been eager in denouncing the excise, and similar riotous meetings had occurred in Morgantown and Martinsburg, Virginia. This had one meaning for Washington: The Whiskey Rebels had been given "every lenient measure"; their continued defiance could only mean that they were actually being manipulated by Genêt and his French minions.

➤ On August 7, Washington issued a proclamation, announcing that "the very existence of Government and the fundamental principles of social order" were in jeopardy and calling for the services of the militias of Pennsylvania, New Jersey, Virginia, and Maryland to assemble at Carlisle, Pennsylvania, where Washington himself proposed to take direct command.

➢ Representative William Findley talked the rebels into appointing him as an emissary to meet with Washington at Carlisle. When Findley arrived there on October 9, as the militia was massing in force, Washington received him with "politeness and attention."

♦ Findley blamed the entire outburst on Hamilton and accused Hamilton of having used the excise to provoke the frontier and "inflame the army in a high degree." But Findley also insisted that he spoke for the majority of western Pennsylvanians in expressing "unfeigned satisfaction" at Washington's response, and assured the president that "in future the laws would be obeyed and the officers protected."

♦ Washington was not entirely mollified, and the march on Pittsburgh began on October 12. At every point, however, Washington encountered, not resistance but cheers and hospitality. On October 20, he had grown sufficiently confident that no fighting would occur that he turned over command to Hamilton and Henry Lee and returned to Philadelphia.

♦ In the meantime, Findley managed to isolate the hotheads and persuade the rank-and-file of the rebels to disperse. Twenty of the rebels were eventually arrested; two were convicted of treason but pardoned by Washington. As he explained to Congress in November, the real culprits were "certain self-created societies," which dissolved in embarrassment over the Whiskey Rebellion.

SUGGESTED READING

McDonald, *Hamilton*, chap. 13.
Slaughter, *The Whiskey Rebellion*, chap. 13.

QUESTIONS TO CONSIDER

1. Why was whiskey so important to rural agriculture?

2. Who was Citizen Genêt?

Lecture 26

BENJAMIN BANNEKER'S SURVEY

*T*he Constitution may well have said nothing about public credit or banks, but it did say something specific about the creation of a national capital: a "District (not exceeding ten miles square) as may, by cession of particular states, and the acceptance of Congress, become the seat of the government of the United States." This was, partly, an attempt to silence a squall of demands that had been blowing since the beginning of the Revolution from more than 30 different locations for the nod as the national capital. It was also, partly, a recognition that designating a national capital involved more than merely an agreement to set up the operations of the new federal government in a particular place.

CHOOSING A LOCATION

- The First Congress had been at work for only four months before the first proposal was made, on August 27, 1789, to select "a permanent residence … for the General Government of the United States." But when the House of Representatives tried to bring the matter to a vote on September 3, the proposal bogged down in three-way debate among advocates for a capital on the Delaware, Potomac, and Susquehanna rivers.

- Not even James Madison could prevail over the tumult. He personally favored a location on the Potomac. It could only have multiplied his irritation that the House, when it finally resolved the matter on September 7, voted to locate the capital "at some convenient place on the banks of the river Susquehanna, in the state of Pennsylvania; and that, until the necessary buildings be erected for the purpose, the seat of Government ought to continue in the city of New-York."

- But Madison was unwilling to take no for an answer, nor were his fellow Virginians. "The business of the seat of Government is become a labyrinth," he wrote to Edmund Pendleton. "We are endeavoring to keep the pretensions of the Potowmac in view, and to give to all the circumstances that occur a turn favorable to it."

THE POTOWMACK NAVIGATION COMPANY

- Madison's fixation on the Potomac was more than just an exercise in Virginian self-importance. Like so much else in the formation of the new government, there was a savvy element of self-interest at work, as well.

- After all, the entire process that created the Constitution began with a conference in 1785 to resolve commercial issues on the Potomac between Virginia and Maryland. Commercial development of the Potomac was the principal feature in the creation of the Potowmack Navigation Company, George

Washington's project for developing Potomac River properties and linking them by a system of canals with the Ohio. Planting the national capital along the Potomac would only make the property investments of the Potowmack Company more valuable.

➢ Washington had invested $12,000 of his own in the Potowmack Company, along with another $22,000 as a gift of the Virginia legislature. Madison, Henry Lee, and former Maryland governor Thomas Johnson had also invested in the Potowmack Company, and Washington eagerly tried to sign up "adventurers" in the project from France.

➢ Washington's plans could be more easily placed within the Potowmack Company's grasp if Congress could somehow be persuaded to stop debating the issue and settle on a Potomac River site for the federal district. The mechanism for securing that agreement came to hand on a June evening in 1790.

   ◆ From the time the first Congress reassembled for its second session in January 1790 until June, the subject that consumed virtually all its time was Hamilton's *Report on Public Credit*. It was a harrowing experience for Hamilton, whose "look was somber, haggard, and dejected beyond description."

   ◆ Much of that dejection was due to James Madison's resolute opposition to Hamilton's plan, especially the provision for takeover of state debts by the federal treasury. But Madison wanted the Potomac, too, and Hamilton had something that he could deliver for Madison: the votes of New York's congressional delegation.

   ◆ Thus, with Jefferson acting as host, Madison and Hamilton met over dinner and cut a deal: Madison would drop his opposition to the takeover of state debts, and Hamilton would line up his congressional allies behind the Potomac scheme.

> Without another word in public, a new bill for locating the capital on the Potomac appeared in the Senate, specifying that the federal government would begin business there on the first Monday of December 1800. This Residence Bill passed both the Senate and the House in July.

> There was a last-minute surge of discontent from several Southern members, led by Aedanus Burke of South Carolina. He saw no purpose in building a new capital from scratch, but he was not willing to let the capital go to Philadelphia, even for a short while.

CREATING THE FEDERAL CITY

> It is one of the delicious ironies of the debate over the capital that, in their eagerness to ensure that the capital moved to the Potomac and not merely stayed in Philadelphia out of inertia, the Southern members of Congress inadvertently threw the work of surveying and laying out the new city into the hands of a free black mathematician, Benjamin Banneker.

> The Residence Bill had actually given Washington a 150-mile stretch of river to use in selecting a site, but he had no doubts where he wanted the federal city built: at the eastern branch (the Anacostia River), only 15 miles upriver from Mount Vernon.

> To survey the new district, he turned to Andrew Ellicott, who had completed the survey of the Mason-Dixon Line in 1784 and been involved in surveying missions in western Pennsylvania and the Northwest Territory. And Ellicott, in turn, hired Benjamin Banneker as his assistant.

♦ Banneker, born on November 9, 1731, was an unusual man. He was noticed from the start as a mathematical prodigy and blessed with total recall. He briefly attended "an obscure and distant country school," but not until 1787, when the Ellicott family began employing him as a clockmaker, did he begin show even more astonishing capacities.

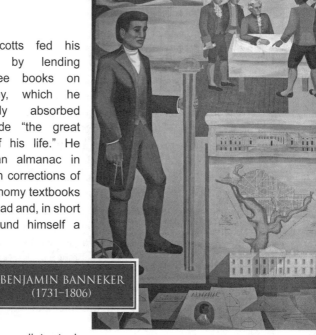

- The Ellicotts fed his curiosity by lending him three books on astronomy, which he effortlessly absorbed and made "the great object of his life." He issued an almanac in 1792 with corrections of the astronomy textbooks he had read and, in short order, found himself a celebrity.

BENJAMIN BANNEKER
(1731–1806)

> Banneker's immediate task in February of 1791 was to join a surveying team headed by Andrew Ellicott and including Pierre L'Enfant, Isaac Roberdeau, and William and Nicholas King. The surveyors set up a temporary base in Alexandria on February 7.

> Together, Ellicott and Banneker laid out the square of the district, starting at Jones Point on the Potomac and laying out four angles. Ellicott finished walking out the first boundary line by February 23, while Banneker checked all sightings by an astronomical regulator. On April 15, they laid the first stone boundary marker at Jones Point, then began marking the remaining boundary lines through the summer.

> The next stages of the creation of the federal city would not go nearly so smoothly. Washington's engineer, L'Enfant, had been commissioned to begin designing the best layout of streets and buildings. What he produced for Washington's inspection on March

28, 1791, was a curious-looking plat of long avenues, meeting at unusual angles to form circles.

- ◆ Compared to the plain and unassuming grid of Philadelphia's streets, L'Enfant's plan looked exotic. But Washington loved it, and L'Enfant went on to select "the most desirable position ... for to erect the Public Edifices."

- ◆ The principal of these locations was Jenkins' Hill, where L'Enfant planned to build the "Congress House"; a mile due west, L'Enfant would construct the "President's mansion." Connecting the two would be a wide boulevard—the present-day Pennsylvania Avenue. North of the president's home, L'Enfant proposed to block out 15,000 building lots, which when auctioned, would provide more than enough revenue for the construction of the city. In deference to the president, Congress decreed in September that the city would bear the name Washington.

- ➤ The first auction of town lots was scheduled for October 17. But at the last moment, L'Enfant decided that the auction was a mistake: The commissioners should borrow the money they needed for L'Enfant's construction projects and hold back the town lots to a later date, when their value would have increased still more. The sale fizzled, and Washington had L'Enfant fired in March 1792.

- ➤ Washington turned next to Samuel Blodget, who proposed to take over management of a second auction in October 1792. Blodget's auction was no more successful than its predecessor. In late September 1793, a third selloff was held, this time, under the direction of James Greenleaf, who had made a fortune during the Revolution as an agent for Dutch bankers.

- ◆ Greenleaf's plan was to buy up as many as 7,325 lots, financed by his Dutch banking friends, but by the time of the auction, the French Revolution had broken out, and with it, war between France and the great European monarchies.

U.S. CAPITOL, WASHINGTON, DC

Investment capital dried up, and by mid-August 1794, Greenleaf and his partners were bankrupt.

- To make matters worse, Washington and the commissioners had given the go-ahead for construction to begin on the Capitol building and the White House; there might not have been cash to pay for the construction, but if the construction was not completed and ready for congressional occupancy by the due date in 1800, the national capital would remain by default in Philadelphia.

➢ Finally, on January 8, 1796, Washington admitted defeat. He addressed a message to Congress, stating with as much dignity as he could muster that the plans for "locating a district for the permanent Seat of the Government of the United States," which he had hoped could "be completed … without aid from the Federal Treasury," had met "new and arduous … difficulties." He now had to submit a request from the commissioners for intervention—a loan from Congress for $500,000.

➤ Naturally, the House of Representatives choked. But, warned Jeremiah Crabb of Maryland, without the loan, Congress "would strongly convey the idea ... that the General Government was not serious, not firmly fixed in their purpose of making the present location the permanent Seat of Congress." On March 31, the House approved the loan.

➤ "By the obstructions continually thrown in its way, by friends or enemies, this city has had to pass through a fiery trial," Washington remarked, "Yet I trust it will ultimately, escape the ordeal with éclat." And it would, in more ways than Washington could have imagined. It would rest on a foundation laid, not by Washington but by a black mathematician and his white employer.

SUGGESTED READING

Bordewich, *Washington*, chaps. 3–4, 7.
Ellis, *Founding Brothers*, chap. 2.

QUESTIONS TO CONSIDER

1. What issues made the selection of a site for the national capital so contentious?

2. How did the work of Benjamin Banneker and Pierre L'Enfant complement each other?

Lecture 27

JOHN JAY'S TREATY

"The Great Rule of conduct for us, in regard to foreign Nations," wrote George Washington, is "to have as little political connection as possible." And certainly the aggravations involved in creating the new government described in the Constitution, putting firm checks on the waywardness of the states, restructuring the feeble public finances, drawing in foreign investment, and managing the talented but fractious personalities who composed the new republic's leadership—these alone would have taxed the patience and wisdom Solomon, much less Washington. He did not welcome foreign distractions. But as we'll see in this lecture, the troubles in the transatlantic world of the 1790s did not give Washington the peace and detachment in foreign affairs that he craved.

TRADE WAR WITH BRITAIN

> In the 1790s, international crises threatened to drag the United States into other peoples' conflicts with demands that foreign armies be allowed free transit over American territory to attack their enemies. The French Revolution posed an even greater threat of disruption.

> There were, for one thing, too many Americans (such as Jefferson) who were convinced that the French Revolution deserved American sympathy and cooperation. They would spend fruitless years discovering this hard truth: that democracies make revolutions, but revolutions do not make democracies.

> There were, to be sure, no shortages of Americans who saw little in common between the French and the American revolutions. Patrick Henry, whom Washington had approached as a successor to Jefferson as secretary of state, feared that the French Revolution was "destroying the great pillars of all government and of social life."

> But what was of more immediate concern to Washington was the reaction of the British, who were now entangled in what would prove to be a war of two decades against the French Republic.

   ◆ The British had proven uncooperative in observing the terms of the Treaty of Paris. They remained an ominous imperial presence on the U.S. northern border, and they placed trade barriers in the path of American shipping to the sugar islands of the British West Indies.

   ◆ To the Francophiles who had made up the democratic-republican societies, these were reasons to put American bets on France; to Washington, these were reasons not to antagonize the British with ill-conceived outbursts of enthusiasm for the French Republic.

➢ The British, of course, had their own view of this situation, which was that any friend of France was the enemy of Great Britain.

   ♦ The British inflamed American outrage by arming and supplying black slave rebellions in the French West Indian islands; by stopping American merchant ships on the high seas and involuntarily pressing American sailors into service; and by issuing orders-in-council that permitted the Royal Navy to seize any neutral ships and cargoes bound to or from France and to confiscate shipping engaged in trade with the French West Indies.

   ♦ These "insults" provoked Washington, in December 1793, to warn Congress that "there is a rank due to the United States, among nations, which will be withheld, if not absolutely lost, by the reputation of weakness." And that meant making it clear "that we are at all times ready for war."

➢ Madison thought he was taking a cue from Washington, and on January 3, 1794, he introduced a series of resolutions that amounted to a declaration of trade war on Great Britain. This would, in turn, have the desirable political result of freeing America from "the influence that may be conveyed into the public councils by a nation directing the course of our trade by her capital" and aligning the United States with France.

➢ But Washington was only rattling his sword, not unsheathing it. The United States had sold the British $8.5 million of goods in 1790–1792, twice what had been sold to France; it imported $15.28 million from Britain and only $2.06 million from France. Moreover, another order-in-council rescinded most of the restrictions on neutral trade, and the prime minister, William Pitt the Younger, insisted that any seizures made under the previous orders were "contrary to instructions given, and that the most ample compensation to the sufferers would be given." Seizing that moment, Washington appointed a special mission to London, headed by John Jay, and sent them off to negotiate a commercial agreement with Great Britain.

JAY AS SECRETARY FOR FOREIGN AFFAIRS

➤ Born in New York City, John Jay was a graduate of Columbia in 1764 and was licensed as a lawyer in the New York courts in 1768. Jay was the youngest member of New York's delegation in the First Continental Congress and sat on the committee for foreign correspondence that sent the first American emissary, Silas Deane, to Europe in search of aid and allies. In 1779, he turned diplomat himself as minister plenipotentiary to Spain. It was in this position that he was named to the team that negotiated the Treaty of Paris.

➤ Jay expected to return to his legal practice once the Treaty of Paris was signed, but he had barely stepped off the boat in New York City in July 1784 when he was notified that the Confederation Congress had nominated him to fill the post of secretary for foreign affairs. This was bound to be a thankless task, as Jay discovered when dealing with the Spanish in 1785.

JOHN JAY (1745–1829)

➤ The frustrations of always dealing the confederation's poor hand convinced Jay that "the construction of our federal government is fundamentally wrong. To vest legislative, judicial, and executive powers in one and the same body of men, and that, too, in a body daily changing its members, can never be wise."

➢ Jay's post as secretary for foreign affairs precluded a seat in the Constitutional Convention but not in the New York ratifying convention. After ratification, Jay stayed on as interim secretary for foreign affairs until the recall of Jefferson from Paris in 1789; as soon as Jay laid down that office, Washington appointed him to another, chief justice of the new Supreme Court. But in April of 1794, it was foreign affairs that reclaimed Jay's attention, and on May 12, he left for England.

➢ Jay was formally presented to King George III on July 2, and for the next four months, Jay and the foreign secretary, William Grenville, pieced together a comprehensive treaty that would address, not only the commercial issues of 1794 but all the unfinished business left over since the Treaty of Paris. A final draft of a treaty was ready as early as August 30, and it was signed on November 19. At its core, the 28 articles of Jay's Treaty involved four major deals:

◆ Britain would complete the evacuation of the military posts it had held onto since the end of the Revolution by June 1, 1796, while debts owed to British merchants since the Revolution would be appraised by a five-member commission and the United States would "make full and complete Compensation."

◆ Disputed boundaries between the United States and British Canada would be resolved by three-member commissions.

◆ There would be "a reciprocal and entirely perfect Liberty of Navigation and Commerce, between their respective People."

◆ Britain would grant most-favored-nation status to the United States in East Indian trade, plus access to the West Indian islands for trade strictly between the United States and the islands.

RESPONSE TO THE TREATY

➤ Given the disparity in power between the United States and the British Empire, the treaty was not a bad arrangement; in fact, one measure of how much it accomplished was the panic that ensued in the minds of Madison and Jefferson when news of the treaty was gradually leaked to the British, French, and American press.

➤ The treaty did not arrive in Philadelphia until March 7, 1795, but until then, suspicion about its contents grew. And that suspicion was more than sufficient to blow the embers of the democratic-republican societies into a flame, roaring that Jay's Treaty could only be a sellout.

➤ Madison was sure that "the bargain is much less in our favor than might be expected" and was nervous that "Jay has been betrayed by his anxiety to couple us with England." When the treaty finally arrived, four days after Congress adjourned, Washington sequestered it until Jay himself could arrive and called for a closed special session of the Senate for June 8, 1795.

   ◆ The actual proceedings in the Senate were comparatively tame. Federalists held a safe majority there, and the Senate took only two weeks of debate before advising and consenting on June 24.

   ◆ The real explosion came once the Senate adjourned and unsympathetic anti-treaty senators released their copies to the newspapers: A Fourth of July parade in Philadelphia turned into a protest riot; a mob in New York City burned a copy of the treaty on Jay's front door; and when Alexander Hamilton offered to debate the treaty publicly, he was greeted with a volley of stones.

➤ It didn't help that Washington was delaying signing, but he ultimately did so on August 18.

SECOND PRESIDENTIAL ELECTION

> A month after signing the Jay Treaty, Washington announced that he would retire from the presidency at the expiration of his second term, in March 1797. This announcement set off "party racers."

> The elections of 1792 were the first intimation of a "struggle between the Treasury department and the republican interest." The uproar over the Jay Treaty only gave party polarization an unlooked-for boost. But the final thread was sewn in the spring of 1796, when the anti-treaty members of Congress, now calling themselves simply Republicans, held their own caucus to endorse candidates for the upcoming presidential election.

> The principal Republican candidate, it was clear, would be Thomas Jefferson; because the Constitution mandated that presidential electors vote for two candidates, the caucus supplied a second name from its newer ranks, Aaron Burr of New Jersey.

AARON BURR
(1756–1836)

> At the same time, the Federalist majority in Congress held their own caucus and produced their own nominees for the presidency, John Adams (the sitting vice president) and Thomas Pinckney of South Carolina. What's more, Adams enjoyed the blessing of Washington.

♦ But balanced against Washington's prestige was the tumult over the Jay Treaty, and one member of the Federalist caucus, William Bingham of Pennsylvania, warned Rufus King, "The

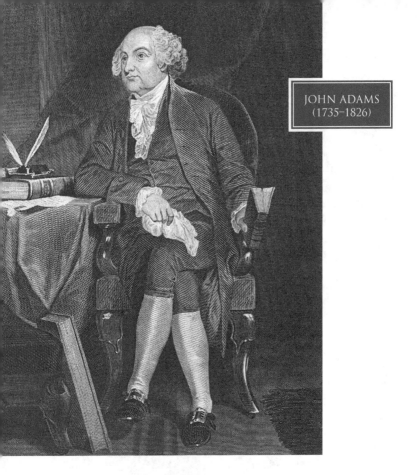

JOHN ADAMS
(1735–1826)

friends of Mr. Adams may calculate on a majority in his favor, but so small, that on so momentous an occasion, it would be risking too much to trust entirely thereto."

◆ When the electoral votes were counted on February 8, 1797, it turned out to have been a near-run after all. Adams won 71 votes, but Pinckney had tallied only 59. Sixty-eight had gone to Jefferson, thus making the two logger-head opponents president and vice president, in what would turn out to be the most unequally yoked presidential administration in American history.

SUGGESTED READING

Combs, *The Jay Treaty*, chaps. 9–11.
Elkins and McKitrick, *The Age of Federalism*, chap. 9.

QUESTIONS TO CONSIDER

1. What were the four deals made with Great Britain by the Jay Treaty?

2. Why was the treaty received in such a hostile fashion?

Lecture 28

JOHN ADAMS'S LIBERTY

*I*f George Washington represented the heart of the American Republic, John Adams aspired to be its brains. And it should be said that few people had better reason for such an aspiration. Born in Quincy, Massachusetts, in 1735, Adams was a fifth-generation New-Englander, son of a deacon and town selectman. He was packed off to Harvard College in 1751, his father expecting that Harvard would make a clergyman of him; instead, it made him a lawyer. He married his third cousin, Abigail Smith, in 1764, a union that lasted for 54 years and produced six children.

ABIGAIL ADAMS
(1744–1818)

BACKGROUND ON ADAMS

> Adams made his first mark politically during the Stamp Act frenzy in 1765, sat in both Continental Congresses, and was a member of the committee appointed to draft the Declaration of Independence in 1776. His first political opus, "A Dissertation on the Canon and Feudal Law," vividly denounced the Stamp Act officers. The 12 essays he published in the winter of 1775 under the penname Novanglus argued that the colonies ought to be thought of as a second part of the British Empire, independent of the Parliament and answerable directly to the king.

> When Lexington and Concord cut short the Novanglus essays, Adams concluded "that there is no good Government but what

is Republican ... If the thirteen Colonies, were all possessed of such Forms of Government, and a Confederation for the above Purposes, was agreed on in Congress and ratified by the Assemblies, they would be unconquerable by all Europe."

➢ Adams was sufficiently imposing as an intellectual that the Continental Congress dispatched him to France along with Benjamin Franklin to represent the new United States; unlike Franklin, however, he made no attempt to accommodate to the free and easy mores of French life. To Count de Vergennes, the French foreign minister, Adams has "an inflexibility, a pedantry, an arrogance, and a conceit which renders him incapable of dealing with political subjects."

➢ But what Adams lacked in popularity, he made up in respect; thus, partly because Adams had been out of the country on diplomatic missions, had not participated in the Constitutional Convention, and had not unduly antagonized anyone in America, he snagged 34 electoral votes in the first presidential election, coming in a distant second to Washington. He was duly installed as Washington's vice president.

➢ Adams's two terms as vice president were politically uneventful, but personally, he continued to blunder from one irritation to another. In April 1790, he began publishing a series of essays, "Discourses on Davila," predicting that the French Revolution would end up in much the same catastrophic way as France's religious civil wars.

➢ This view, of course, astounded James Madison: "J. Adams has made himself obnoxious to many ... by the political principles avowed in his book." Even Alexander Hamilton was not "without apprehensions" that Adams would end up embarrassing the Federalists "and give additional weight to the opposition to the Government."

> But Adams had the blessing of Washington, and he was certainly more acceptable for the presidency in 1796 to Hamilton and other suspicious Federalists than the alternative, which was Jefferson. Adams was also fortunate in the appalled reaction of the French Republic to the Jay Treaty, in which the French inadvertently made him the most popular man in America.

ADAMS AND THE FRENCH

> By 1796, the Reign of Terror had collapsed, and the French Republic was now ruled by a five-man Directory that was still embroiled in war. The Directory regarded the Jay Treaty as a stab in the back of a fellow republic and responded by declaring open season on American shipping.

> During the controversy over the British orders-in-council, Congress had authorized the construction of six large frigates for the U.S. Navy, only to suspend construction once the Jay Treaty was signed. Now, in March 1797, Congress authorized the completion of the first three. On March 25, Adams called for a special session of Congress to consider what other measures he should take. "My entrance into office is marked by a misunderstanding with France," he wrote to his son, John Quincy Adams, "which I shall endeavor to reconcile, provided that no violation of faith, no stain upon honor, is exacted."

> In pursuit of reconciliation, Adams nominated a three-man commission—Charles Cotesworth Pinckney, Elbridge Gerry, and John Marshall—"to conduct a negotiation with the French Republic" for "a removal of prejudices, a correction of errors, a dissipation of umbrages, an accommodation of all differences, and a restoration of harmony and affection."

> But from the beginning, nothing went well for this mission. The Directory kept the commissioners waiting for weeks before granting them an interview with its sleazy foreign minister, the turncoat aristocrat Talleyrand.

- Talleyrand, curiously, was not necessarily prepared to demand hard bargains of the Americans. He "never disputed the right of the United States to make even a shameful commercial treaty with Great Britain provided it does not violate their stipulations to us."

- But Talleyrand had been receiving reports from the French consul in New York that France need be in no hurry to sign an agreement of its own with the United States. "Mr. Adams," the French consul had been told, "is vain, suspicious, and stubborn … but his presidency will only last five years; he is only President by three votes, and the system of the United States will change with him."

- If the commissioners continued to press for an agreement, then Talleyrand concluded that they ought to be willing to pay for it—an immediate "gratification" of $240,000 to Talleyrand and a subsidy of $10 million to the Directory in the form of a loan. The commissioners were dumbfounded, but Talleyrand's intermediaries made it clear: "It is money—it is expected you will offer money."

- The diplomatic back-and-forth dragged on into the spring of 1798, when Marshall and Pinckney gave up and broke off the negotiations; Gerry alone would remain in Paris to keep an American ear to the ground.

RESPONSE TO THE XYZ AFFAIR

> In Philadelphia, Adams received his first dispatches from Pinckney, Marshall, and Gerry on the evening of March 4, 1798, and the next day he sent a notice to Congress that they had been received and were being decoded. Despite mounting public demands for publication, Adams wanted to be sure that the commissioners were safely away from Paris before finally, on April 3, sending the dispatches to Congress.

> Even then, Adams declined to reveal the names of the French officials involved—substituting the letters X, Y, and Z—but the impact remained staggering. When the texts were released to the newspapers, they reacted in anti-French fury. "To be lukewarm after reading the horrid scenes is to be criminal," screamed the *New York Gazette*, "and the man who does not warmly reprobate the conduct of the French must have a soul black enough to be fit for treasons, stratagems, and spoils." Pinckney's angry outburst of refusal became "Millions for defense, but not one cent for tribute"; Adams became the hero of the hour; and France, the mortal enemy.

> No actual declaration of war was issued, but naval combat—Quasi-War—broke out wherever French and American warships collided. Nearly 80 French vessels were gobbled up by the American ships.

> When John Marshall arrived in Philadelphia on June 18, he was greeted with parades and banquets as a hero. "Such a shock on the republican mind," admitted Jefferson, "as has never been seen since our independence." Everywhere, Republicans hid their heads, while Federalism flourished as patriotism.

ADAMS'S BLUNDERS

> And then, with staggering ineptitude, Adams proceeded, through two catastrophic blunders, to bobble away all the political advantages he had acquired. The first blunder was the passage of a series of acts, fueled by the public panic, that were to eliminate the possibility that the French would use French sympathizers in America to undermine the administration. The acts, known collectively as the Alien and Sedition Acts, were really four separate bills that dealt with immigration and permitted the arrest of those who spoke out or wrote against the government.

> ♦ But the enforcement of these laws backfired. Its principal victims were not French secret agents but Americans who

did nothing more than disagree a little too vocally with the Federalists.

♦ Jefferson and Madison capitalized on Adams's blunder by drafting two sets of anti-administration resolutions for the legislatures of Virginia and Kentucky to adopt in defiance of the acts. Let these acts stand, warned the Virginia and Kentucky resolutions, and it might be necessary for the individual states of the Union to declare them "void and of no force." Madison hinted even more darkly that the ultimate remedy might have to be secession of states from the Union.

➢ Adams might have been able to withstand the wave of revulsion that followed the Alien and Sedition Acts if the Quasi-War had finally climaxed, as almost everyone expected it would, in a full-scale war with France. But in August 1798, the Royal Navy, under the direction of Admiral Horatio Nelson, destroyed the core of the French republican navy at the battle of Aboukir Bay and, thus, removed much of the Directory's means for disturbing American shipping.

➢ The Directory itself was on shaky political ground, and in November 1799, its most successful general, Napoleon Bonaparte, would overturn it in a coup d'etat and install himself as de facto ruler of France. Desperate to shore up its political position at home, the Directory now struggled to convince Americans that it was "sincerely desirous of restoring harmony between this country & the United States."

➢ This gave Adams the opportunity to reproduce for his administration the kind of diplomatic success Washington had achieved in the Jay Treaty, and on February 18, 1799, he announced that he was appointing William Vans Murray, the current U.S. minister to the Dutch, "to be minister plenipotentiary of the United States to the French republic … to discuss and conclude all controversies between the two republics by a new treaty."

> By the time Murray finally had a treaty ready for signing, Napoleon was in charge, and the French refused to offer compensation for losses suffered by American merchant ships. Murray signed it anyway, on September 30, 1800. But it did nothing to promote Adams's political standing.

> Adams still had enough control over the Federalist caucuses to control their endorsement for reelection but not in the country at large. Thomas Jefferson, in his second bid for the presidency, garnered 73 electoral votes, along with Aaron Burr, who would become his vice president; Adams won only 65.

SUGGESTED READING

Elkins and McKitrick, *The Age of Federalism*, chap. 12.
Toll, *Six Frigates*, chaps. 1–2.

QUESTIONS TO CONSIDER

1. Why did so many people dislike John Adams, even as they admired him?

2. Why did the XYZ Affair enrage American public opinion?

3. What political mistakes cost Adams any political advantage he would have gained from the XYZ Affair?

Lecture 29

HECTOR SAINT JOHN DE CRÈVECOEUR'S AMERICANS

*I*f Americans found dealing with Europeans a torturous proposition, Europeans were no less perplexed by Americans. The great dictionary-maker Samuel Johnson told James Boswell: "I am willing to love all mankind, except an American"; they were "Rascals—Robbers—Pirates." Nor did the American experiment in popular sovereignty gain much applause from John Wesley, the founder of Methodism and otherwise the great proponent of free will: "No governments under heaven are so despotic as the republican." As for culture, Thomas Cooper, in *Some Information Respecting America* in 1794, scorned American literature as nothing more than commercialism. The French were no less dismissive, excepting perhaps Hector Saint John de Crèvecoeur.

THE "NEW MAN"

> Born in Normandy in 1735, Hector Saint John de Crèvecoeur had served as an officer in the French Canadian militia, and after France's defeat and the surrender of Canada to Great Britain, he stayed on in America. Briefly marooned in Britain during the latter part of the Revolution, Crèvecoeur published *Letters from an American Farmer*, which frankly contradicted the viewpoint Europeans held at the time of Americans.

> "The American is a new man," Crèvecoeur wrote. Partly, this new man was a product of republican government and the abolition of aristocracy. America "is not composed, as in Europe, of great lords who possess everything and of a herd of people who have nothing. … We have no princes, for whom we toil, starve, and bleed: we are the most perfect society now existing in the world. Here man is free; as he ought to be."

> But a great deal of what made the American new was the newness of the space he occupied. In Europe, vast numbers of people were crowded into a small amount of land and were organized around varying creeds, kings, and languages. But America had an apparently infinite amount of space and comparatively few people, and as Madison had anticipated in *Federalist* 10, that vast space allowed the competing identities of the old nations and dogmas to dissolve.

> "Zeal in Europe is confined; here it evaporates in the great distance it has to travel." Hence, Crèvecoeur triumphantly concluded, "He is an American, who, leaving behind him all his ancient prejudices and manners, receives new ones from the new mode of life he has embraced, the new government he obeys, and the new rank he holds."

> It would be easy to wave away Crèvecoeur's love affair with America as the passion of a convert. But Jefferson included him in his circle of correspondents; Washington cited him in his projects

for land development; and Franklin had him elected as a member of the American Philosophical Society. Any picture of Americans at the end of the 18th century that emerges from the statistics gathered by the first national census gives Crèvecoeur more than a little credit for correctly understanding the newness of the "new" American, for we were already a people who looked like no other nation on earth.

THE 1790 CENSUS

- ➤ All told, the American population in 1790 numbered a little more than 3.9 million. Population density in the United States was 4.5 people per square mile, while England, with a population of 7.5 million and 50,000 square miles, had a density of 150 people per square mile.

- ➤ Americans were also overwhelmingly young. At the time of the Philadelphia Convention, something close to half of all Americans were too young to remember the Declaration of Independence; the median age was 16, and life expectancy at birth was in the low 30s.

- ➤ Americans were more or less evenly spaced into three zones: New England, the Mid-Atlantic states, and the South, and fully 90 percent were of English or Scottish and Scots-Irish extraction, followed by 8 percent German.

BLACK AMERICANS

- ➤ One demographic group not so evenly spread was the nearly 700,000 (mostly enslaved) Africans. In fact, African Americans would make up a higher percentage of the American population than they ever would at any later time in American history, even subtracting those who left with the end of the Revolution. Those who remained behind now took the struggle for freedom into their own hands.

- In 1781, an enslaved woman in Sheffield, Massachusetts, known as Mum Bett recruited a Stockbridge lawyer, Theodore Sedgwick, to assist her in bringing a suit for her freedom, on the grounds that the 1780 Massachusetts state constitution had declared "all men are born free and equal and have certain natural, essential, and unalienable rights; among which may be reckoned the right of enjoying and defending their lives and liberties." The case took all of one day for the jury to hear and find in Bett's favor.

    - A similar case was filed on behalf of a male slave, Quok (or Kwaku) Walker, this time working its way up to the Massachusetts Supreme Judicial Court in 1783. "Our Constitution of Government," announced Chief Justice William Cushing, "sets out with declaring that all men are born free and equal—and that every subject is entitled to liberty, and … this being the case, I think the idea of slavery is inconsistent with our own conduct and Constitution."

    - Slavery thus had its legal underpinnings erased in Massachusetts, and by 1790, there were no slaves remaining in the state. In 1783 and 1784, New Hampshire, Connecticut, and Rhode Island began the process of emancipating their slaves, followed by New York in 1799 and New Jersey in 1804. The pattern for all these abolition movements was established in Pennsylvania, where the Pennsylvania legislature had adopted a gradual emancipation program in 1780.

- The free black population of Maryland rose from 1,800 in the mid-18th century to 20,000 by 1799; in 1782, Virginia's free black population amounted to only 1,800, but by 1800, it had swollen to 13,000. Manumission societies sprang up in New York, as well as North Carolina, Virginia, and Maryland.

- Even when passing from slavery to freedom, however, life for black Americans was not as free as it might be for whites. Whatever other traditional restraints and hierarchies the Enlightenment had thrown off, the bugaboo of race remained persistent. David Hume, like Jefferson, could insist that all men are created equal; like Jefferson, however, Hume could not rid himself of the belief that "Negroes" are "naturally inferior to the whites."

GROWING POLITICAL POWER

➤ In the 1790s, few Americans lived alone. Whether as working households or blood-related dynasties, Americans conceived of themselves as parts of networks, and even slaves on plantations were governed by expectations of belonging to a household. Strangers were viewed with fear and suspicion.

➤ Between 8 and 9 out of every 10 Americans lived and worked in the countryside. Only about 5 percent of the population lived in urban centers of more the 2,500 inhabitants. A quarter of all town-dwellers were concentrated in and around Philadelphia, New York, Boston, and Baltimore. Within these, the most obvious division was skilled and unskilled workers.

- ◆ Skilled workers included everything from apprentice tailors to master carpenters and goldsmiths. Laborers, merchant sailors, shoemakers, and tailors made up between one-quarter and one-half of all urban workmen. The rest were unskilled and manual laborers—the "working poor."

- ◆ There were substantial numbers of blacks in these urban centers, but most of them were consigned to the lowest rungs on the economic ladder. Nevertheless, these urbanites considered themselves as "unfettered and unrestrained" as Crèvecoeur the farmer. Johann David Schoepf, who had served during the Revolution, wrote that "the inhabitants of Philadelphia … think, act, and speak here precisely as it prompts them."

➤ Moreover, these same people, urban or rural, were acquiring an increasing say in who spoke for them politically. Although even Pennsylvania's open-ended 1776 Constitution only enfranchised "free men having a sufficient evident common interest with and attachment to the community," this still opened voting privileges far more widely for Americans than for Britons.

- In America, widespread land ownership in fee simple and the addition of non-landholding taxpayers to voting rolls opened access to unprecedented numbers of ordinary citizens. For a brief moment in the 1780s, even free blacks in 8 of the 13 states could vote. By the time of Washington's reelection in 1792, as many as 80 percent of white males were eligible to vote.

- On the national level, this growth in voting rights was muted by the electoral process; in 1792, state legislatures still chose the presidential electors, and the people could be said to vote for a president only in an indirect way. But even that was yielding to change: In the election of 1796, 8 states permitted casting a direct vote for presidential electors. The Constitution had framed a republic, not a mass democracy, but it was a republic that was becoming increasingly democratic within the Constitution's framework.

WOMEN AND MARRIAGE

➤ One category of free Americans who did not have the vote was, of course, American women. In hierarchical societies, women scarcely had any independent existence, either socially or legally; married women were legally classified as *femmes couvertures* and could not be sued or sue, draft wills, make contracts, or deal in property.

➤ But the solvent of liberty ate away even at these traditional restraints. Jefferson might think that American women were "too wise to wrinkle their foreheads with politics," but women thought otherwise. "The Sentiments of an American Woman," announced a broadside posted in 1779 in Philadelphia, were "born for liberty."

- In a society of political equals, marriage itself was the first institution to be reconceived—although, as with so much else in the new republic, it was not the model of virtuous republicanism that was pursued. If so, American women would have recast themselves after the women of classical Rome, which meant no equality, no natural rights, and an obligation to raise their sons as warriors. American women of the 1790s had a far more Lockean set of objectives in view.

- No longer would men be kings, nor would marriage be a kind of domestic diplomatic arrangement between the fathers of brides. Women began to consider themselves as the partners of their husbands, and marriage itself was to be built on companionship and affection, rather than the strategic placement of heirs.

- The road to equal rights, property, and access to power lay through education. Benjamin Rush argued, "The cultivation of reason in women is alike friendly to the order of nature and the private as well as the public happiness." Several "academies" for women were opened in the 1780s and 1790s, and their graduates were not shy about claiming a larger role for themselves in American life.

SUGGESTED READING

Glover, *Founders as Fathers*, chap. 5.
Nash, *The Unknown American Revolution*, chap. 8.

QUESTIONS TO CONSIDER

1. What factor did Crevecoeur believe made Americans distinctive?

2. How widely were voting rights established in the American states?

Lecture 30

TIMOTHY DWIGHT'S RELIGION

As men of the Enlightenment, the Founders sought a natural order in politics, just as Newton and Galileo sought a natural order in the physical world. But a republic did not operate in the same way as gravity. Locke had suggested a little too simplistically that self-interest and self-preservation would compel people to cooperate. But societies cannot be built only on the self-serving impulse to cooperate. The character and spirit of a republican people could be preserved only if they were persuaded to practice public virtue for the common good. Madison had warned the Virginia ratifying convention, "To suppose that any form of government will secure liberty or happiness without any virtue in the people is a chimerical idea."

VIRTUE AND RELIGION IN THE REPUBLIC

➤ To the great chagrin of the Founders, virtue did not pop automatically out of the American hat. It was bad enough, under the confederation, that the new state legislatures passed one self-serving measure after another. It was worse, after the smoke had cleared for the Revolution's first native-born historian, David Ramsay, to discover that "our morals are more depreciated than our currency."

➤ By 1783, Ramsay was convinced that "This revolution has introduced so much anarchy that it will take half a century to eradicate the licentiousness of the people." One of Washington's correspondents complained that "Selfishness has so far prevailed over that patriotic spirit which at first wrought wonder through the Continent that I have little dependence on the virtue of the people." How was virtue to be replenished? What was virtue anyway?

➤ George Washington thought he knew what formed and shaped virtue: religion. But Washington was not himself what we might call a sterling model of piety. He was a practicing Episcopalian and probably believed in a God who maintained some sort of active control of human affairs. But more than that, Washington was too reticent to reveal.

➤ Bear in mind, though, that there were a number among the Founders who would have been happy to offer more fervent religious credentials and who expected religion to play a larger role in the formation of America's republican virtue. Roger Sherman, for example, was a serious convert to the same evangelical Awakeners who had played so large a role in Patrick Henry's life and subscribed to the full menu of Puritan Calvinism.

➤ Patrick Henry was anxious, too, about ensuring a role for evangelical Christianity in public life. Henry was infuriated by the publication of Thomas Paine's *Age of Reason* in 1794, which popularized what was known as *deism*: the minimal belief "in one

God, and no more," a hope "for happiness beyond this life," and "the equality of man." Henry wrote, "The view which the rising greatness of our country presents to my eyes, is greatly tarnished by the general prevalence of deism; which, with me, is but another name for vice and depravity."

➢ But it was the evangelical Awakeners who lost the most in the Revolution's outcome. New Jersey and North Carolina eliminated all state funding for churches in 1776, and New York followed suit in 1777. By 1790, membership in evangelical churches founded during the Great Awakening had waned to as little as 14 percent of the white population.

➢ In 1785, Madison persuaded the Virginia legislature to drop all public funding for religion. And although the First Amendment was crafted by Madison to prevent the federal government from making any "law respecting an establishment of religion," he had a much more expansive notion of what *no establishment* meant than Roger Sherman.

- ◆ He had opposed, in the Confederation Congress, the plan to set aside public lands for the support of religion in the Northwest Ordinance. Madison also opposed counting ministers, as ministers, on the federal census, lest this lead the government into the business of "ascertaining who, and who are not ministers of the gospel." He went on to oppose the hiring of chaplains for Congress and for the American military and urged Congress to tax church property.

- ◆ Jefferson summed up his own attitude toward public religion succinctly in 1802: "I contemplate with sovereign reverence that act of the whole American people which declared that their legislature should 'make no law respecting an establishment of religion ...' thus building a wall of separation between church and state."

BACKGROUND ON DWIGHT

> Timothy Dwight was born on May 14, 1752, in Northampton, Massachusetts. Northampton was the Congregationalist parish once presided over by the great theologian of the Awakening, Jonathan Edwards, and had been its intellectual epicenter. Dwight's mother, moreover, was Edwards's third child, and his father, Major Timothy Dwight, had been one of the pillars of support for Edwards when the congregation turned against him in 1750.

> As befitted a grandson of Edwards, Dwight toddled into learning, mastering Latin sufficient to pass the Yale College entrance exam at age 8, although not actually matriculating at Yale until age 13. At Yale, he formed one angle of a trio of ardent Federalists who became known as the "Connecticut Wits."

> By the time the cloud of war had passed over, the colleges were more enamored with deism and the French Revolution's cult of the supreme being than with orthodox piety. At Yale, the youthful Lyman Beecher recalled that when he began as a student in 1793, "The college church was almost extinct."

DWIGHT AT YALE

> At some point after the war, Dwight became convinced he should enter the Congregational ministry and, in 1783, was ordained as minister of Greenfield parish, in Fairfield, Connecticut. He at once took up cudgels against "infidelity," using poetry in defense of the Great Awakener's piety.

> Not poetry, however, but somber analysis formed the address he delivered to the General Association of Connecticut, and he made it clear that there could be no national virtue without national religion. "The whole end singly aimed at in the New Testament, is manifestly to make mankind virtuous," Dwight said, and nothing will promote virtue better throughout society than Christianity.

> That was enough to convince the powers in Connecticut that Dwight was the man to muck out the intellectual stables at Yale, and after the death of Yale president Ezra Stiles in 1795, Dwight was duly installed as his successor. From there, Dwight went on the offensive, denouncing unbelief as "the genuine source, the Vesuvius" of the French Revolution. "There can be no halting between two opinions," he demanded, "Will you enthrone a Goddess of Reason before the table of Christ? Will you burn your Bibles? Will you crucify anew your Redeemer?"

> In short order, Yale was moved by an outbreak of religious revival that confirmed that the grandfather's mantle had descended on the grandson's shoulders. "The whole college was shaken," wrote Heman Humphrey, one of the college converts. "It seemed for a time as if the whole mass of the students would press into the kingdom."

> But Dwight was shrewd, as well as pious. America was now a republic, and if he really wanted to undercut "infidelity," he was not going to do it in the old tones of hierarchy. He cultivated a "conciliating" manner, wrote the son of one of Dwight's faculty. The students he "addressed and treated as young gentlemen."

  ◆ Student ranking, which in colonial days had been done on the basis of social status, was now based on academic performance; hazing of freshmen was abolished; and in place of fines "for neglect of study and other violations of duty, he substituted private remonstrance" and "appeals … to the conscience of the delinquent."

  ◆ Nor was Dwight an anti-intellectual enthusiast. He shunned the more radical followers of Jonathan Edwards, and he began hiring new faculty who were not theologians, including the chemist Benjamin Silliman. In a republic where ordinary citizens were free to choose their own affiliations, Dwight understood that wooing, not commanding, was the new order of the day.

➤ Dwight had more trouble translating his hostility toward the French into practical politics. As president of Yale, Gardiner Spring thought Connecticut Federalism "revolved around him as the centre of that circle of intelligence and excellence." Upon his ascent to the Yale presidency, Dwight began purging pro-French— and pro-Republican—faculty. He turned his rhetorical guns on the democratic-republican societies in 1798, denouncing them as "nothing but infidelity, irreligion, faction, rebellion, the ruin of peace, and the loss of property."

➤ But the prospect of Jefferson as president was the worst omen of all. "Unless you make some exertions," Dwight exhorted Connecticut's Federalist senator, James Hillhouse, "you will lose perhaps the only and certainly best, opportunity of securing the public safety. … Mr. Jefferson will ruin the Republic."

➤ Nevertheless, Dwight found that he could not stop the Jeffersonian juggernaut in 1800; he could not, in the end, even command Yale's students to toe the Federalist line. But Jefferson's victory did not mean the doom of virtue, either. Dwight stayed at the helm of Yale until his death in 1817. In the process, he mentored a generation of virtue-hungry activists and scholars, all of whom stood at the headwaters of a second Great Awakening that would break over the republic in the 1820s and all of them joined in a campaign that, if it did not successfully Christianize American government, certainly Christianized American culture.

➤ While Jefferson and Madison ensured public sponsorship for Christianity would never get so far as actual federal tax support, the disciples of Dwight would orchestrate a number of indirect gestures of support for Christian institutions in the form of local and state laws punishing Sabbath-breaking and blasphemy, the introduction of religious exercises in state schools, restrictions on the movement of the mail on Sundays, and proclamations calling for days of public thanksgiving.

- And beyond government, the heirs of Timothy Dwight would create an interlocking empire of voluntary societies and associations for foreign missions, Bible distribution, and moral improvement that Madison would complain were really "Ecclesiastical Bodies … lurking under plausible disguises."

- But Madison's complaints didn't matter. By 1825, the American Bible Society was distributing the Bible in 140 languages; the American Board of Commissioners for Foreign Missions had a budget twice the size of Harvard College; and between 1780 and 1820, American religious denominations built 10,000 new churches and created 50 seminaries to train new volunteers for the ministry. By defining Christianity as virtue, Christianity could be treated as a necessary component of republican government, whether Jefferson liked it or not.

SUGGESTED READING

Hall, *Roger Sherman*, chaps. 2 and 6.
Wells, *The Devil and Doctor Dwight*, chap. 4.

QUESTIONS TO CONSIDER

1. Were Protestant evangelicals the big losers of the American Revolution?

2. How did Dwight persuade Yale College to embrace religion as the source of virtue?

Lecture 31

JAMES McHENRY'S ARMY

*N*ever was a worry more misplaced than the one which had haunted Elbridge Gerry at the Constitutional Convention—that of a Congress creating a permanent, regular army that would quickly turn into a latter-day Praetorian Guard, threatening the very life of the republic. For whatever Gerry's anxieties about the power granted to Congress to "raise and support Armies ... provide and maintain a Navy" and "make Rules for the Government and Regulation of the land and naval Forces," the army and navy that Congress actually called into being in the 1790s was so absurdly small as to be unthreatening, not just to the republic but to anyone else.

POSTWAR MILITARY FORCES

➤ The 86 regiments and battalions that had composed the army of the United States during the Revolutionary War—the Continental Army—technically ceased to exist as of June 3, 1784, when it was ordered to disband. But Washington had warned Congress that it should not fool itself into thinking that it needed no professional military force. Washington hoped that Congress would retain at least 2,631 long-service infantry and artillerymen, a nucleus of trained professionals that could be expanded as needed.

➤ But all that the Confederation Congress voted to create was a minuscule military force—only 700 men and 37 officers. The states reserved the authority to commission the officers and recruit the troops. Washington sighed: "a large standing Army in time of Peace has ever been considered dangerous to the liberties of a Country," and so only the thought of "a few Troops" would even be tolerated. "Fortunately for us, he added, "our relative situation requires but few."

➤ Washington could at least console himself with the thought that army affairs had ended up better than those of the navy. The Continental Navy had to be scraped into being from the purchase of odds-and-ends of ships, and its expeditions generally did not end well.

➤ For a brief moment, in response to Shays's Rebellion, the frightened Confederation Congress sluggishly moved to triple the size of its diminutive army. But the states did little to recruit the new force, and after the rebellion was put down, Congress happily went back to the same comfortable policies it had been following and disbanded its newly recruited soldiers.

➤ Perhaps Congress imagined it could get by with the services of the state militias, although this wouldn't be true of the navy. As soon as the Treaty of Paris made it clear that American merchant shipping was no longer protected by the mantle of the Royal Navy, pirates from the coasts of North Africa began feasting on hapless American merchantmen in the Mediterranean. They not only raided American ships but held their crews as slaves until ransomed.

DOMESTIC CONFLICT

➤ Even the state militias might not be equal to more domestic troubles. On the northern and northwestern frontier, the powerful Indian tribes of the Iroquois federation were willing to concede that their allies, the British, had been defeated in the Revolutionary War, but they were much less willing to admit that they had been defeated.

- ◆ Thus, when American commissioners and Iroquois chiefs met at Fort Stanwix in 1784 to create a peace settlement, the Iroquois balked at being treated as a conquered people. However, the entire Indian population east of the Mississippi amounted to little more than 160,000 people, and in the end, the Seneca sachem Cornplanter bargained away land in New York and Ohio in order to get peace.

- ◆ Similar treaties with the Iroquois' western allies followed in 1785 at Fort McIntosh and in 1786 at Fort Finney, while to the South, the Cherokees and Creeks made similar bargains in the treaties at Augusta and Hopewell.

- ◆ But the bargains angered dissidents, who eyed the agreements with suspicion. In 1785, low-level warfare broke out with Indians in the Ohio country and Kentucky. When the confederation proved unable to respond, the extended North Carolina settlements made motions toward proclaiming themselves the state of Franklin and began conducting backdoor negotiations to put themselves under the sovereignty—and protection—of Spain.

➤ Even though the convention authorized Congress to "raise and support Armies … provide and maintain a Navy," what Congress actually raised and supported was not much of an improvement on the confederation's version of an army and navy. A Department of War was created on August 7, 1789, to be headed by Henry Knox.

- But when Knox introduced Washington's plan for a "legionary corps" of 2,000 men whose cadres would absorb the state militias in times of emergency, the new Congress stiffened; when Congress finally approved a plan on September 29, 1789, it provided for only a single regular regiment of 840 men. A year later, Congress grudgingly authorized a modest expansion to 1,200 men.

- They might have saved themselves that small trouble: In 1790, three companies of the First Regiment, under the command of Lieutenant-Colonel Josiah Harmar, along with 1,500 Pennsylvania and Virginia militia, attempted to track down marauding Shawnee and Miami Indians along the Maumee River in Ohio. The Indians instead turned on Harmer's force, sending the militia fleeing in panic and allowing the regulars to stand and be massacred.

- Congress was galvanized into authorizing a second regiment of regulars. But when the governor of the Northwest Territory, Arthur St. Clair, tried to lead them in a second expedition, St. Clair blundered into an Indian ambush at the headwaters of the Wabash River, and his forces were nearly annihilated.

- Finally, in March 1792, Congress voted to reconstitute the two existing infantry regiments and recruit three further infantry regiments and four troops of mounted infantry. Armed with the independent financial powers given by the Constitution, Congress did not have to beg the states for money for these troops; in fact, Congress passed a national militia bill in May 1792 that spelled out the federal government's authority over the state militias in explicit terms. With those resources finally in force, revolutionary veteran Anthony Wayne brought the Shawnee and Miami to bay at the battle of Fallen Timbers on August 20, 1794, and ended at least that threat—for the moment.

JAMES MCHENRY

JAMES MCHENRY
(1753–1816)

> It took the eruption of the Quasi-War with France under President Adams before Congress would take its obligations to "raise and support Armies" and "provide and maintain a Navy" with real seriousness, and it would take Adams's secretary of war, James McHenry, to put them into play for the first time.

> McHenry was Irish-born but immigrated to America in 1771 and became a physician, served as a surgeon in the Revolution, and after the war, went into business and politics as a member of the Maryland legislature. He became part of Alexander Hamilton's Federalist circle, and Hamilton actually recommended McHenry to Washington after the disgrace of Edmund Randolph as a likely secretary of state in 1796. But Washington posted McHenry instead to the War Department, and when John Adams succeeded Washington in the presidency a few months later, Adams kept McHenry in place.

> McHenry at once announced that his priorities would be to "create a navy and always maintain a formidable army." This, for McHenry meant an army of not less than 12,000 regulars and a navy with at least 12 line-of-battle ships. In this, his most unlooked-for friend was the French Republic, because once news of the XYZ Affair broke, Congress was ready to give McHenry and Adams anything they wanted.

> McHenry did not consider himself a navy man, and at his prompting, Congress authorized the creation of an entirely separate Navy

Department under McHenry's fellow-Maryland Federalist, Benjamin Stoddert. McHenry's attention was devoted to recruiting the new "additional army," and at its head, he wanted no one less than the retired 66-year-old former president, Washington.

- ◆ Surprisingly, Washington agreed, but with a provision that made Adams choke: that Alexander Hamilton would be appointed as his second-in-command.

- ◆ As much as Adams wanted Washington in command in order to fend of Republican critics who would accuse him of creating the provisional army for a coup against Congress, he was certain that Hamilton wanted to use the provisional army to undermine his own presidential authority. But Adams really had no choice: He signed a commission for Washington as lieutenant-general; Hamilton would join him as the army's inspector-general, with the rank of major-general.

➢ Adams was right about Hamilton's ambitions, and in fact, Hamilton started by bestowing unwanted advice on McHenry about the reorganization of the War Department staff. He then proposed to Congress the recruitment of a further 24 regiments of infantry, battalions of riflemen, artillerists, and engineers and 3 regiments of cavalry. But while Hamilton was lighting a fire in McHenry's front, President Adams was lighting another in his rear, pressuring McHenry to get Washington to change his mind about designating Hamilton as his second-in-command; when Washington refused, Adams blamed McHenry for conspiring against him.

➢ And yet, for all the backstairs maneuvering, McHenry launched recruiting for the additional army, along with a revived military staff; new fortifications were to be built, new uniform styles were adopted, and a new weapons-manufacturing arsenal was begun at Harpers Ferry, Virginia.

EXPLAINING THE BUILD-UP

> What no one among the Federalists seemed to have stopped to ask themselves was an obvious question: Why the build-up? McHenry was sincerely convinced that France "intends ... to bring the United States, or a part of them, by her arms, added to her intrigues, into the same state of vassalage."

> It was only left, in McHenry's thinking, for Adams to "recommend to Congress ... an immediate declaration of war, against that nation." But did anyone seriously think that the French Republic's army was poised to conquer its American counterpart? Even Washington half-heartedly admitted that such an outcome seemed difficult to believe.

> McHenry unwittingly fed Republican paranoia by asserting that the additional army was needed because France's policy is "to prepare the country she designs to subdue by previous divisions, among its citizens, before she strikes it." McHenry was aghast when, far from declaring war, Adams announced in February 1799 that he was sending William Vans Murray to France to reopen the negotiations that the XYZ Affair had closed down. When Murray's mission produced an agreement with the French, Congress cheerfully slashed funding for McHenry's army.

> Congress only deprived McHenry of funding, however. In May 1800, the New York state legislative elections went against the Federalists, and Adams interpreted this a devious plot by Hamilton to undercut Adams's upcoming battle for reelection against Thomas Jefferson. On May 5, Adams summoned McHenry for a meeting "of one minute," which in fact turned into a maniacal tirade, accusing McHenry of complicity with Hamilton in "indecorous & at times outrageous" language. McHenry resigned as secretary of war the next day.

SUGGESTED READING

Lambert, *The Barbary Wars*, chap. 5.
Robbins, *James McHenry*, chaps. 8 and 12–18.

QUESTIONS TO CONSIDER

1. What made Congress so allergic to maintaining a regular army?

2. What was the additional army?

Lecture 32

THOMAS JEFFERSON'S FRUSTRATION

*J*efferson had never been sure, in the first place, that the Constitution was a good idea. He had been in Paris during the Constitutional Convention and had returned to the United States to find the political mechanics of the Constitution already in full operation. But the Constitution did not strike him as an improvement on the Articles of Confederation. "I think all the good of this new constitution might have been couched in three or four new articles to be added to the good, old, and venerable fabrick." Twelve years of Federalist rule—especially 12 years of dealing with Hamilton and his onetime friend John Adams—had only made the defects of the Constitution glare more harshly.

JEFFERSON AS PRESIDENT

➤ To Jefferson, the American Revolution had begun with the purpose of introducing "a just & solid republican government" that would become a model for other countries. But it had been betrayed by the machinations of the Federalists into copying much too closely the trappings of a centralized British monarchy. At length, however, Americans had come to realize their peril. And they had elected Jefferson to correct the course of the republic.

➤ Surprisingly, Jefferson's inaugural address was an eloquent appeal for reconciliation after the turmoil of the Whiskey Rebellion, the Jay Treaty, and the Quasi-War. "Let us ... unite with one heart and one mind. ... Every difference of opinion is not a difference of principle. We have called by different names brethren of the same principle. We are all republicans: we are all federalists."

➤ But unrepentant Federalists saw an iron hand inside the velvet glove. "That speech," snorted one Federalist newspaper, "was but a net to ensnare popularity." Nor was this just the customary Federalist paranoia. In 1799, Jefferson wrote to the Elbridge Gerry to outline exactly the plan he meant to follow if elected president:

- ◆ First, he would dismantle the administrative apparatus developed by Hamilton in his series of reports as secretary of the treasury.

- ◆ Second, he would not only demobilize the additional army but slice spending on national defense as a whole, because such spending only created tax burdens that erased the independence of virtuous farmers.

- ◆ Third, he would show no favoritism in foreign policy, particularly to the British.

➤ What Jefferson really meant by in his speech by "all republicans," "all federalists" was actually no parties at all. "If we can hit on the true line ... which may conciliate the honest part of those who were called federalists," Jefferson wrote to Horatio Gates, "I should hope to ... obliterate ... the names of federalist & republican." But whether the Federalists went willingly or not, Jefferson was determined "by the establishment of republican principles ... to sink federalism into an abyss from which there shall be no resurrection for it."

JEFFERSON'S STRATEGIES

➢ Jefferson's first strategy for creating the Federalist abyss was to evict Federalists from federal officeholding, which he did with gusto. Tax collectors and inspectors, and the whiskey excise they had tried to collect, were also eliminated; the Sedition Law was allowed to expire; and individuals who had been indicted under the other anti-French acts were pardoned. The diplomatic corps was reduced to just three missions, to Britain, France and Spain.

➢ Jefferson then turned his eye on the federal judiciary. In the last weeks of the Adams administration, the Sixth Congress adopted a Judiciary Act that reorganized the structure of the federal judiciary, reducing the number of Supreme Court justices to five and dividing the federal appeals courts into 19 district courts and 6 circuit courts.

- ◆ What made this reorganization something less than a mere reshuffling was the opportunity the Judiciary Act provided to John Adams, first for more active enforcement of the Alien and Sedition Acts, and then to appoint a full slate of Federalists to fill 13 of the new judgeships.

- ◆ Jefferson could not, constitutionally, dismiss federal judges. But with a 65-to-40 majority in the House and only 2 votes shy of a majority in the Senate, Jefferson was able to get the Judiciary Act repealed by the Seventh Congress and replaced in April 1802 with a new Judiciary Act. The jobs of some judges thereby simply ceased to exist.

➢ Jefferson was even determined to republicanize the style of the presidency. The Executive Mansion was still only "scantily furnished with articles brought from Philadelphia," and Jefferson was disinclined to spend much money changing that, even closing down the East Room entirely.

➢ When Jefferson decided to run for reelection in 1804, his victory was even more smashing than the one of 1800, winning 162 out of 176 electoral votes for himself and his new vice president, the inveterate New York Federalist-hater, George Clinton.

JEFFERSON'S SECOND TERM

➢ Although he could kick Federalist officeholders into the Federalist abyss, Jefferson could not kick Hamiltonian fiscal policy there quite so easily. Despite his persistent shyness, Jefferson spent virtually all of his life from 1774 in one form or other of public service. But apart from the Enlightenment eloquence he poured into the Declaration of Independence, he had accomplished surprisingly little.

◆ He had been governor of Virginia during the Revolution and failed to keep the British from chasing him out of office; he had been minister to France and Washington's secretary of state—mostly without distinction. Jefferson's electoral victories were due more to "the

THOMAS JEFFERSON

popularity of his doctrines, than by his strength of personal character, or by the practical wisdom of his public measures."

- ◆ Now, as president, the pattern repeated itself. As much as he hated Hamilton's Bank of the United States and the decision to fund the national debt in full, Hamilton had pledged the nation's honor to paying the debt, and to change that now would hurt Americans who owned federal securities and destroy American credit abroad.

- ➤ Nor did matters abroad cooperate with Jefferson's wishes. No sooner had Jefferson cancelled the remainder of the navy's frigate-building program in favor of building a fleet of 100 coast-defense gunboats, than the Barbary pirates cheerfully renewed their demands for bribes.

  - ◆ When Jefferson refused, Yusuf Karamanli, the pasha of Tripoli, declared war, and Jefferson was forced to send the decommissioned frigates to the Mediterranean to teach the pirates a lesson, except of course, that the pirates proved recalcitrant learners.

  - ◆ In 1805, Karamanli finally signed an agreement to end the war, but only after Jefferson had pledged $60,000 to ransom American sailors whom Karamanli was holding.

- ➤ And then there was France. In 1799, the last façade of the revolutionary republic crumbled as Napoleon Bonaparte overthrew the Directory and, in 1804, crowned himself emperor of France. Jefferson wrote, "To whine after this exorcised demon is a disgrace to republicans, and must have arisen either from want of reflection, or the indulgence of passion against principle."

  - ◆ Nevertheless, he was more than willing to barter with Napoleon if opportunity beckoned, which it did in 1803, when Napoleon offered to sell the Louisiana province to the United States for $15 million in cash.

- The Louisiana Purchase was approved by Jefferson before consulting with Congress and justified afterward on grounds very close to the invocation of necessary-and-proper powers Hamilton had used for the Bank of the United States. The Senate ratified the agreement in October, and American officials took possession of Louisiana on December 20, 1803.

➤ The British were not amused by these dealings because they had hoped to seize New Orleans for themselves and, thus, control the Mississippi River valley. The great British naval victory at Trafalgar in 1805 wrecked Bonaparte's hopes of challenging British preeminence at sea, but that only produced a whipsaw response for American shipping.

- Bonaparte declared a continental embargo of Britain in 1806 and threatened to seize any American ships in European waters whom he suspected of trading with Britain; the British responded with fresh orders-in-council that demanded search privileges of American shipping they suspected of trading with France. Ground between both stones, American shippers lost 1,500 ships to British and French seizure over nine years.

- Nor did the British stop with merchant vessels: On June 22, 1807, the U.S. frigate *Chesapeake* was hailed by the British frigate HMS *Leopard* off the Virginia capes. The British demanded to search the *Chesapeake*'s crew for deserters. The *Chesapeake*'s senior officer, Commodore James Barron, stalled, but the British didn't wait: A broadside from the *Leopard* killed 3 American sailors and wounded 18.

- Jefferson wrote that he had "never ... seen this country in such a state of exasperation as" it was over the *Chesapeake* outrage. But Jefferson, through his own parsimony, had no fleet at hand for retaliating against the Royal Navy. Instead, he proposed a boycott on commerce with both Britain and France.

- Jefferson's secretary of the treasury, Albert Gallatin, counseled Jefferson that war would be preferable to a "permanent embargo." Nevertheless, when the Tenth Congress assembled in December 1807—six months after the *Chesapeake* affair—Jefferson recommended, in his annual message, a unilateral embargo. After four days of deliberation, Congress obligingly passed an Embargo Act on "any ship or vessel bound … to any foreign port or place."

- The congressmen quickly had reason to regret their decision. Jefferson liked to believe that an economy based on the independent farmer had no need of imports or exports, but this was an illusion. Britain lost 58 percent of the value of its exports to the United States, but American exporters suffered a catastrophic wipeout of 73 percent.

- Ironically, the domestic manufacturing Jefferson despised actually blossomed behind what was, in effect, an unlimited tariff wall; there were 15 cotton mills in the United States in 1808, and by 1809, 87 had been built. But otherwise, the impact was horrendous. Despite protests, Jefferson refused to admit that the embargo had been a mistake, even though, by the end of his second term, he had quietly given up trying to enforce it.

➢ By the end of that term, Jefferson had grown weary of fighting Hamilton's incubus. "I am tired of an office where I can do no more good than many others who would be glad to be employed in it," he sighed. "To myself personally it brings nothing but unceasing drudgery & daily loss of friends. … My only consolation is in the belief that my fellow citizens at large give me credit for good intentions."

SUGGESTED READING

Elkins and McKitrick, *The Age of Federalism*, chap. 15.
Wood, *Empire of Liberty*, chap. 17.

QUESTIONS TO CONSIDER

1. What were Jefferson's principal aims as president?

2. How did pirates, bankers, newspapers, the British, and his own shortcomings sabotage Jefferson's intentions?

Lecture 33

AARON BURR'S TREASON

No one could claim a more distinguished intellectual lineage in the Founders' generation than Timothy Dwight, the grandson of Jonathan Edwards, unless it was Aaron Burr, Dwight's cousin and also a grandson of Edwards. But from that point, no two paths in the early Republic diverged further. His father, Aaron Burr, Sr., was a devoted disciple of the great Edwards and became president of Princeton College in 1747. However, the senior Burr died when the boy was less than two years old, followed in the next few years by Burr's grandfather, his mother, and grandmother. The boy ended up in 1760 in Stockbridge, Massachusetts, in the care of his aunt and uncle but with £3,000 for his education.

BACKGROUND ON BURR

➤ Burr joined the Continental Army early on and was attached to the staff of General Richard Montgomery for Montgomery's ill-fated attempt to capture Quebec. Montgomery's death left him without a sponsor, but he found his footing again as an aide to Connecticut general Israel Putnam, was promoted to lieutenant-colonel, survived the winter at Valley Forge, and finally left the army in 1779. He turned to the study of law, married a wealthy widow, and moved to New York City as the British evacuated it in 1783.

➤ Burr clashed almost at once with another newly minted New York City lawyer, Alexander Hamilton, over the confiscation of property from one-time Tory loyalists.

   ◆ Given that the war was over, Hamilton reasoned, these people were useful to the new republic. Why impoverish them and the republic by punishing them further?

   ◆ Burr looked at the question from the other end of the telescope: Confiscated Tory properties could be sold and used to compensate impoverished patriots for their sacrifices—especially such impoverished patriots as Aaron Burr.

➤ In 1784, Burr was elected to the New York Assembly, where he allied himself with George Clinton and won appointment as state attorney-general. Burr increasingly served as Clinton's foil to Hamilton in New York politics, and in 1791, Clinton muscled Burr's election to the U.S. Senate through the state assembly, unseating Hamilton's father-in-law, Philip Schuyler. By 1796, Jeffersonian Republicans were already talking of Burr as a possible candidate to run for president against Adams.

➤ Yet Burr was already sending uneasy currents of anxiety through even Republican ranks. His political ideas, if he had any, were glib and mostly concentrated on his own self-advancement.

JEFFERSON VERSUS BURR

➢ In 1800, Burr was picked to run as the Republicans' candidate for vice president with Jefferson. The problem was that the presidential itch was now about to drive him over the line.

➢ Jefferson easily outscored Adams in the Electoral College, 73 to 65. But Burr, running on Jefferson's coattails, had also tallied 73 electoral votes, and this meant that the House of Representatives would have to sort out who would serve as president. Jefferson wrote uneasily to Burr on December 15, 1800, to suggest that this was simply an oversight, but it turned out to be an oversight of near-fatal proportions.

➢ Hamilton would have preferred the devil to Jefferson as president, and he did not hesitate to lay out suggestive snares in Burr's path that Federalists in the House might be willing to unload their votes on him; for his part, Burr scooped up the snares with unbecoming greed. He did not openly campaign against Jefferson, but he coyly declined to issue any statement promising support for Jefferson, and he allowed his allies to seduce Republican congressmen to vote for Burr.

➢ When the House of Representatives convened on February 11, 1801, 19 ballots were cast without a clear majority before an exhausted House recessed after midnight. Three more ballots followed over the next two days. After seven days of haggling, James Bayard, a Federalist and the lone representative of Delaware, withheld his vote, and the election was finally over.

➢ But Burr, said Bayard, "had completely forfeited the confidence and friendship of his party." He enraged them still further by obstructing Jefferson's replacement Judiciary Act in 1802. By the time Jefferson was ready for his second presidential campaign, he was anxious to be rid of Burr, and in January 1804, called him to the Executive Mansion to tell him as much. When the congressional

Republican caucus met on February 25 to renominate Jefferson, not a single vote was cast for Burr to continue as vice president.

THE DUEL

➢ This ended Aaron Burr's career as a public man but not his ambitions or his thirst for revenge. Denied the vice presidency, Burr threw his hat into the ring for the governorship of New York in the spring of 1804. He lost and blamed Hamilton for it. He sent Hamilton a letter claiming that Hamilton had defamed him during the campaign and, ultimately, challenged Hamilton to a duel.

➢ The two met on July 11, on the bluffs overlooking the Hudson River. Hamilton fired his pistol into the air; Burr, however, took deliberate aim and hit Hamilton in the right hip, penetrating the liver and striking the spine. He died at 2:00 the next afternoon.

➢ Burr was denounced as an "assassin" and indicted for murder in August but slipped out of New York before he could be arrested, heading southward. The charges were eventually dropped on technicalities.

➢ With astonishing brass, even for Burr, the lame-duck vice president showed up for the lame-duck session of the Eighth Congress in Washington as though nothing remarkable had happened. He had the impudence to give a farewell speech in the Senate on March 2, and then, in April, set off overland to Pittsburgh, arriving later in New Orleans.

BURR IN LOUISIANA

➢ For 20 years after the Treaty of Paris, the American Republic had squirmed in anxiety over what might happen along its distant western borders. Indeed, the United States had nothing that guaranteed that its boundary on the Mississippi River could be protected from interference by foreign powers. The Louisiana

Purchase gave title to the whole region, including New Orleans, but enforcing that title did not become any easier.

➢ Jefferson opened up every possible encouragement to western settlement, but even at the best reckoning, there were only 50,000 settlers in the Northwest Territory, and only 9,000 in the southwest outside of New Orleans. Let any of the European powers resolve to recolonize in North America, and there would be little the United States could do to stop it.

➢ As early as the summer of 1804, while he was still the vice president of the United States, Burr began dropping hints to the British minister in Washington, Anthony Merry, about his interest in helping the British stir up trouble for the French in the Caribbean by recruiting American mercenaries for clandestine operations.

   ◆ The talks matured, and in short order, Burr revealed that he was prepared to aid in "effect[ing] a Separation of the Western Part of the United States from that which lies between the Atlantic and the Mountains."

   ◆ All the British needed to do was back him with £110,000 and a Royal Navy squadron to secure the mouth of the Mississippi river, and the deed would be done.

➢ Merry was not without a certain incredulity at this proposition, and rightly so, because Burr was also negotiating simultaneously with the Spanish to deliver exactly the same western lands to them. Still, Burr was doing more than just talk: he had recruited between 4,000 and 5,000 volunteers and established a base on Blennerhassett Island in the middle of the Ohio River. To all of them, he confided that he had been specially commissioned by Jefferson to lead an expeditionary force to conquer Mexico.

➢ But Burr had not counted on the double-crossing propensities of General James Wilkinson. In October 1806, just before Burr was ready to spring his plan, Wilkinson recalculated the odds of Burr's success, then wrote to President Jefferson, betraying every detail of Burr's plan that he knew. Jefferson promptly issued a cease-and-desist proclamation on November 27, and Ohio and Virginia militia staged a rowdy occupation of Blennerhassett Island.

AARON BURR

➤ Burr, however, eluded them. For all his swollen promises, he had only 16 boats and 60 men at hand. He did not find about Wilkinson's betrayal until January 10, whereupon he scattered his pathetic force and took to the hills. He didn't get far. Federal troops arrested him on February 19 as he tried to slip across the border into Spanish West Florida.

PROTECTION OF THE CONSTITUTION

➤ It was at this moment that the Founders' Constitution revealed one of its most unsuspected strengths, and that was its willingness to throw the arms of protection around the liberties even of the people who meant it harm. Article III, Section 3, defines "treason" as "only ... levying War" against the United States, "or in adhering to" its "Enemies." That in itself pulled the punch of anyone eager to convict someone else of treason, because treason had to be an act rising to the very high level of war and its concomitants.

> It did not lighten the prosecution's burdens to discover that the case against Burr was not nearly so transparent as it seemed. The constant crisscrossing of his intentions allowed Burr's defense to confuse the issues, and though Jefferson provided his prosecuting attorney, George Hay, with blank pardons to induce Burr's co-conspirators to turn state's evidence, too many of them turned out to be suspicious and unreliable characters. Further, though a number of Burr's men had been assembled and armed on Blennerhassett Island, Burr had not actually been there himself, thus undercutting the actual association of Burr with an armed plot.

> Hay tried to invoke the more expansive English common-law definition of *constructive treason*, but Burr's counsel insisted that the Constitution's narrower definition had superseded English common law. Burr himself insisted that his party of armed travelers were simply employees whom he was planning to use on new lands he had bought in Louisiana.

> On August 31, after two weeks of trial, Marshall instructed the grand jury that the treason indictment was groundless, because it did not meet the technical definition and because Burr had not been present on Blennerhassett Island where the plotters had assembled. The grand jury deliberated for only a few minutes and announced that they found Burr not guilty.

> Burr thus walked away a free man, and after several months of dodging his creditors, boarded a packet-ship under the name H. G. Edwards and sailed for England. He returned from Europe in 1812 and, boldly opened up a law office at 9 Nassau Street. He made only a scanty living, and people pointed him out on the streets of New York City as "the greatest villain on earth."

SUGGESTED READING

Isenberg, *Fallen Founder*, chaps. 1 and 9.
McDonald, *Alexander Hamilton*, epilogue.

QUESTIONS TO CONSIDER

1.   How did Aaron Burr trigger a constitutional crisis in 1800?

2.   Was Burr really guilty of treason?

Lecture 34

JOHN MARSHALL'S COURT

*I*t was at Valley Forge that John Marshall got his first taste of the law. On February 5, 1778, Marshall was detailed to assist the judge-advocate of the army as a "deputy judge-advocate." He evidently had the sort of mind that feasts on the fine distinctions of law and arbitration. In 1779, Marshall was sent home and put himself under the tutelage of George Wythe at William and Mary for a course in legal studies. At the end of actual campaigning at Yorktown in 1781, Marshall resigned his commission and took up law practice in Richmond.

BACKGROUND ON MARSHALL

➤ In 1782, John Marshall won a seat in the Virginia legislature, where his eyes were opened to the cause of the suffering of the Continentals at Valley Forge: While the soldiers suffered, gaseous politicians exhaled platitude-laden speeches in state assemblies about the glories of liberty, then gutted every initiative on the national level for victory.

➤ Elected to the state ratifying convention for the Constitution, Marshall boldly bearded Patrick Henry in his own den. "The

JOHN MARSHALL
(1755–1835)

supporters of the constitution," and not the Antifederalists, such as Henry and George Mason, "claim the title of being sincere friends of liberty and the rights of mankind." Marshall continued:

> What are the favourite maxims of democracy? A strict observance of justice and public faith, and a steady adherence to virtue. These, sir, are the principles of a good government. ... Would to Heaven that these principles had been observed under the present government! Had this been the case, the friends of liberty would not be so willing now to part with it.

➤ This astonished Henry, who thought what Marshall was advocating revolution. But it delighted James Madison, who thought Marshall had shown "a great deal of ability" in the ratifying convention. It was not that Marshall was an eloquent orator, but the force of his reason carried the day.

➤ By the mid-1790s, he had become a principal figure in Virginia Federalism. Washington offered him the post of attorney-general in 1795; Adams tagged him as one of the three XYZ commissioners in 1797 and then as Adams's secretary of state; and when Oliver Ellsworth resigned as chief justice of the Supreme Court in 1800, Adams nominated Marshall as his replacement.

DEBATING THE LAW

➤ Before the Revolution, lawyers' primary duties involved supervising community morals, determining tax assessments, issuing licenses, appointing road commissioners, and the like. Judges had been Crown appointees, settling disputes through the invocation of English common law and its great interpreter, Sir William Blackstone.

➤ The Revolution, however, was nowhere more revolutionary than its overthrow of these practices. Common law, which was little more than the accumulated precedents set by English courts, was now anathema to the new American order. Blackstone, whose whole theory of law was based on the sovereignty of the monarch and the glories of Parliament, was rejected as a holdover of Toryism. Every dictate of Enlightenment reason and every respect for America as a republic demanded a completely new kind of jurisprudence for Americans, free from all-powerful judges, deferential to the right of juries to interpret the law, and based on clearly written statutes adopted by the legislatures as the voice of the people.

➤ The principal difficulty with this overthrow of common law was that it was easier said than done. An entirely new republican jurisprudence could not be invented by even the most diligent state legislature, and none of them would tolerate the federal government doing it. Moreover, Federalists, such as Alexander Addison, suspected that Jeffersonian Republicans had other motives in eliminating the common law.

  ◆ "The common law is founded on the law of nature and the revelation of God, to which all men are subject," Addison wrote in 1800, and though "the declaration of independence ... annulled the power of Britain over the colonies," the colonies "carried with them all the common law of England" in their everyday operations.

  ◆ Hamilton took this one step further in *Federalist* 78 by casting the courts in the role of restrainers of state legislative foolishness. "The courts," he wrote, "were designed to be an intermediate body between the people and the legislature, in order, among other things, to keep the latter within the limits assigned to their authority."

➤ The Jeffersonians feared both the extension of common law and the authority of judges in using it. And this fear became all the more urgent because the Constitution was never more vague than in describing where the line lay between state and federal judicial authority.

  ◆ One of Jay's cases, *Chisholm v. Georgia* in 1793, unwisely declared that the state of Georgia could be sued by citizens of other states; the state legislatures howled in protest, and in 1798, an Eleventh Amendment was added to the Constitution, preventing the federal judiciary from claiming authority in "any suit in law … against one of the United States by Citizens of another State."

♦ But they would not be able to go to the amendment pump every time an aggressive chief justice tried to clip the states' wings, and John Marshall was nothing if not aggressive. He would devise a national judicial sovereignty to match the national constitutional sovereignty envisioned by Madison and the national economic sovereignty proposed by Hamilton.

MARSHALL'S DECISIONS

➢ Just how aggressive he would be in this regard became apparent in the Marshall court's first major decision, *Marbury v. Madison*. The case involved the delayed appointments of some justices of the peace (JPs) after Jefferson took office.

♦ One of these JPs, William Marbury, a Federalist, filed suit on December 21, 1801, directly in the U.S. Supreme Court, requesting a *writ of mandamus* (an order to correct an oversight) to force delivery of his commission. Marshall handed down his response for a unanimous court on February 24, 1803.

♦ Marbury's suit was technically invalid because it had been filed at the wrong court level. As for the nub of the suit— that Marbury had been entitled to an appointment that the Jefferson administration had wrongly denied him—Marshall was entirely in agreement, and "having this legal right to the office, he has a consequent right to the commission."

♦ Thus, Marshall established the principle that the federal courts have review power over the actions of both the presidency and Congress.

➢ Marshall's next step was to bring the state courts to heel. The Reverend Denny Martin was the heir of the Fairfax family, whose holdings on the Northern Neck of Virginia had been confiscated by the state of Virginia from Lord Thomas Fairfax in 1777, and portions sold to a land speculator, David Hunter, in 1789; Hunter, in turn, moved to eject Martin's tenants.

   ◆ Because both the Treaty of Paris and the Jay Treaty required an end to confiscations of Loyalist property, Martin won the first round in the Virginia district court in 1794 and, in 1796, an out-of-court settlement with an investors' consortium (which included John Marshall) that purchased title to Martin's property.

   ◆ But Spencer Roane, Patrick Henry's son-in-law and the most ardent Jeffersonian judge on the Virginia Court of Appeals, was determined to make the case a test of federal judicial authority. Roane insisted that the Fairfax properties did not fall under the treaty protections and reversed the 1794 ruling and out-of-court settlement.

   ◆ The consortium then turned to the U.S. Supreme Court, which in a decision delegated by Marshall to Joseph Story, overturned the Virginia decision. But Roane refused to recognize the Supreme Court's jurisdiction in a state matter; thus, the case went back to the Supreme Court as *Martin v. Hunter's Lessee*.

   ◆ This time, Story (acting as Marshall's mouthpiece) delivered a slap to state judicial authority. "It has been argued that such an appellate jurisdiction over state courts is inconsistent with the genius of our governments, and the spirit of the constitution," Story wrote. "We cannot yield to the force of this reasoning. ... It is a mistake" to think that "the constitution was not designed to operate upon the states." To the contrary, "the courts of the United States can, without question, revise the proceedings of the executive and legislative authorities of the states, and if they are found to be contrary to the constitution, may declare them to be of no legal validity."

- If Virginia possessed the power to nullify the provisions of treaties, then there would be no hindrance to nullifying acts of Congress, and the Constitution would collapse. Once again, the Marshall Court had placed the authority of the federal government, and the ghost of Alexander Hamilton, over that of any of their rivals or critics.

McCulloch V. Maryland

- But in no case did Marshall come more decisively to the defense of Hamilton's agenda than in *McCulloch v. Maryland*, because that case offered a direct and unambiguous challenge to Hamilton's creation, the Bank of the United States, and the power of the federal government to have established it in the first place.

- In 1816, the Bank of the United States, which operated branches in nine American cities, opened a branch in Baltimore without applying to the Maryland legislature for a corporate charter. As a federal entity, there seemed to be no reason to need a state charter. But the Maryland legislature, teeming with Jeffersonians, thought otherwise.

- On February 18, 1818, the Maryland General Assembly passed a bill to limit the issuance of the bank's notes to bills between $5.00 and $1,000.00 and to have a Maryland revenue stamp fixed to each. The chief cashier of the bank's Baltimore branch, James William McCulloch, refused to purchase the stamps and was promptly sued by the state of Maryland.

- McCulloch, in turn, appealed to the federal courts, and Marshall began hearing the case on February 22, 1819. It may have been the single greatest assembly of legal talent in one spot: not only Marshall and Joseph Story on the bench, but George Washington's nephew Bushrod, as well; Luther Martin for the state of Maryland;

and William Wirt and Daniel Webster as counsel for McCulloch and the bank.

> *McCulloch v. Maryland* was argued for nine days, with Luther Martin arguing that it had exceeded the enumerated powers of the federal government. But Marshall, with equal skill, reduced all of Martin's arguments to nitpicking. Of course, the federal government may establish a bank as an exercise of its necessary-and-proper authority. He could not tell what was more perverse: Luther Martin insisting that every detail of the federal government's responsibilities as a government had to spelled out or the Maryland General Assembly's refusal to read the words that the Constitution did spell out—that the document was the "supreme law of the land."

SUGGESTED READING

Newmyer, *John Marshall and the Heroic Age of the Supreme Court*, chap. 5.
Smith, *John Marshall*, chaps. 2 and 13.

QUESTIONS TO CONSIDER

1. What experiences made John Marshall a Federalist?

2. How did Marshall respond to arguments in favor of judicial deference to the legislature?

3. In one sentence each, what were the principal lessons of *Marbury v. Madison, Martin v. Hunter's Lessee,* and *McCulloch v. Maryland?*

Lecture 35

JAMES MADISON'S WAR

*T*he election of John Adams to the presidency in 1796 and the Quasi-War with France seemed to be the nadir of the Republicans. Even though Jefferson, as Adams's unwilling vice president, would preside over the Senate, Jefferson himself was certain that Adams intended to exclude him from "participating in the administration" as much as possible. But no one felt the discouragement of the Republicans more than James Madison. From his position as the de facto floor leader of the opposition, he had been forced to watch as, one by one, Hamilton's plans were implemented, as Washington became increasingly chilly and distant, and as Madison's own influence gradually declined.

MADISON IN JEFFERSON'S ADMINISTRATION

➤ In Madison's eyes, the Jay Treaty was "full of shameful concessions, of mock reciprocities, and of party artifices, that no other circumstances than the peculiar ones which mark our present political situation, could screen it from universal execration." Further, there seemed no point in protesting that "the bill for establishing a national bank" was "not warranted by the constitution," because there were other members of the Constitutional Convention sitting in the same House who insisted exactly the opposite.

➤ In December of 1796, Madison decided not to seek reelection to Congress and stayed in Virginia for the next four years. However, the sudden collapse of Federalist political fortunes in the last two years of the Adams administration and the election of Jefferson to the presidency seemed suddenly to have brought the sun from behind the clouds. The day after his inauguration, Jefferson offered Madison the post of secretary of state, and together, they plan to restore strict republicanism.

➤ Together with Jefferson's secretary of the treasury, Albert Gallatin, the three men believed that they were called to rescue the republic from the grasping hands of would-be aristocrats. Madison's day-to-day responsibilities were more hum-drum: dealing with passports, diplomatic correspondence, ships' cargo manifests, and patents.

➤ Madison's chief problem was how to deal with British arrogance on the high seas. He composed a dense treatise on the subject in 1805. But treatises were little answer to the broadsides of HMS *Leopard*, and rather than face the prospect of outright war, Madison endorsed Jefferson's embargo.

➤ What surprised Madison was how little credit he, Jefferson, and Gallatin received for their labors. John Randolph of Roanoke, as the new floor leader of the Republicans in the House and chairman of the Ways and Means Committee, denounced the

Louisiana Purchase, Madison's interest in land speculation, and nearly everything else the administration did as "apostacies" from true republicanism.

- He gathered around him a dissident Republican faction, and yet another faction, the War Hawks, blamed Jefferson and Madison for doing too little to punish Great Britain.

- Their most talented figurehead was the Virginia-born Henry Clay, who was outraged that "the injuries we have received from Great Britain remain unredressed." But the War Hawks' chief preoccupation was with the British, and their inevitable answer to the British menace was to annex Canada.

HENRY CLAY
(1777–1852)

MADISON AS PRESIDENT

➢ Neither Randolph's nor Clay's factions could assemble enough political mass to oppose the administration successfully. Thus, when Jefferson announced that his second term as president would be his last, the Republican caucus gave Madison its blessing as the next Republican nominee for the presidency. And he won handsomely. However, the Federalist vote had improved by 30 percent over the 1804 election, and Federalist candidates for Congress picked up 24 new seats.

➢ But Madison was less worried by the Federalists than he than he was by the War Hawks of his own party, and not only because he feared the consequences of a war with the greatest naval power on earth, but also because he was determined not to be dictated to by the upstart Henry Clay. Despite the appearance of "submission to Foreign Edicts," the embargo was allowed to expire and was replaced by a much weaker Non-Intercourse Act.

  ◆ Unhappily for Madison, the British clumsily undid every one of his efforts to maintain a respectable peace. Madison had hardly taken office as president in the spring of 1809 when the new British minister in Washington, David Erskine, unrolled a new British policy initiative that offered to mollify American grievances over the *Chesapeake-Leopard* incident and secure noninterference with American trade on the seas.

  ◆ Madison was delighted at the offer, and Congress promptly dropped the new military appropriations bill it had been mulling over. However, Erskine, who was eager to placate American interests, had exceeded his instructions from London, and when the news of the agreements reached the desk of the British foreign minister, they were angrily repudiated.

➢ The following spring, it was the turn of the French minister to present an offer from Bonaparte that, in like manner, proposed to ease French harassment of American trade. Madison took

Bonaparte at his word, and reinstated an embargo on trade with Britain. To Madison's embarrassment, Bonaparte then insisted that his offer could not be fully implemented until the British also agreed to lift their restrictions on American shipping. Once again, Madison was left out in the cold.

➤ While these diplomatic insults boxed the American Republic on one ear, two major military crises in 1811 boxed it on the other. The first of these was the Tecumseh confederation, which the War Hawks treated as nothing but a stalking-horse for British recolonization of America. The second was the clash between the American frigate *President* and the British sloop-of-war *Little Belt*, which was won by the Americans.

➤ "Are we upon the eve of a declaration of our independence upon G[reat] Britain being repeated ... not by the pen, or by a general Suffrage but by the mouths of our Cannon?" asked Benjamin Rush at the end of August 1811. Light-Horse Harry Lee now confronted Madison with the demand that Madison "take us out of the odious condition ... of half war ... by drawing the sword."

  ◆ In mid-May, the Republican congressional caucus met to select its presidential nominee for elections in the fall of 1812, and led by Henry Clay, the caucus "plainly told" Madison "that his being supported as the party candidate for the next Presidency depended upon his screwing his courage to a declaration of war."

  ◆ On June 1, Madison finally yielded: He sent a message to Congress, reviewing the situation with the British and asked Congress for a declaration of war. The House responded promptly with a 79-to-49 vote in favor of the declaration; Federalists in the Senate slowed the measure down but could not stop it, and the war bill passed the Senate on June 17. The next day, Madison signed it.

THE WAR OF 1812

➤ The United States was no better prepared to go to war against England than it had been to go to war against the pasha of Tripoli, only now the Americans were squaring off against the most powerful empire on the globe. It is one of most obscure wars, and with good reason, because there is much in it we can only look back on with regret.

➤ The United States was disastrously unprepared for war: The Royal Navy possessed 219 ships-of-the-line and 296 frigates; the United States had 5 frigates and a flock of sloops, schooners, and privateers. Some feverish prewar preparations had set the size of the U.S. Army at 10,000 men, but by the time of the declaration of war, only 6,750 had been recruited.

➤ And then there was the ballyhoo about seizing Canada. Admittedly, the entire British garrison for Canada counted no more than 5,600 regular British infantry. But the War Hawks would have more difficulty than they imagined convincing skeptics that a war declared in defense of "Free Trade and Sailors' Rights" had anything to do with invading Canada. And it certainly gave no cheer to Republican hearts when Albert Gallatin announced that the war should be financed by excise taxes.

➤ As it was, Canada turned out to be a more difficult nut to crack than anyone had imagined. Madison's secretary of war, William Eustis, drew up a comprehensive plan for invading Upper Canada, but it fizzled ingloriously, as did the invasion of Lower Canada.

➤ To the disappointment of the War Hawks, it was the navy that won the laurels. Oliver Hazard Perry, a lieutenant sent to take charge of the tiny base at Presque Isle on Lake Erie in March 1813, managed to build a flotilla of 10 small ships, led by two 20-gun brigs, *Lawrence* and *Niagara*, and defeated a British lake squadron on Lake Erie.

➤ But American victories were only pinpricks in the hide of a Royal Navy. When the American frigate *Essex* captured the British sloop *Alert* and took 15 British merchantmen, the Royal Navy pursued and sank the Essex off the cost of Chile.

➤ Nor did the Navy's frigates do much to compensate for American failures on land. In 1814, a reorganized American army commanded by Major General Jacob Brown once again crossed into the Niagara peninsula and, this time, soundly defeated the British at Chippewa on July 5. But Brown had no resources with which to exploit this achievement, and in three weeks, the American invasion was almost back where it had begun.

➤ What was worse, Napoleon had finally been cornered, defeated, and exiled to the Mediterranean island of Elba, thus freeing up troops and ships to undertake offensive campaigns against the American coastline.

♦ In a campaign of revenge for the destruction of York, a combined British naval and army expedition, under the command of Vice Admiral Alexander Cochrane and Major General Robert Ross, lunged up the Chesapeake Bay, landing 4,000 infantry.

♦ Cochrane prepared to land at Benedict, on the Patuxent River, brushing aside a hastily assembled American defense force at Bladensburg, and descending on Washington itself. There, on August 24, the British burned the Executive Mansion, the Capitol, the Treasury, and numerous other public buildings.

♦ The fiasco might have been worse if the British had managed to add the city of Baltimore to their bag. But an unexpectedly stout defense put up by Major George Armistead and the garrison of Fort McHenry, guarding Baltimore harbor, forced them to abandon any more ambitious efforts to occupy the Chesapeake Bay.

FORT McHENRY,
BALTIMORE, MD

> The initial war enthusiasm guaranteed Madison's reelection to the presidency in 1812, but in mid-1813, he nearly died of an attack of malaria. Cockburn earnestly hoped he could capture Madison during the attack on Washington "and carry him to England for a curiosity." But Madison went no nearer the fighting than a hilltop above Bladensburg; he had simply lost heart.

> Madison was relieved when, in February 1815, the British offered to end the war and return to the prewar status quo. Like Jefferson, he would accept no third term.

SUGGESTED READING

Hickey, *The War of 1812*, chaps. 2 and 11.
Ketcham, *James Madison*, chaps. 18–20.

QUESTIONS TO CONSIDER

1. Who were the tertium quids? Who were the War Hawks?

2. How deeply did the British humiliate the United States in the War of 1812?

Lecture 36

ALEXIS DE TOCQUEVILLE'S AMERICA

On May 11, 1831, two French travelers, Alexis de Tocqueville and Gustave de Beaumont, stepped off the 500-ton brig *Le Havre* in New York and proceeded to conduct one of the most interesting journeys ever conducted across the face of America. They were not explorers in the usual sense of the term. They were in pursuit of something more elusive, and that was the set of fundamental principles that allowed the American Republic to survive.

THE REPUBLICAN DREAM

➤ Republicanism might have been the darling political theory of the Enlightenment, but after the American founding, it had enjoyed a rocky and disappointing career as an idea of government. The republic created by the French revolutionaries in 1789 in imitation of the American one had declined swiftly into the hands of a dictator. And when Bonaparte's empire itself collapsed under the blows of Europe, the victorious allies insisted on turning the clock of French politics back to 1789 and placing a king, Louis XVIII, on a restored French throne in 1815.

➤ Meanwhile, the political ideals of the Enlightenment were challenged and succeeded by a violent gust of reaction known as the Romantic Revolt. Not reason, insisted the Romantics, but passion formed nations; not logic, but race and blood gave identity to peoples. Thus, as Europeans planted themselves all over the world, they did so at the behest of aristocratic governments, gathering new strength from the practical failures of republicanism and the stormy winds of Romanticism; only the United States remained as the one large-scale example of a republic in the world.

➤ Yet the republican dream lived on, and Tocqueville was one example of its persistence. Tocqueville's forebears were local aristocrats from Normandy, but Alexis grew up with few starry-eyed illusions about aristocrats. As a student at the Sorbonne from 1829 to 1830, he came under the spell of the French liberal republican François Guizot, from whom he learned that history was a record of the movement of progress and that progress had equality as its goal.

➤ Tocqueville caught a fleeting glimpse of that future for France in 1830, but then a new monarch was installed, and Tocqueville reluctantly took an oath of allegiance to him. No one seemed to believe any more that a republic was a viable alternative; thus, Tocqueville began casting around for an example that would convince people otherwise. And that, in 1832, was what brought him to the United States.

ALEXIS DE TOCQUEVILLE
(1805–1859)

> Tocqueville and his friend would actually stay in America for only slightly more than nine months, where they considered their real tasks to be "researching statistics on the conditions of the population, on public institutions, and on all the political questions that concern us." They journeyed upriver to Albany; west to Niagara Falls; across the Great Lakes to Detroit, Quebec, and Montreal, then doubled back to Boston, Philadelphia, and Baltimore. By January, 1832, they had visited Cincinnati, Nashville, Memphis, and New Orleans and made one last turn through Washington and New York before departing in February. Along the way, they met John Quincy Adams, Andrew Jackson, Albert Gallatin, John Marshall, Henry Clay, and many others.

JAMES MADISON

> By 1832, the ranks of the Founders had grown exceedingly thin. Of the 39 who had signed the Constitution, 4 of them died in 1790, including the tottering Benjamin Franklin. Washington himself died in 1799, and the decade also saw the loss of Robert Sherman, James Wilson, and Patrick Henry. The 1800s witnessed the losses of John Rutledge, James McHenry, William Findley, Jefferson, Adams, Rufus King, and John Marshall.

> That left, at the end, only one man standing: James Madison, the last survivor of the Constitutional Convention. Now at age 80,

he had come out of retirement only once, in 1829, to serve as a delegate from Orange County to the new Virginia Constitutional Convention, and in the only speech he delivered at the convention, he might have been summarizing in advance for Tocqueville what he would have told the Frenchman face-to-face:

> The essence of Government is power; and power, lodged as it must be in human hands, will ever be liable to abuse. In monarchies, the interests and happiness of nil may be sacrificed to the caprice and passions of a despot. In aristocracies, the rights and welfare of the many may be sacrificed to the pride and cupidity of the few. In republics, the great danger is, that the majority may not sufficiently respect the rights of the minority.

➤ Madison had never flagged in his belief that the great danger to liberty was power. But it was an enemy without which liberty could not survive, if only for the purpose of self-protection. In monarchies and tyrannies, we always know in what direction power acts—from the top down. The novelty in republics is that it can just as easily operate from the bottom up, and all the labors Madison had devoted to the Constitutional Convention had been aimed at preventing bottom-up power from creating lawless local despotisms.

➤ Madison also took the opportunity to ask for a correction to the one great oversight of the summer of 1787, and that concerned slavery.

◆ Emancipation was the one remaining stone that would complete the wonderful edifice of liberty, Madison asserted. "Other nations are surprised at nothing so much as our having been able to form Constitutions in the manner which has been exemplified in this country. Even the union of so many States, is, in the eyes of the world … a miracle."

◆ If Americans had been able to do so much so quickly, then Madison was confident that, even "without a miracle," we could end slavery.

SELF-INTEREST

> In his travels through the United States, the one word that Alexis de Tocqueville did not hear was *virtue*. "In the United States, it is almost never said that virtue is beautiful." What he heard about instead was self-interest. "The doctrine of self-interest well understood … has been universally accepted," Tocqueville wrote, "one finds it at the foundation of all actions; it pierces into all discussions."

> Americans had not formed communities in search of righteousness but in search of profits. Karl Marx, in the next decade, would write about society and economics as a war between classes, in which profits were the chief cause of personal alienation and conflict the ceaseless order of the day. But the only conflict Tocqueville saw in America was between profit-seeking individuals who were, ironically, entirely in agreement with each other about the pursuit of self-interest.

> Even more ironically, it was the pursuit of wealth that produced virtue, rather than the other way around. "The doctrine of self-interest well understood does not produce great devotion," Tocqueville acknowledged, "by itself it cannot make a man virtuous; but it forms a multitude of citizens who are regulated, temperate, moderate, farsighted, masters of themselves." The great exception to this self-mastery was, of course, American slavery. But even among the enslaved, as Frederick Douglass would later say, what the slave wanted most in freedom was the free pursuit of self-interest.

> But the substitution of self-interest for virtue did have this drawback: It made equality more important than liberty. No single individual—no matter how wise, well-educated, or authoritative—was entitled to more of a say in public affairs than any other self-interested individual. This created an atmosphere in which only numbers, not truth, were the effective force in American life. What kept democracy from degenerating into mere mob rule were, as

Tocqueville noted, two uniquely American institutions: newspapers and voluntary organizations.

- Newspapers make "political life circulate in all sections of this vast territory" and force "public men … to appear before the court of opinion."

- Voluntary associations—organizations of citizens, collected at their own prompting— performed much of the social work that governments in Europe took unto themselves and formed a

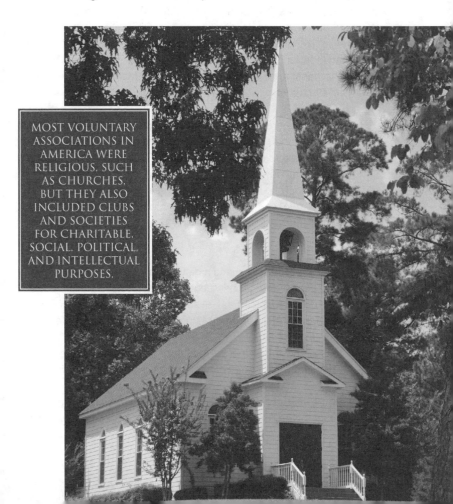

MOST VOLUNTARY ASSOCIATIONS IN AMERICA WERE RELIGIOUS, SUCH AS CHURCHES, BUT THEY ALSO INCLUDED CLUBS AND SOCIETIES FOR CHARITABLE, SOCIAL, POLITICAL, AND INTELLECTUAL PURPOSES.

layer of resistance to government forcing a tyrannical authority downward or from a mob imposing a tyrannical force upward on the government.

- ◆ Most of these voluntary associations were religious. But Americans also have "a thousand other kinds": In fact, where "at the head" of any "new undertaking" in France or England you see the government or "a great lord," in America, "you will find an association."

➢ Tocqueville was not being censorious. When he published his observations as *De la démocratie en Amérique* (*Democracy in America*), he did not believe that "the perils that equality brings to human independence" were "insurmountable." But he was worried that the passion of equality was draining American democracy of any art or culture.

- ◆ He met "a great quantity of individuals who are interested in things of the mind" but the "least occupied with literature" of any "civilized country of our day." The passion for equality exerted a downward pressure on intellectual freedom, not by aristocratic censorship from above, but from a spirit of democratic conformity that resented intellectual superiority and demanded conformity to the lowest common denominator of thought.

- ◆ Judgment, taste, and distinction become suspect; a cheapened and debased public opinion rules self-righteously. Each citizen becomes "a stranger to the destiny of all the others; his children and his particular friends form the whole human species for him." At that moment, government steps in to assume "an immense tutelary power" which "takes charge of assuring their enjoyments and watching over their fate."

➢ It was the rise of voluntary associations, especially the religious ones, that saved Americans from despotism; when the day arrived that these associations ceased to function, then a new form of despotism—a soft despotism—would have arrived, in which people thoughtlessly chained their own shackles to themselves.

➢ In an odd way, Tocqueville and Madison complement each other. Both of them understood that free government is an awkward and constantly adjusting dance between liberty and power; both understood that the threat of power can come from below as well as from above; both hoped that by divvying up power and distributing it broadly (whether between branches of government or in the form of voluntary associations), power could be made to serve liberty's purposes.

  ◆ This might not make for efficiency, and in the modern world, efficiency has become one of the principal disguises power takes unto itself. But the Founders were not concerned with efficiency; they were concerned with liberty. And they knew that its life was always precarious.

  ◆ Emerging from the locked doors of the Constitutional Convention in September 1787, a voice called out to Benjamin Franklin, "What is it? Republic or monarchy?" Franklin stopped to reply, hopefully with a twinkle in his still-mischievous eye: "A republic, if you can keep it." The question, and its answer, are still with us.

SUGGESTED READING

Diggins, *On Hallowed Ground*, chap. 4.
McCoy, *Last of the Founders*, chaps. 6–7.

QUESTIONS TO CONSIDER

1. How important in Tocqueville's observation was self-interest to Americans?

2. What kept democracy from degenerating into mob rule?

3. What did Madison always believe was the relationship of liberty and power?

BIBLIOGRAPHY

GENERAL HISTORIES OF THE FOUNDING

Beeman, Richard. *Plain, Honest Men: The Making of the American Constitution*. New York: Random House, 2009. The most thorough one-volume history of the Constitutional Convention.

Berkin, Carol. *A Brilliant Solution: Inventing the American Constitution*. New York: Harcourt, 2002.

Collier, Christopher, and James Collier. *Decision in Philadelphia: The Constitutional Convention of 1787*. New York: Ballantine Books, 2007.

Elkins, Stanley, and Eric McKitrick. *The Age of Federalism: The Early American Republic, 1788–1800*. New York: Oxford University Press, 1993. An extraordinary reconstruction of the personalities and policies of the Federalists.

Kaminski, John P., ed. *The Founders on the Founders: Word Portraits from the American Revolutionary Era*. Charlottesville: University of Virginia Press, 2008.

McDonald, Forrest. *Novus Ordo Seclorum: The Intellectual Origins of the Constitution*. Lawrence: University Press of Kansas, 1985. A virtuoso introduction to the basic political principles of the Founders.

Stewart, David O. *The Summer of 1787: The Men Who Invented the Constitution*. New York: Simon and Schuster, 2007. A vigorously written popular history of the Constitutional Convention.

COLLECTIONS OF PRIMARY DOCUMENTS

The most often-cited source on the Constitutional Convention is the record kept by James Madison, which appears as (a) "Debates in the Federal Convention of 1787 as Reported by James Madison," in *Documents Illustrative of the Formation of the Union of the American States*, edited by C. C. Tansill (Washington: Government Printing Office, 1927)—a volume that has the attraction of including in its single, mammoth bulk most of the other relevant documents for the founding—and (b) in *The Records of the Federal Convention of 1787*, edited by Max Farrand (New Haven: Yale University Press, 1911). As much as Madison's notes stand apart as a primary source, Madison forbade their publication until after his death, and the notes themselves show evidence of Madison's own tinkering and editing of what was ultimately published.

On the ratification of the Constitution, see *The Debates in the Several State Conventions on the Adoption of the Federal Convention*, edited by Jonathan Elliott (Philadelphia: J. B. Lippincott, 1836) and its modern and much more expansive counterpart, *The Documentary History of the Ratification of the Constitution*, edited by Merrill Jensen, et al. (Madison: State Historical Society of Wisconsin, 1976, 27 vols.).

OTHER PRIMARY DOCUMENTS ON THE FOUNDING

Crevècoeur, Hector Saint John de. *Letters from an American Farmer and Sketches of Eighteenth-Century America*. Edited by Albert Stone. New York: Penguin, 1981.

Gales, Joseph, ed. *Debates and Proceedings in the Congress of the United States: With an Appendix Containing Important State Papers and Public Documents*. Washington: Gales & Seaton, 1834.

Hyneman, C. S., and D. S. Lutz, eds. *American Political Writing during the Founding Era, 1760–1805*. Indianapolis, IN: Liberty Fund, 1983. An outstanding two-volume collection of political documents of the founding era, outside the orbit of the founders themselves.

Storing, Herbert J., ed. *The Complete Anti-Federalist*. Chicago: University of Chicago Press, 1981.

Tocqueville, Alexis de. *Democracy in America*. Edited by Harvey C. Mansfield and Delba Winthrop. Chicago: University of Chicago Press, 2000.

Warren, Mercy Otis. *History of the Rise, Progress, and Termination of the American Revolution*. Boston: Manning & Loring, 1805.

Wootton, David, ed. *The Essential Federalist and Anti-Federalist Papers*. Indianapolis, IN: Hackett, 2003.

EDITIONS OF PAPERS AND WRITINGS OF THE FOUNDERS

Abbot, W. W., ed. *The Papers of George Washington: Confederation Series*. 6 vols. Charlottesville: University Press of Virginia, 1997.

Allen, W. B., ed. *George Washington: A Collection*. Indianapolis: Liberty Fund, 1988.

———. *Works of Fisher Ames*. 2 vols. Indianapolis, IN: Liberty Fund, 1983.

Boyd, Julian P., ed. *The Papers of Thomas Jefferson*. 21 vols. Princeton: Princeton University Press, 1950–2006.

Butterfield, Lyman H., ed. *The Adams Papers. Cambridge, MA: Harvard University Press, 1961.*

Butterfield, Lyman H. et al, eds. *The Book of Abigail and John: Selected Letters of the Adams Family, 1762–1784*. Boston: Massachusetts Historical Society, 1975.

Cohn, Ellen R. et al, eds. *The Papers of Benjamin Franklin*. 41 vols. New Haven: Yale University Press, 1959–2011.

Dillon, J. M., ed. *John Marshall: Complete Constitutional Decisions.* Chicago: Callaghan & Co., 1903.

Ferguson, E. J., et al, eds. *The Papers of Robert Morris 1781–1784.* 9 vols. Pittsburgh: University of Pittsburgh Press, 1973.

Hall, K., and M. D. Hall, eds. *Collected Works of James Wilson.* 2 vols. Indianapolis: Liberty Fund, 2007.

Rutland, Robert A., ed. *The Papers of George Mason, 1725–1792.* 3 vols. Chapel Hill: University of North Carolina Press, 1970.

Rutland, Robert, A. et al, eds. *The Papers of James Madison.* 38 vols. Chicago: University of Chicago Press & Charlottesville: University of Virginia Press, 1962–2016.

Syrett, Harold C., ed. *The Papers of Alexander Hamilton.* 27 vols. New York: Columbia University Press, 1961.

Twohig, Dorothy, ed. *The Papers of George Washington: Presidential Series.* 18 vols. Charlottesville: University Press of Virginia, 1987–2015.

BIOGRAPHIES: SOCIAL AND POLITICAL HISTORIES

Banning, Lance. *The Jeffersonian Persuasion: Evolution of a Party Ideology.* Ithaca: Cornell University Press, 1978.

———. *The Sacred Fire of Liberty: James Madison and the Founding of the Federal Republic.* Ithaca: Cornell University Press, 1995. The best one-volume introduction to Madison's political ideas.

Beeman, Richard. *Patrick Henry: A Biography.* New York: McGraw-Hill, 1974.

Bernstein, Richard B. *The Founding Fathers Reconsidered.* New York: Oxford University Press, 2009.

Bodenhamer, David J. *The Revolutionary Constitution*. New York: Oxford University Press, 2012.

Bordewich, Fergus. *Washington: The Making of the American Capital*. New York: HarperCollins, 2008. A sprightly history of the creation of the District of Columbia.

Broadwater, Jeff. *George Mason: Forgotten Founder*. Chapel Hill: University of North Carolina Press, 2006.

Brookhiser, Richard. *Gentleman Revolutionary: Gouverneur Morris, the Rake Who Wrote the Constitution*. New York: Simon & Schuster, 2003.

Buel, Richard. *America on the Brink: How the Political Struggle over the War of 1812 Almost Destroyed the Young Republic*. New York: Palgrave Macmillan, 2005.

Burnett, Edmund Cody. *The Continental Congress: A Definitive History of the Continental Congress from Its Inception in 1774 to March, 1789*. New York: Macmillan, 1941. Although creaking with age, still the best overall history of the Confederation years.

Chapin, Bradley. *The American Law of Treason: Revolutionary and Early National Origins*. Seattle: University of Washington Press, 1964.

Chernow, Ron. *Alexander Hamilton*. New York: Penguin Press, 2004. A highly successful and popular biography of Hamilton that became the basis for Lin-Manuel Miranda's hip-hop musical, *Hamilton*.

Clarkson, Paul S., and R. Samuel Jett. *Luther Martin of Maryland*. Baltimore: Johns Hopkins University Press, 1970.

Combs, Jerald A. *The Jay Treaty: Political Battleground of the Founding Fathers*. Berkeley: University of California Press, 1970.

Diggins, John Patrick. *On Hallowed Ground: Abraham Lincoln and the Foundations of American History*. New Haven: Yale University Press, 2000.

Drez, Ronald J. *The War of 1812, Conflict and Deception: The British Attempt to Seize New Orleans and Nullify the Louisiana Purchase*. Baton Rouge: Louisiana State University Press, 2014.

Ellis, Joseph J. *Founding Brothers: The Revolutionary Generation*. New York: Alfred A. Knopf, 2000.

Ernst, Robert. *Rufus King: American Federalist*. Chapel Hill: University of North Carolina Press, 1968.

Estes, Todd. *The Jay Treaty Debate, Public Opinion, and the Evolution of Early American Political Culture*. Amherst: University of Massachusetts Press, 2006.

Fleming, Thomas. *Duel: Alexander Hamilton, Aaron Burr, and the Future of America*. New York: Basic Books, 1999.

———. *The Louisiana Purchase*. Hoboken, NJ: John Wiley & Sons, 2003.

Freeman, Joanne B. *Affairs of Honor: National Politics in the New Republic*. New Haven: Yale University Press, 2001.

Glover, Lorri. *Founders as Fathers: The Private Lives and Politics of the American Revolutionaries*. New Haven, CT: Yale University Press, 2014.

Hall, Mark David. *Roger Sherman and the Creation of the American Republic*. New York: Oxford University Press, 2013.

Hickey, Donald R. *The War of 1812: A Forgotten Conflict*. Chicago: University of Illinois Press, 2012.

Holton, Woody. *Unruly Americans and the Origins of the Constitution*. New York: Hill & Wang, 2007. A strikingly written account of the economic motivations of the founders, harking back to progressive interpreters of the Constitution in the early 20th century.

Isaacson, Walter. *Benjamin Franklin: An American Life*. New York: Simon & Schuster, 2003.

Isenberg, Nancy. *Fallen Founder: The Life of Aaron Burr*. New York: Viking Penguin, 2007.

Israel, Jonathan. *Democratic Enlightenment: Philosophy, Revolution, and Human Rights, 1750–1790*. New York: Oxford University Press, 2011. This massive tome, one of a series written by Israel on the Enlightenment, sets the American political experiment in an international 18th-century context.

Jensen, Merrill. *The Articles of Confederation: An Interpretation of the Social-Constitutional History of the American Revolution, 1774–1781*. Madison: University of Wisconsin Press, 1940. The most thorough analysis of the creation and content of the first American constitution.

———. *The New Nation: A History of the United States during the Confederation, 1781–1789*. New York: Vintage, 1965.

Kaminski, John P. *George Clinton: Yeoman Politician of the New Republic*. Madison: Madison House, 1993.

———. *The Great Virginia Triumvirate: George Washington, Thomas Jefferson, and James Madison in the Eyes of Their Contemporaries*. Charlottesville: University of Virginia Press, 2010.

Ketchum, Ralph L. *James Madison: A Biography*. Charlottesville: University Press of Virginia, 1990. An extraordinary one-volume survey of the life of Madison.

Kidd, Thomas. *Patrick Henry: First among Patriots*. New York: Basic Books, 2011.

———. *The Great Awakening: The Roots of Evangelical Christianity in Colonial America*. New Haven: Yale University Press, 2007.

Labunski, Richard. *James Madison and the Struggle for the Bill of Rights*. New York: Oxford University Press, 2006.

Lambert, Frank. *The Barbary Wars: American Independence in the Atlantic World*. New York: Hill & Wang, 2005.

Lyons, Jonathan. *The Society for Useful Knowledge: How Benjamin Franklin and Friends Brought the Enlightenment to America*. New York: Bloomsbury Press, 2013.

Maier, Pauline. *Ratification: The People Debate the Constitution, 1787– 1788. New York: Simon & Schuster, 2010. A wonderful single-volume overview of the state ratifying conventions.*

Main, Jackson Turner. *The Antifederalists: Critics of the Constitution, 1781–1788*. Chapel Hill: University of North Carolina Press, 2004. First published 1961.

Malone, Dumas. *Jefferson and His Time: Jefferson the President, First Term, 1801–1805*. Boston: Little, Brown, 1970.

Matthews, Marty D. *Forgotten Founder: The Life and Times of Charles Pinckney*. Columbia: University of South Carolina Press, 2004.

McCoy, Drew R. *Last of the Founders: James Madison and the Republican Legacy*. Cambridge: Cambridge University Press, 1989. Looks back on Madison's participation in the founding from the perspective of his last years in retirement.

McDonald, Forrest. *Alexander Hamilton: A Biography*. New York: W. W. Norton, 1979. The finest scholarly biography of Hamilton.

———. *The Presidency of George Washington*. Lawrence: University Press of Kansas, 1974.

———. *We the People: The Economic Origins of the Constitution*. Chicago: University of Chicago Press, 1958. A comprehensive reply to Progressive Era denigrations of the Constitution.

Miller, William L. *The Business of May Next: James Madison and the Founding*. Charlottesville: University Press of Virginia, 1992.

Morris, Richard B. *Seven Who Shaped Our Destiny: The Founding Fathers as Revolutionaries*. New York: Harper & Row, 1973.

Myerson, Michael I. *Liberty's Blueprint: How Madison and Hamilton Wrote the Federalist Papers, Defined the Constitution, and Made Democracy Safe for the World*. New York: Basic Books, 2008.

Nash, Gary B. *The Unknown American Revolution: The Unruly Birth of Democracy and the Struggle to Create America*. New York: Viking 2005.

Newmyer, R. Kent. *John Marshall and the Heroic Age of the Supreme Court*. Baton Rouge: Louisiana State University Press, 2001.

O'Brien, Conor Cruise. *The Long Affair: Thomas Jefferson and the French Revolution, 1785–1800*. Chicago: University of Chicago Press, 1996. A no-holds-barred attack on Jefferson's naiveté about the French Revolution.

O'Connor, John E. *William Paterson: Lawyer and Statesman, 1745–1806*. New Brunswick, NJ: Rutgers University Press, 1979.

Rael, Patrick. *Eighty-Eight Years: The Long Death of Slavery in the United States, 1777–1865*. Athens: University of Georgia Press, 2015.

Rakove, Jack. *Original Meanings Politics and Ideas in the Making of the Constitution*. New York: Knopf, 1996.

———. *The Beginnings of National Politics: An Interpretive History of the Continental Congress*. Baltimore: Johns Hopkins University Press, 1979.

Randall, Willard Sterne. *George Washington: A Life*. New York: Henry Holt, 1997. The best single-volume life of Washington.

Rappleye, Charles. *Robert Morris: Financier of the American Revolution*. New York: Simon & Schuster, 2010.

Richards, Leonard L. *Shays's Rebellion: The American Revolution's Final Battle*. Philadelphia: University of Pennsylvania Press, 2002.

Robbins, Karen E. *James McHenry: Forgotten Federalist*. Athens: University of Georgia Press, 2013.

Sheehan, Colleen A. *James Madison and the Spirit of Republican Self-Government*. New York: Cambridge University Press, 2009.

Slaughter, Thomas P. *The Whiskey Rebellion: Frontier Epilogue to the American Revolution*. New York: Oxford University Press, 1986.

Smith, Jean Edward. *John Marshall: Definer of a Nation*. New York: Henry Holt, 1996.

Stahr, Walter. *John Jay: Founding Father*. New York: Palgrave Macmillan, 2005.

Szatmary, David P. *Shays' Rebellion: The Making of an Agrarian Insurrection*. Amherst: University of Massachusetts Press, 1980.

Thach, Charles C. *Creation of the Presidency, 1775–1789: A Study in Constitutional History*. Indianapolis, IN: Liberty Fund, 2007. First published 1969.

Toll, Ian W. *Six Frigates: The Epic History of the Founding of the U.S. Navy*. New York: W. W. Norton, 2006.

Vogel, Steve. *Through the Perilous Fight: Six Weeks That Saved the Nation*. New York: Random House, 2013.

Wells, Colin. *The Devil and Doctor Dwight: Satire and Theology in the Early American Republic*. Chapel Hill: University of North Carolina Press, 2002.

Wood, Gordon S. *Empire of Liberty: A History of the Early Republic, 1789–1815*. New York: Oxford University Press, 2009. A Pulitzer Prize–winning survey of the early republic.

———. *The Creation of the American Republic, 1776–1787*. Chapel Hill: University of North Carolina Press, 1969. One of the great books on the ideas that ruled the minds of the founders, focusing on the domestic sources of the revolution's ideology.

———. *The Idea of America: Reflections on the Birth of the United States*. New York: Penguin, 2011. A collection of Wood's finest essays.

———. *The Radicalism of the American Revolution: How a Revolution Transformed a Monarchical Society into a Democratic One Unlike Any That Had Ever Existed*. New York: Knopf, 1997. Alongside Forrest McDonald's *Novus Ordo Seclorum*, a marvelous account of the transformation of the political ideas of the founding from monarchy to democracy.

IMAGE CREDITS

Notes

Notes

Notes

Notes

Notes